THE LEADERSHIP WISDOM OF SOLOMON

28 ESSENTIAL STRATEGIES *for* LEADING *with* INTEGRITY

PAT WILLIAMS
with JIM DENNEY

Standard®
PUBLISHING

Cincinnati, Ohio

Published by Standard Publishing, Cincinnati, Ohio
www.standardpub.com

Printed in: United States of America
Editors: Dale Reeves and Lynn Lusby Pratt
Cover design: The DesignWorks Group
Interior design: Dina Sorn at Ahaa! Design

ISBN 978-0-7847-2128-5

Library of Congress Cataloging-in-Publication Data

Williams, Pat, 1940-
  The leadership wisdom of Solomon : 28 essential strategies for leading with integrity / Pat Williams with Jim Denney.
     p. cm.
  ISBN 978-0-7847-2128-5 (perfect bound)
  1. Leadership--Biblical teaching. 2. Leadership--Religious aspects--Christianity. I. Denney, Jim, 1953- II. Title.
  BS1199.L4W55 2010
  158'.4--dc22

                          2010008516

15 14 13 12 11 10   1 2 3 4 5 6 7 8 9

I gratefully dedicate this book to

Bob Vander Weide,
Alex Martins,
and Otis Smith—

who provide leadership
for the Orlando Magic
the Solomon way.

Robert −

Good luck with your new responsibilities.
Hopefully you will find some useful
takeaways to help guide your leadership
journey.

Bryan

CONTENTS

One Sunday morning I was sitting in church, thumbing through the book of Proverbs in *The Message,* Eugene Peterson's contemporary paraphrase of the Bible. (I know what you're thinking—and in fact I *was* paying attention to the minister. I can listen to the sermon and look through the Bible at the same time. It's called multitasking.)

As I turned the pages of Proverbs, I noticed that the words *leader* and *leadership* appeared again and again:

- *"A good leader motivates, doesn't mislead, doesn't exploit"* *(Proverbs 16:10).*
- *"Sound leadership has a moral foundation" (v. 12).*
- *"We don't expect eloquence from fools, nor do we expect lies from our leaders" (17:7).*

As I scanned the pages, I encountered one great leadership insight after another—and I underlined each one. Then it hit me: These are the leadership lessons of Solomon—the most successful leader in history, the man who transformed a small tribal kingdom into a superpower!

People everywhere speak of "the wisdom of Solomon," but how many of us grasp what a role model of leadership this dynamic, visionary leader was? How he transformed his society? How he led ancient Israel into a golden age of peace and prosperity? How his wisdom has influenced human lives down through the ages?

It was a eureka moment.

I suddenly realized that I'd never read a book on the leadership wisdom of Solomon. And believe me, with a six-hundred-book leadership library in my home, I feel like I've read every leadership book ever written. I've underlined and highlighted and scribbled in the margins of all of them. I own books on leadership written by (or about) presidents, generals, coaches, CEOs, and management gurus.

So as I sat in church, flipping through the Bible, I could hardly believe it: the leadership insights of the greatest leader of all time have lain largely ignored for some three thousand years. I decided to do something about it.

I left church feeling energized, my brain cells humming with ideas, my synapses glowing like St. Elmo's fire. I couldn't stop thinking about Solomon. The next day I called my writing partner, Jim Denney, and told him my idea. He listened, then said, "Wow, Pat, this is big! This is a powerful idea!"

Jim pulled up *The Message* on his computer and did a quick search.

"I find twenty-eight passages in Proverbs and Ecclesiastes that focus on leadership," he said. "Each one deals with a distinct facet of the leadership role. We could do a short chapter on each passage, and people could either read the book straight through or read one chapter a day for a month. Or they could work through it with a group at their own pace. Pat, let's do it."

And that's how this book was born.

We introduce the book with a concise two-chapter biography of Solomon. The first of those will examine Solomon's immense achievements. In the second, we take the measure of his most famous character trait, his wisdom.

Then we plunge into the heart and soul of Solomon and explore the twenty-eight leadership insights he left to us in Proverbs and Ecclesiastes. And finally, we sum up what we have learned from this incomparable leader.

There are questions for reflection and discussion after each chapter. Use them to guide your own study of Solomon's leadership principles—or better yet, use them to trigger a spirited conversation in a leadership discussion group.

As you read, keep your pen and journal handy to record important insights. Use this book as bedtime reading if you like—but I suspect that, as you encounter the greatest leader who ever lived, you're going to want to read it sitting upright and attentive, with both feet on the floor.

So get ready, my friend. Let me take you on an exciting leadership cruise, conducted by the wisest, most successful leader history has ever known.

You're about to be mentored by Solomon himself.

Pat Williams
Orlando, Florida

INTRODUCING THE MOST SUCCESSFUL
LEADER IN HISTORY

A s the election of 1944 approached, President Roosevelt's health was failing. White House insiders knew there was a good chance that the president, if reelected, would die during his next term. They worried that Roosevelt's vice president, Henry A. Wallace, wasn't seen as capable of leading America in wartime. So for the reelection campaign, the party replaced Wallace with a little-known Missouri senator, Harry S. Truman. The Roosevelt-Truman ticket won handily.

On April 12, 1945, about three months after the inauguration, Roosevelt died of a massive cerebral hemorrhage. With fewer than a hundred days' vice presidential experience to his credit, Harry Truman suddenly found himself commander in chief of a nation at war. As vice president, he had been largely kept in the dark. Only after Roosevelt's death was he briefed about America's new secret weapon, the atomic bomb, which would soon be used against the Japanese mainland.

The day after taking office, Truman told reporters, "Boys, if you ever pray, pray for me now. I don't know whether you fellows ever had a load of hay fall on you, but when they told me yesterday what had happened, I felt like the moon, the stars, and all the planets had fallen on me."[1]

A few days later, when Truman delivered his first address before a joint session of Congress, he summoned the memory of another leader, King Solomon. "At this moment," Truman said, "I have in my heart a prayer. As I have assumed my duties, I humbly pray Almighty God, in the words of King Solomon: 'Give therefore Thy servant an understanding heart to judge Thy people, that I may discern between good and bad: for who is able to judge this Thy so great a people?' I ask only to be a good and faithful servant of my Lord and my people."[2]

It was an apt comparison. Just as King Solomon ascended to power in a time of crisis, feeling ill equipped to replace the beloved King David, President Truman felt unprepared to replace the much-beloved FDR. At such times, wise leaders know they need an extra measure of wisdom to face the challenges ahead.

‖ A ROLE MODEL FOR EVERY LEADER ‖

Our world today cries out for leaders. Our national leaders, corporate leaders, and religious leaders face crises on every hand. They are tested by threats of war and terrorism, economic upheaval and social collapse, moral corruption and spiritual malaise. Again and again we see leader after leader fail those tests. Our government is paralyzed by political division. Our society seems rudderless. Our corporations are failing. Our religious leaders are falling to scandal. The people around us are like sheep without a shepherd. They look for leaders to follow . . . and find none.

There are few issues more important to our daily lives than the issue of leadership. And there is no greater example of leadership than King Solomon. He is a role model for every leader, in every age, in every leadership arena. Solomon was no passive monarch, sitting on a throne, waiting to be served by his loyal subjects. Solomon was a dynamic, proactive leader who led with a bold vision for his nation. He dramatically transformed the world in which he lived.

Solomon was a *chief executive,* a master financier . . . the CEO of Israel, Incorporated. His brilliance as a broker of international commerce created untold prosperity and brought twenty-five tons of gold into Israel's treasury every year. He transformed the tiny tribal nation of Israel into a great sea-spanning imperium.

He was also a *military mastermind,* the commander in chief of Fortress Israel, the leader who secured the nation's borders and brought four decades of peace and plenty to the land. He expanded Israel's military forces and established fortified cities on key transportation routes into the nation. He never had to fight a war; he achieved "peace through strength."

Solomon was also a *philosophical leader,* an author and poet, a deep thinker whose writings continue to inspire and instruct us three thousand years later.

He was a *master architect and urban planner* who built entire cities; surrounded Jerusalem with fortified walls; designed grand palaces; and oversaw the construction of the crowning achievement of his reign, the great temple of Jerusalem.

The Age of Solomon was truly a golden age—Israel's Camelot. There were four glorious decades during which the splendor of Israel equaled that of Egypt, Babylon, Persia, Arabia, and the other great kingdoms of the world. Israel was never as great before the reign of Solomon—or after.

Following his death, the kingdom split in two. The splendor of Solomon's Israel was lost forever.

‖ SUCCESS BEGINS WITH A VISION ‖

The account of Solomon is recorded in 1 Kings 1–11; 1 Chronicles 28, 29; and 2 Chronicles 1–9. Solomon is remembered by Christians and Jews as the wisest and most successful leader in Scripture. In the Islamic Koran, he is called Sulayman and is revered as a prophet. And people of other faiths (or no faith at all) study his life and his writings in order to acquire the secrets of his wisdom.

Born the son of King David and Bathsheba, Solomon succeeded his father as king in approximately 967 BC, while King David still lived.[3] It was not an orderly succession. One of Solomon's half brothers, Adonijah, attempted to thwart Solomon and usurp the throne.

While King David was on his deathbed, he received news that Adonijah had declared himself king, in violation of the line of succession David had established. So David sent Solomon to the spring at Gihon, where Zadok the priest anointed him king over Israel (1 Kings 1).

Solomon began his reign by removing disloyal advisers who would undermine his leadership. He then appointed new advisers—people he could trust—to key positions in the government, the military, and the religious institution. He solidified his leadership position and demonstrated his ability to meet problems head-on.

We can't be sure of Solomon's age when he became king. According to 1 Kings 2:12 in the Septuagint (the Greek translation of the Hebrew Bible, dating back to the second or third century BC), Solomon was a mere *twelve years old* when he became king. This seems rather young for a man who already had a one-year-old son at the time (compare 2 Chronicles 9:30 with 1 Kings 14:21). Many scholars don't speculate on his age at all, though some put Solomon at age twenty (or even somewhat older) at the time.

One source reminds us that even though Solomon refers to himself in 1 Kings 3:7 as "a little child," his actions in 1 Kings 2 fit someone who is older than twelve.[4]

Regardless of his precise age, it's hard to believe that any young adult could grasp the intricacies of statecraft—and in particular, do so to the satisfaction of people in a culture that prized the wisdom of the "elders." But we must remember that young Solomon was undoubtedly well instructed by his illustrious father, King David.

The greatest demonstration of Solomon's early wisdom was his deep awareness that he still had much to learn. He was not your typical brash, know-it-all young leader. Solomon knew he was inadequate to such a great leadership challenge. So he went to the city of Gibeon, north of Jerusalem, and offered sacrifices to God. That night God appeared to him in a dream and said, "Ask for whatever you want me to give you."

In reply, Solomon thanked God for his kindness and said, "Now, O LORD my God, you have made your servant king in place of my father David. But I am only a little child and do not know how to carry out my duties. Your servant is here among the people you have chosen, a great people, too numerous to count or number. So give your servant a discerning heart to govern your people and to distinguish between right and wrong. For who is able to govern this great people of yours?" (1 Kings 3:4-9).

In Solomon's vision and his conversation with God, we see the secret of his success: he had an insatiable hunger for wisdom. God was pleased with young Solomon because he had asked for wisdom and discernment. God said:

> Since you have asked for this and not for long life or wealth for yourself, nor have asked for the death of your enemies but for discernment in administering justice, I will do what you have asked. I will give you a wise and discerning heart, so that there will never have been anyone like you, nor will there ever be. Moreover, I will give you what you have not asked for—both riches and honor—so that in your lifetime you will have no equal among kings. And if you walk in my ways and obey my statutes and commands as David your father did, I will give you a long life (vv. 11-14).

Solomon then woke up and realized that this conversation had taken place in a dream. All of Solomon's marvelous accomplishments occurred after this encounter with God.

All genuine success begins with a vision.

‖ PEACE AND PROSPERITY ‖

Under Solomon's leadership, Israel became a nation of immense wealth and power. He established a standing army that included a force of fourteen hundred chariots and twelve thousand horse soldiers (1 Kings 10:26). The once-embattled nation, which had fought off invasions by the Philistines and other tribes for centuries, now controlled all the territory west of the Euphrates River.

One of Solomon's military fortresses was the hilltop town of Megiddo, which overlooked the Jezreel Valley and guarded the highway that ran along the Mediterranean coastal plain from Egypt in the south to Damascus in the north. Archaeologists have uncovered fortified city walls, palaces, administrative buildings, storehouses, barracks, a sophisticated water system, and stables to accommodate 450 horses, plus garages for Solomon's battle chariots.[5]

Solomon established colonies throughout his empire to protect Israel's military and commercial interests in the region. He established trade with nations near and far. As a result, he enjoyed peace along his borders throughout his long tenure as king.

He formed an alliance with Hiram, the Phoenician king of Tyre, a seaport city-state on the Mediterranean coast. The Phoenicians were expert shipbuilders and sailors. The Israelites had no maritime skills. Solomon looked to Hiram to supply what his own people lacked, and Hiram became an essential ally in converting the once-landlocked nation of Israel into a seafaring empire.

With Hiram's assistance, Solomon established seaports at Elath and Ezion Geber on the gulf (known as Eilat, or Aqaba) east of the Sinai Peninsula. The gulf opens into the Red Sea. From there Solomon could send his merchant fleet southward to East Africa and eastward to Persia, and perhaps even to India and beyond. Israel's merchant ships brought enormous wealth back to the land.

The first voyage of Solomon's merchant fleet returned from the fabled land of Ophir with immense wealth—about sixteen tons of gold. Later voyages returned with more gold, plus silver, ivory, and rare exotic animals. Solomon also collected tribute from neighboring nations, totaling about twenty-five tons of gold per year, as well as tax revenue from the merchants and traders who came from distant lands (1 Kings 9:26-28; 10:14, 15; 2 Chronicles 8:17, 18; 9:21).

Solomon understood how societies become successful, how wealth is created through specialized production and trade, and how international alliances and trading partnerships benefit everyone. The principles he used to turn Israel into a peaceful, prosperous empire are the same principles that lead to peace and prosperity today. When a leader follows these principles of leadership, there are no limits to what he can achieve.

‖ SOLOMON'S GREATEST ACHIEVEMENT ‖

The vast influx of wealth enabled Israel to finance numerous construction projects. In the center of Jerusalem, Solomon built a palace out of massive cedar beams from Lebanon. He constructed a great hall of justice, from which he dispensed his famed legal wisdom. He built a palace for his wife, Pharaoh's daughter. Other construction projects during Solomon's tenure included the defensive terraces and fortified walls of Jerusalem; the fortress cities in the plains and deserts—Hazor, Megiddo, Gezer, Lower Beth Horon, Baalath, and Tadmor; and a series of cisterns and pools used to irrigate Jerusalem's wooded gardens (1 Kings 7:1-8; 9:15-19; Ecclesiastes 2:6).

But the most famous symbol of Solomon's success was the great temple in Jerusalem.

Solomon's father, King David, had dreamed of such a temple as a permanent house for the ark of the covenant, the centerpiece of Israel's religious devotion. Solomon began building the temple in the fourth year of his reign (1 Kings 6:1). This was an amazing leadership challenge for one so young.

Before Solomon could begin construction, he first had to make sure that Israel was militarily strong, secure, and at peace. So he spent his first four years as king—the same length of time as a U.S. president's first term—preparing the nation for its greatest challenge, the building of the temple. He created military alliances and trade partnerships so that he could import the materials needed for the temple's construction. He led Israel into a new era of unparalleled prosperity and productivity. At the end of that four-year period, he began building his masterpiece.

The temple was constructed of stone and imported cedar. The stone was painstakingly measured, cut, and exactingly finished at the quarry. When the stone was transported to the temple, it was fitted into place without the use of any hammer, chisel, or iron tool. The temple interior was paneled with intricately carved cedar. The inner sanctuary was overlaid with pure gold. Artists carved statues of angels and images of trees and flowers. The entire structure took seven years to build; read all the details in 1 Kings 6.

When the project was completed, Solomon experienced a second vision, much like the vision he had experienced at Gibeon. Again God spoke to him: "I have consecrated this temple, which you have built, by putting my Name there forever. My eyes and my heart will always be there" (9:3). God then commanded Solomon to lead the nation with integrity, obeying his laws.

Solomon's success began with the vision at Gibeon. His success was confirmed by a second vision, in which God gave Solomon's temple his divine stamp of approval and blessing—a statement that said, in effect, "Solomon, you are a success in my eyes. I approve of your achievements. I take full ownership of the temple you have built, and I am pleased to put my Name on it."

Solomon accepted the leadership role not to serve himself but to serve God and the people of his nation. He served with humility and a desire to do what is right. At the beginning of his tenure, he asked God to give him a gift—not long life or wealth or power over his enemies, but the gift of wisdom. That was the secret of his success. The *wisdom* of Solomon produced the *success* of Solomon.

|| THE SEVEN SIDES OF LEADERSHIP ||

Leadership has been one of the themes of my life since I was a boy. Over my five-decade career in professional sports and corporate management, I have identified seven principles that form the essence of leadership. I call them the Seven Sides of Leadership. King Solomon possessed all seven sides of leadership in abundance.

1. Vision

Solomon envisioned a bright future for Israel—a future of expansion, commerce, and prosperity. Not only did he have great vision, he was able to mobilize the nation and turn that vision into a shining reality.

2. Communication skills

Solomon was a man who could think deeply, then communicate his thoughts in persuasive, inspiring language. Great leaders can move people to action through the power of words alone.

3. People skills

Solomon motivated and empowered people to work together toward a common goal. He crossed barriers of culture and language to form alliances with King Hiram and the leaders of other nations.

4. Good character

Most of Solomon's writings deal with matters of character. Solomon's exemplary character enabled him to gain the trust and support of his people so that he could accomplish great things.

5. Competence

Solomon was a learned and accomplished leader. When he removed disloyal advisers and solidified his leadership team, he demonstrated from the outset that he was competent to lead.

6. Boldness

Solomon enacted a bold vision for transforming the nation. He undertook audacious construction projects. He established trade with many nations and formed a merchant fleet to boldly expand Israel's reach across the seas.

7. Servanthood

A great leader is a servant, not just a boss. (Throughout this book, we'll use the word *boss*—for lack of a better term—to indicate a person who has authority over people but isn't a true leader.) Solomon didn't seek to advance himself or be served by others. He saw himself as a servant of God and of his people. His servant's heart was probably the single most important aspect of his greatness as a leader.

Solomon not only exemplified these seven qualities of great leaders but also wrote about them in the books of Proverbs and Ecclesiastes.

We will examine everything Solomon had to say about leaders and leadership, and we will discover how Solomon achieved such astonishing success as a leader. Most important of all, we'll learn how to apply Solomon's leadership lessons to our own leadership styles.

Throughout the four decades during which King Solomon led Israel, his kingdom increased in size, power, and prosperity. By the time of his death, Israel had become an empire stretching north and east to the Euphrates River and southward to Egypt. Solomon's fleets plied the waters of distant seas. He commanded mighty armies and maintained secure and peaceful borders. Rulers from around the world paid him honor and tribute.

Solomon succeeded like no other leader in history. And the key to his success was his wisdom.

GET WISDOM, GET UNDERSTANDING
QUESTIONS FOR PERSONAL REFLECTION OR GROUP DISCUSSION

1 || Do you agree with the characterization of Solomon as "the most successful leader in history"? Why or why not?

2 || Is there another leader you consider as successful as Solomon? If so, who? What accomplishments do you point to as support for your choice?

3 || How do you define success for your own life? What would success look like to you?

4 || Early in his leadership career, Solomon went to the city of Gibeon and had a dream in which God offered him anything he asked. Solomon asked only for wisdom. That vision was a turning point in Solomon's life as a leader. Have you ever had a dramatic turning point in your leadership experience? If so, describe it and note how that experience changed your life. If not, what could you do to dynamically refocus your leadership role?

5 || The centerpiece of Solomon's leadership career was the construction of the great temple in Jerusalem. Do you have a single great goal that could be the masterpiece of your career? What steps are you taking today to turn that dream into a reality?

6 || Of the Seven Sides of Leadership (p. 18), which traits do you consider to be your strengths? Which are your weaknesses?

7 || What steps can you take to become more complete and well-rounded as a leader?

8 || If you're studying with group members who know one another well enough, talk about the strengths you see in each other, referring to the Seven Sides of Leadership.

INTRODUCING THE WISEST
LEADER IN HISTORY

Who was the wisest leader in American history? I would nominate our sixteenth president, Abraham Lincoln. He held the Union together, ended human slavery in America, and guided our nation through the most perilous war in its history.

President Lincoln reminds me of many leaders from biblical history. He was a liberator like Moses and a warrior like Joshua. But above all, he was a man of deep wisdom like Solomon. Lincoln was keenly aware of his inadequacy for the challenge of leading America through the crisis of the Civil War. He once said, "I have been driven to my knees over and over again because I have nowhere else to go."[1]

Nineteenth-century lecturer James F. Murdock recalled a time when he stayed in the White House for three weeks in the summer of 1861 as a guest of President Lincoln. One night Mr. Murdock was tossing and turning, suffering from insomnia, when he heard a low voice from down the hall. He got up to investigate and found himself at the door of a private room. The door was ajar, and Murdock could see the president kneeling before an open window.

"Oh, Thou God that heard Solomon in the night when he prayed for wisdom, hear me," Lincoln prayed. "I cannot lead this people; I cannot guide the affairs of this nation without Thy help. I am poor and weak and sinful. Oh, God, Who didst hear Solomon when he cried for wisdom, hear me and save this nation."[2]

Like Solomon, Lincoln prayed for an extra measure of wisdom so that he could be a wise leader of his war-torn nation. History shows that Lincoln's prayer, like Solomon's, was answered.

Because Solomon prayed for wisdom, he became the most successful leader in history. Under his leadership, Israel embarked on a golden age. The biblical account tells us that Solomon's prayer was answered in still more amazing ways. His wisdom and insight were "as measureless as the sand on the seashore . . . greater than the wisdom of all the men of the East, and greater than all the wisdom of Egypt." Solomon "spoke three thousand proverbs and his songs numbered a thousand and five. He described plant life, from the cedar of Lebanon to the hyssop that grows out of walls." Word of his wisdom spread throughout the known world, so that people from all nations came to hear his wise words (1 Kings 4:29-34).

Many people mistakenly think that wisdom is simply a by-product of getting older. Nothing could be further from the truth. I've known many young people who were wise beyond their years—and I've known some very old people who were as foolish as children. Advice columnist Abigail Van Buren said, "Wisdom doesn't automatically come with old age. Nothing does—except wrinkles. It's true, some wines improve with age. But only if the grapes were good in the first place."[3]

Solomon, remember, was a young man when he became king of Israel. Nevertheless, he was wise enough to ask God for even greater wisdom. The wisest people are those who know their own limitations. They are wise enough not to deceive themselves into thinking they are wiser than they are. That is the wisdom of Solomon—and of men like Abraham Lincoln.

True wisdom begins with an attitude of humility.

‖ THE FIRST TEST OF SOLOMON'S WISDOM ‖

The first test of Solomon's wisdom took place soon after the death of his father, David—and it occurred *immediately* after Solomon, in his vision, had asked God for the gift of wisdom. The chronology is crucial. Solomon asked God for wisdom, God granted Solomon's request for wisdom, and almost instantly Solomon's wisdom was tested and displayed for the whole nation to see.

Solomon's wisdom was demonstrated by a legal dispute, a child custody case. In ancient Israel, the king was the living personification of the law, so Solomon's leadership role required him to settle legal disputes.

Two prostitutes who lived as roommates came to Solomon's court with a dispute over a baby. The two women had given birth three days apart. One said, in effect, "During the night, this woman rolled over on her baby and smothered him. Then she got up while I slept and stole my baby."

The other woman told a contradictory story—the living baby was hers, the dead baby belonged to her roommate. Since the science of DNA testing was thirty centuries in the future, Solomon had no physical evidence to go by. So he used psychology to settle the case.

"Bring me a sword," he said. When his servants had brought the sword to him, he said, "Cut the living child in two and give half to one and half to the other."

One woman said, "Neither I nor you shall have him. Cut him in two!"

The other said, "Please, my lord, give her the living baby! Don't kill him!"

Solomon had his answer. He had proven who was the true mother and who was the liar. He gave the baby to the woman who demonstrated genuine love for the child (1 Kings 3:16-28).

Solomon approached the problem like a chess game: "If I do *this,* she will do *that.* If I threaten the baby with a sword, the real mother will seek to protect the child." Solomon had to peer into the future and anticipate the actions of both women. Leadership often requires that we do more than simply *react* to circumstances; leaders must sometimes provoke a crisis and see how *others* react.

This was more than a mere child custody case. The much-beloved King David had recently died. The people of Israel mourned their late king and wondered whether Solomon was up to the task. Would he be as wise and fair as King David? Solomon's career as king depended on the decisions he made at the outset.

Young Solomon's ruling was announced throughout Israel—and the people were in awe of his wisdom. Now they could be sure that

King Solomon possessed the wisdom to firmly and fairly administer justice in the land. His reputation for wise leadership spread and laid the foundation for all of Israel's future success and splendor.

A reputation for wisdom is leadership capital that a wise leader can spend to achieve great things. People will follow a wise leader. They will trust his decisions. They will buy into his vision for the future.

|| HIS WISDOM TOOK HER BREATH AWAY ||

Years passed. Under Solomon's leadership Israel built new cities, including fortress cities along the main trade routes. Solomon built his merchant fleet and sent it on trade missions to distant lands. Gold and other precious cargoes poured into Israel by the ton. Solomon built his masterpiece, the temple of Jerusalem.

The fame of Solomon and tales of his wisdom spread to distant lands. Copies of his writings—Proverbs, Ecclesiastes, and Song of Songs—may well have circulated beyond the borders of Israel. Word of Solomon's achievements spread wherever Israel's merchant ships put into port.

Tales of Solomon's deeds reached the land of Sheba, on the southernmost tip of the Arabian Peninsula, where Yemen is today. Sheba was rich in mineral wealth, spices, and agricultural goods. The kingdom of Sheba sent trade caravans throughout the known world. When the queen of this rich land heard of the wisdom and success of King Solomon, she had to meet this man and see whether the reality of Solomon matched the incredible legend.

Riding at the head of a trade caravan, the Queen of Sheba made the difficult journey from the southern tip of the Arabian Peninsula to Jerusalem—a distance of more than twelve hundred miles (as the crow flies). It was "a very great caravan—with camels carrying spices, large quantities of gold, and precious stones" (1 Kings 10:2). The Queen of Sheba came bearing gifts of inestimable value.

King Solomon received her and "answered all her questions; nothing was too hard for the king to explain to her" (v. 3). Some suggest that the Queen of Sheba posed riddles to Solomon to test his wisdom. But I don't believe her questions were riddles. As I read the accounts of the queen's visit (vv. 1-13; 2 Chronicles 9:1-12), I see a woman seeking answers to the troubling questions of her life. She traveled a great distance for those answers—and Solomon gave them to her.

When the Queen of Sheba had plumbed the depths of Solomon's wisdom and beheld the splendor of the temple and the nation of Israel, she was overwhelmed. The original Hebrew language tells us that there was no more *ruach* (literally, "spirit" or "breath"[4]) left in her. The wisdom and success of Solomon took her breath away!

The reality of Solomon *exceeded* the legend. The queen exclaimed, "I did not believe these things until I came and saw with my own eyes. Indeed, not even half was told me; in wisdom and wealth you have far exceeded the report I heard" (1 Kings 10:7). And she went on to praise Solomon's God.

The Queen of Sheba gave King Solomon more than four tons of gold, plus costly spices and precious stones. In turn, Solomon gave *even greater* gifts to the queen. Was Solomon simply being generous when he gave the queen more than she gave him? No. I believe Solomon was employing a wise leadership strategy. If the queen had given the greater gift, then Solomon and Israel would have been indebted to her. Solomon's generosity to the queen kept Israel in the dominant position in this international relationship.

‖ THE AUTHOR OF WISDOM LITERATURE ‖

Solomon was a prolific author of wisdom literature (1 Kings 4:32). Proverbs 1:1 gives us the title and author of that book: "The proverbs of Solomon son of David, king of Israel." Ecclesiastes 1:1 opens that book similarly: "The words of the Teacher, son of David, king in Jerusalem." Song of Songs 1:1 also begins with a statement of Solomon's authorship: "Solomon's Song of Songs."

The book of Proverbs is a collection of life teachings with a fatherly tone; many of the wise sayings and principles in that book are addressed to "my son." The book of Ecclesiastes is more philosophical in tone and reflects a somber sense of life's brevity and the futility of striving after things that do not last. Both Proverbs and (to a lesser degree) Ecclesiastes contain profound advice for leaders who seek to follow in Solomon's footsteps. The Song of Songs is a poem of romantic love, with allegorical overtones.

I'm grateful that Solomon recorded these profound nuggets of wisdom that still apply to our lives in this Internet age. Genuine wisdom is timeless—and always timely, essential to effective leadership. Solomon concluded, "The quiet words of the wise are more to be heeded than the shouts of a ruler of fools. Wisdom is better than weapons of war" (Ecclesiastes 9:17, 18). In the remaining chapters of this book, we will explore the leadership wisdom found in Proverbs and Ecclesiastes. I challenge you to read a chapter a day for the next month.

In the ancient Scripture texts, Solomon left a manual for leadership greatness. These are not bland, meaningless, fortune-cookie proverbs but time-honored principles for becoming a wise, effective, successful leader. Meditate on Solomon's leadership principles and put them into action, and you will be able to lead your company, your military unit, your nonprofit organization, your religious organization, your church, or your family to a "golden age" of success.

‖ A WORD OF WARNING ‖

But before we move on to Solomon's leadership principles, a final word of warning is in order. The story of Solomon does not end on a happy note.

As was often the case in that ancient Middle Eastern culture, Solomon was married to many women from foreign cultures—seven hundred wives in all, plus three hundred concubines. The biblical account explains that these wives led him astray: "As Solomon grew old, his wives turned his heart after other gods, and his heart was not fully devoted to the LORD his God, as the heart of David his father had been. He followed Ashtoreth the goddess of the Sidonians, and Molech the detestable god of the Ammonites. So Solomon did evil in the eyes of the LORD; he did not follow the LORD completely, as David his father had done" (1 Kings 11:4-6).

Another Old Testament book confirms this diagnosis of Solomon's failure of wisdom and leadership at the close of his life: "Was it not because of marriages like these that Solomon king of Israel sinned?

Among the many nations there was no king like him. He was loved by his God, and God made him king over all Israel, but even he was led into sin by foreign women" (Nehemiah 13:26).

Tragically, in his old age Solomon departed from his former faith—and yes, he departed from the wisdom he himself set forth in Proverbs and Ecclesiastes. He knew what wisdom was. He literally wrote the book on it! He had seen the prosperity and splendor that wisdom had brought into his own life and into the national life of Israel. Yet he turned away from wisdom.

Near the end of his life, enemies rose up against him. Rebels took up arms against him. Though Solomon remained in control of his kingdom until the end of his days, the kingdom was troubled. Soon after his death, Israel split in half. The glory of Israel's golden age passed into history and never returned.

———————————

The success of Solomon is instructive—but the failure of Solomon may well be *more* instructive. The lesson of his life is clear: Listen to wisdom. Learn it. Apply it. Meditate on it. And above all, never let go of it. Wisdom is the key to success, and its rejection leads to failure.

GET WISDOM, GET UNDERSTANDING
QUESTIONS FOR PERSONAL REFLECTION OR GROUP DISCUSSION

1 || The author nominates Abraham Lincoln as the wisest leader in American history. Who personifies wisdom to you? A public figure? A personal friend or mentor? Explain your answer.

2 || Solomon's wisdom was "as measureless as the sand on the seashore." It was displayed through his writings (proverbs and songs), his understanding of the natural realm (plant and animal life), and his international influence as a statesman (the kings of the world had heard of his wisdom). Solomon

was a "Renaissance man" whose curiosity and insight knew no bounds. He didn't confine himself to the study of politics alone. He was a scientist, a philosopher, and a poet, as well as a leader. How does the broad range of Solomon's interests challenge and inspire you? What steps can you take to become a more well-rounded individual, seeking wisdom in various fields and interests?

3 || Can you imagine being in Solomon's shoes regarding the child custody case? Think about how he must have anticipated each woman's reaction. Does this story give you any new insights into your own everyday leadership experience? Have you ever had to solve a leadership problem by trying to anticipate how others would react? How did that situation turn out?

4 || What can you learn from Solomon's wise solution to the case of the quarreling mothers?

5 || The Queen of Sheba traveled twelve hundred miles to find out whether the tales of Solomon's wisdom were true. Imagine that you are the Queen of Sheba. What questions would you like to ask Solomon? What are the great unanswered questions that disturb you? Do you think Solomon would have the answers? Why or why not? Do you think the answers exist? What are you doing to seek wisdom so that you can know the answers to those questions?

6 || After a lifetime of triumph and achievement, Solomon defected from his faith and from wisdom. What lessons do you derive from the sad ending of Solomon's story? What safeguards can you take to ensure that you will finish strong?

"I, WISDOM"

|| Proverbs 8:15-18 ||

Frederick II was King of Prussia from 1740 to 1786. He became known as an "enlightened despot," a ruler who used his dictatorial powers for the good of his people. He improved the efficiency of the Prussian bureaucracy, promoted religious tolerance, and supported the work of artists and philosophers. With a reputation for wise judgment, he endeared himself to the people and became known as Frederick the Great.

One day as he toured a prison in Berlin, scores of prisoners shouted to him, protesting that they were innocent and wrongly imprisoned. They all knew that this man had the power to pardon them and set them free.

As the king passed by, he noticed one man sitting in the corner, strangely silent. Intrigued, Frederick singled the man out and said, "You there. Why are you here?"

"Armed robbery, Your Majesty."

"And are you guilty?"

"Yes, indeed, Your Majesty. I entirely deserve my punishment."

Frederick called to the prison guard. "Release this guilty wretch at once," he said. "I will not have him kept in this prison where he will corrupt all the fine innocent people who occupy it."[1]

Frederick's response to those guilty men—the many who denied their guilt and the one who confessed it—reminds me of the wisdom of Solomon. Frederick's wisdom was like a sword slashing away deception, cutting to the bone of truth, exposing reality.

Solomon is not only our role model but also our leadership mentor. The theme of Solomon's first law of leadership, as recorded in Proverbs 8:15-18, is clear: *Listen to the voice of wisdom.*

‖ WISDOM SPEAKS TO LEADERS ‖

Solomon spoke of wisdom as a lady with a pleasant voice who calls to us: "Does not wisdom call out? Does not understanding raise her voice? On the heights along the way, where the paths meet, she takes her stand; beside the gates leading into the city, at the entrances, she cries aloud: 'To you, O men, I call out; I raise my voice to all mankind'" (vv. 1-4).

What does wisdom say to us as leaders? She has a special message for those in positions of influence and authority. I like the way *The Message* paraphrase expresses the meaning of verses 15-18. Wisdom says to us: "With my help, leaders rule, and lawmakers legislate fairly; with my help, governors govern, along with all in legitimate authority. I love those who love me; those who look for me find me. Wealth and Glory accompany me—also substantial Honor and a Good Name."

You may be thinking, *I'm not a king, a ruler, a prince, or a noble.* All right, you're not royalty. But you're a leader, aren't you? You may be a CEO or a middle-level manager, a general or a sergeant, a committee chairman or the head of a family. You have a leadership role in some arena of your life, or you wouldn't be reading this book. Whatever your leadership role may be, listen to the voice of wisdom.

Leaders cannot envision the future, communicate their vision, and inspire their followers until they have first heard the voice of wisdom. Lawmakers cannot make fair and just laws unless those laws are aligned with the principles of wisdom. Presidents, prime ministers, governors, CEOs, board chairmen, coaches, pastors, military officers, and parents cannot make high-quality leadership decisions without listening to wisdom.

Authority without wisdom is dictatorship. A leader who rejects wisdom is simply a poor boss—and he will drag his people into failure, scandal, and disgrace. The leadership landscape is littered with the remains of leaders who rejected wisdom. All leaders would do well to remember the tragedies of the past: Watergate, the Keating Five, Ivan Boesky, Marion Barry, the Lewinsky scandal, Adelphia Communications, Enron, Tyco International, Fannie Mae, Freddie Mac, AIG, and on and on.

Those who refuse to heed the voice of wisdom are doomed to failure. But those who seek wisdom will find her—and with her, they will find honor, prosperity, and a good reputation.

Do you have to be smart to be wise? Not at all. Some of the smartest, savviest, cleverest, most knowledgeable people in the world are completely devoid of wisdom. And some of the simplest, most humble, and uneducated people in the world are truly wise. If wisdom corresponded to intelligence, you could give people a WQ test and score their "wisdom quotient" the same way you score their IQs. Bookstores could sell how-to-become-wise books with titles like *Wisdom for Dummies*.

Being *smart* and being *wise* are two very different things. In fact, sometimes intelligence and education get in the way of genuine wisdom.

In the 1980s, Harvard Business School established a new academic chair, the Chair on Ethics. Many in the media praised Harvard for addressing the problem of corruption in American business. But after a few years, graduates of the Harvard course complained that they were not being taught how to make wise, ethical decisions based on right and wrong. Rather, they were being taught how to avoid getting caught. It was not an ethics course. It was a course in pragmatism and public relations.

Charles Colson, the former Watergate conspirator who became an author and crusader for faith and prison reform, wrote an editorial about the Harvard course. He observed that it might be impossible to teach ethics at Harvard, because ethics are based on wisdom—a fundamental understanding of what is right and what is wrong. He concluded, "Harvard's philosophical relativism precluded the teaching of real ethics. No wonder the best they could offer was a course in pragmatics."[2]

Not long after Colson's views appeared in print, the Harvard Business School surprised him by inviting him to speak at the school as part of its Distinguished Lecturer series. Colson accepted, expecting to be booed or shouted down. But the students were attentive and polite. At the end of his talk, Colson invited questions from the audience and expected a tough grilling. Instead, he received a few bland comments and no questions. When he asked why no one questioned his views, one student replied that he and his fellow students didn't know the right questions to ask. They had never been exposed to ethics before. They had no foundation in matters of wisdom.[3]

You cannot take Wisdom 101 at any university in the world. Yet wisdom is essential to effective leadership. If you're going to be an effective leader, you must learn to hear the voice of wisdom.

‖ SEEKING WISDOM ‖

Where do you go to listen to the voice of wisdom? Here are some practical ways to seek wisdom and make her your friend for life.

Become a sponge for wisdom.

Cultivate a thirst for wise sayings, especially from the Bible's wisdom literature. Start a file of articles and quotations that speak of wisdom, and keep them in a file drawer or on your computer for ready reference. Post wisdom proverbs on the wall in your bedroom, bathroom, kitchen, office, and on the dashboard of your car. Meditate on those words and soak up all the wisdom you can absorb.

Memorize wisdom.

Memorization is an excellent mental discipline. By locking wise sayings into your brain, you'll always have a reservoir of wisdom to dip into whenever you face an ethical dilemma. The ability to store up nuggets of wisdom that can be dispensed at just the right moment is a key leadership skill.

Seek out wise counsel.

Great leaders usually have wise mentors, a circle of wise counselors to give advice, provide a reality check, and hold them accountable to keep their commitments. Wise leaders hunger for constructive criticism more than praise because criticism instructs; praise does not.

When someone asks you a question, never bluff.

Admit candidly that you don't know—then go find the answer. Give credit to those who add to your knowledge.

When crises arise, don't panic.

Get the facts so you can act wisely. Never let people or circumstances stampede you into hasty and ill-considered action. Face every problem squarely, gather as many facts as you can, think it through, and then act decisively.

Embrace change.

A leader who embraces the status quo is not leading at all—he's resting on his laurels. A leader's job is to move an organization forward, encourage innovation, and manage change. When change is on the horizon, consider with kindness and humility how others will be affected. Consult your advisers and your own moral compass. Then embrace change confidently.

The search for leadership wisdom is a lifelong quest. Make it a relentless quest. Solomon calls us to seek wisdom every day of our lives. Wisdom points the way to leadership success, saying, "I, wisdom, dwell together with prudence; I possess knowledge and discretion" (Proverbs 8:12).

What is the voice of wisdom saying to you today?

GET WISDOM, GET UNDERSTANDING
QUESTIONS FOR PERSONAL REFLECTION OR GROUP DISCUSSION

1 || In Proverbs 8, Solomon personified wisdom as a lady who calls to us in a sweet and gentle voice. Can you think of a time when wisdom seemed to speak to you in a voice (the voice of your conscience, the voice of a friend or counselor, the voice of God)? What happened?

2 || Describe your leadership role. What are the toughest challenges and burdens of your leadership role? What are the hardest decisions you face?

3 || How does this image of wisdom offer insight into ways to face your challenges and decisions? How does it help you to imagine, as you face these leadership problems, that wisdom is speaking to you and advising you?

4 || Have you ever known someone who was extremely wise without possessing a high IQ or being well educated? What traits or behaviors do you recall about that person that stand out to you as evidence of genuine wisdom?

5 || Look through the list of practical suggestions for seeking wisdom on page 33. In which of those areas are you the strongest? Why?

6 || When it comes to hearing the voice of wisdom, what are your weak areas? Do you lack mentors and counselors to advise you and hold you accountable? Do you have a problem treating subordinates kindly or sharing credit? Do you struggle with keeping your composure under stressful conditions? What steps can you take to become a better listener to the voice of wisdom? Identify at least two or three suggestions you could implement right now to seek wisdom in a more intentional way.

7 || Is there an area of your life where wisdom is speaking to you and trying to get your attention? Have you closed your ears? What attitude or habit holds you back from doing what wisdom pleads with you to do?

TWO

WHO'S FOLLOWING?

‖ Proverbs 14:28 ‖

In 1803, President Thomas Jefferson sent Meriwether Lewis and William Clark, along with thirty soldiers and frontiersmen, to explore the recently acquired Louisiana Purchase. Their mission was to map the Missouri River and seek a waterway to the Pacific Ocean. In June 1805, the expedition reached a fork in the river. Which way should they go, left or right? Which was the true course of the Missouri River?

Lewis and Clark were convinced that the left fork was the true Missouri, but all the other men believed it was the right fork. The two leaders argued their case, but their followers—every man without exception—remained unconvinced. Yet the men had such respect for the leadership of Lewis and Clark that (as Meriwether Lewis later recorded) they said "very cheerfully that they were ready to follow us [anywhere] we thought proper to direct but that they still thought that the other was the river."[1] Later, when it turned out that Lewis and Clark were right, these men were glad that they trusted their leaders instead of their own instincts.

Isn't that amazing? The followers *unanimously* thought the leaders were wrong, yet they were willing to follow Lewis and Clark wherever they led. Lewis and Clark were leaders—not because they could *force* others to carry out their will but because their men were willing to follow them anywhere, right or wrong.

Solomon wrote, "The mark of a good leader is loyal followers; leadership is nothing without a following" (Proverbs 14:28, *The Message*). As someone once said, "If you think you're leading and no one is following, you're just out for a walk."

|| THE MEASURE OF A LEADER ||

You might say, "I run a taut ship. I say, 'Jump!' and my people say, 'How high?'" But are they really followers? And are you truly their leader?

If you give orders and people obey them, then you're at least a boss. You have authority, and you use that authority to get things done. But a boss is not necessarily a leader, and the people you boss around are not necessarily followers.

A leader needs to understand from the start that followers don't have to follow your leadership. Real followers willingly place themselves under your authority so that they can learn from you and emulate you. But they are also free to reject your leadership. You can't demand that people follow your leadership. You have to earn your following.

High-caliber leadership attracts high-caliber followers—and dysfunctional followers indicate dysfunctional leadership. Organizations tend to take on the personality of their leaders. Those leaders who demonstrate integrity, commitment, and an intense work ethic are likely to inspire those same qualities in their followers. But if an organization is dispirited and riddled with laziness and corruption, it is probably a reflection of the leader. The way you measure yourself as a leader is by measuring the people you lead.

Captain Queeg was at the helm of the minesweeper USS *Caine* in the novel *The Caine Mutiny* by Herman Wouk. Captain Queeg (portrayed by Humphrey Bogart in the 1954 film version) was not a likable man. He had a number of eccentric habits—such as compulsively clacking metal balls in his hand. When he made a mistake, he shifted the blame to subordinates. Soon his men were talking behind his back and ridiculing him. Captain Queeg's crisis of leadership occurred when the ship was caught in a typhoon and nearly sank.

Queeg's subordinates, who never trusted his leadership, mutinied and relieved him of command.

All leaders face the same challenge that confronted Captain Queeg. We must earn the following of our subordinates every day. We can't demand that people follow us; we must *inspire* their loyalty. If we fail to earn their followership, we risk a breakdown of command in times of crisis.

‖ THE QUALITY OF YOUR FOLLOWERS ‖

General W. L. "Bill" Creech, former commander of Tactical Air Command, once said, "The first duty of a leader is to create more leaders."[2] Listen to the general. If you want to be an effective leader, you must raise up *more* leaders. You must inspire, motivate, and train your followers to become effective leaders in their own right.

We see this principle in the life of Solomon. In 1 Kings 4:1-21 (*The Message*), we read, "King Solomon was off to a good start ruling Israel. These were the leaders in his government . . ." The text goes on to name his secretaries, the priests, the royal historian, the commander of the army, and so forth. Then we read, "Solomon had twelve regional managers distributed throughout Israel. They were responsible for supplying provisions for the king and his administration." And the text names the various regional managers and their areas of responsibility.

Finally, we read, "Judah and Israel were densely populated—like sand on an ocean beach!" Despite Israel's vast population, no one went hungry. Solomon organized the government so that there was strong, effective leadership at every level, in every village and town. Solomon's followers were also leaders. By entrusting power and authority to his followers down the line, Solomon made sure the people received what they needed. The text tells us, "All their needs were met; they ate and drank and were happy. Solomon was sovereign over all the kingdoms from the River Euphrates in the east to the country of the Philistines in the west, all the way to the border of Egypt."

One of my mentors, Fred Smith Sr., was vice president of operations for the Gruen Watch Company, a consultant to Mobil and

Caterpillar, and a leading Dallas-based food broker. He once wrote, "A leader is not a person who can do the work better than his team; he is a person who can get his team to do the work better than he can."[3] That's the kind of leader Solomon was.

Question: How can you get your followers to do the work of the organization better than you can?

Answer: By training them and empowering them to be leaders. Make sure your organization is bursting at the seams with leadership ability.

Advertising executive David Ogilvy has been called the Father of Advertising. He once said, "I admire people who hire subordinates who are good enough to succeed them. I pity people who are so insecure that they feel compelled to hire inferiors as their subordinates."[4] Recruit people with leadership potential. Look within your ranks and promote those who have the capability to achieve even greater things than you can. Train your followers to become leaders, and they will take your organization to unimaginable heights.

‖ A FOLLOWER'S POINT OF VIEW ‖

Learn to see leadership from a different perspective; that is, from a *follower's* point of view. Ask yourself: "What are my followers and subordinates thinking? What questions are they asking? What questions are they *afraid* to ask?"

Let me suggest some questions your followers and subordinates would like to ask you—if they dared.

"What does the leader expect from me?"

Followers want to know what they should and shouldn't do. They want to know what actions will make them successful in your organization—and what actions will get them into trouble. As leaders, we need to provide clarity.

"How much authority do I have to make decisions?"

Followers want to know if their decisions will be reversed or, worse, punished. Learn to let your followers make decisions (including *wrong* decisions), tolerate their mistakes, and treat their errors as learning experiences—not failures.

"Will you help me when I have problems or questions?"

Followers want to know if you have an open-door policy or a closed-door policy. My advice: take the door off the hinges. Make sure your followers know you welcome their questions. You won't solve their problems for them, but you'll gladly point them in the right direction.

"How will I know how I'm doing?"

Followers want your feedback on their performance. Give them regular feedback, both informally ("Good job!") and formally (a regular performance review). Don't leave your followers wondering where they stand. Praise in public; correct in private.

"How will I benefit?"

Followers want to know they are an essential part of the overall effort of the organization. They want to know how they will be rewarded when the organization succeeds, when the team meets its goals, when the shared vision is finally realized. Make sure every follower feels invested—and knows that the investment of time, energy, and sweat will pay big dividends.

In October 2009, the Orlando Magic hosted a luncheon featuring Dan Cathy, president of the Chick-fil-A restaurant chain and son of Truett Cathy, the company's eighty-eight-year-old founder. Also at the luncheon was Ross Cathy, the twenty-eight-year-old grandson of Truett Cathy. I asked Ross to name his grandfather's most important leadership skill.

"My grandfather has always known when to lead and when to back off," Ross said. "As a result, he allowed his people to have significance in the company and to feel that they were an integral part of the Chick-fil-A team."

"Why should I follow this leader?"

Do you inspire them with your personal charisma? motivate them with your stirring speeches? or terrorize them into obedience with strict rules and angry demeanor?

Let me suggest a better way to get followers to follow you: show them you care. If your followers know you care about them, that you're interested in their success, that you see them as human beings and not just cogs in a machine, they will not only follow you; they will lift you on their shoulders and carry you around.

Several years ago I spoke on the phone with Seth Greenberg, the men's basketball coach at Virginia Tech. I asked him, "How do you get players to play hard for you every night?"

He replied, "That's not very complicated. If they know you care about them as people, they'll play hard for you."

┠━━━━━━━━━┨

In *Be a People Person,* John C. Maxwell relates a story about Ralph Waldo Emerson, the nineteenth-century poet. Emerson lived on a farm by Walden Pond, not far from the home of his friend, Henry David Thoreau. One day Emerson and his son were struggling with a strong-willed calf, trying to drag her into the barn. Emerson and his son were soaked in sweat, and the poet was running out of patience.

Just then a servant girl came by, saw Emerson's predicament, and offered to help. Emerson didn't see how she could succeed where he and his son had failed, but he let go of the calf, told his son to do the same, and invited the girl to try.

The girl thrust her index finger into the calf's mouth. To the calf, the girl's finger seemed exactly like that maternal appendage from which she received nourishment. Emerson and his son had tried to force the calf into the barn by sheer muscle power. The servant girl simply showed the calf a gesture of caring—and the calf followed her contentedly into the barn.[5]

The servant girl was a leader. Why? Because she had a follower. King Solomon's question for you and me is simply this: Who is following you?

GET WISDOM, GET UNDERSTANDING
QUESTIONS FOR PERSONAL REFLECTION OR GROUP DISCUSSION

1 || Why do your subordinates follow your leadership? Is it because they admire you? trust you? are inspired by you? want to be like you? fear you? Or for some other reason? Explain your answer.

2 || Organizations tend to take on the personality of their leaders. What do your followers tell you about the way you lead? about your leadership strengths? about your leadership weaknesses?

3 || Do you tend to recruit inferior talent to your organization so that your subordinates won't make you look bad? Or do you recruit people whose talents and abilities exceed your own? Explain your answer and cite an example, if possible.

4 || If you were laid up in the hospital for three months, could your followers run your organization without you? Have you empowered them to make decisions in your absence? Explain your answer.

5 || List three reasons (positive qualities you possess or actions you exhibit) why your subordinates should follow you.

6 || What is one thing you've been prompted to do to become a more inspiring leader—the kind of leader people want to follow? What changes do you need to make in your life in order for that to happen?

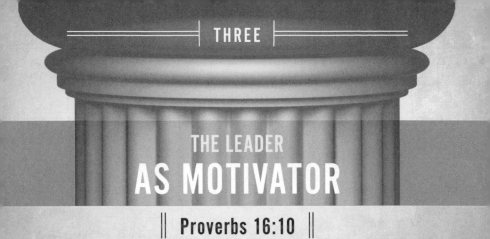

THREE

THE LEADER
AS MOTIVATOR

|| Proverbs 16:10 ||

On September 1, 1939, Nazi Germany invaded Poland, triggering World War II. Great Britain declared war on Germany two days later, yet the British prime minister, Neville Chamberlain, did little to back up the declaration with action. From the fall of 1939 through the winter and spring of 1940, the British government engaged in what came to be known as the Phoney War, or the Sitting War (*der Sitzkrieg*).

In early May 1940, Germany invaded Norway and prepared to attack France. Realizing that his diplomatic attempts to restrain Adolf Hitler's ambitions had failed, Chamberlain resigned as prime minister. On May 10, Winston Churchill was chosen to serve as prime minister of an all-party government.

At the time, Britain's foreign secretary, Lord Halifax, and much of the British public favored a negotiated peace with Hitler. But Churchill believed Hitler could not be trusted to keep his word. So he utilized his leadership ability to galvanize public opinion against a negotiated peace with Nazi Germany. In his speeches, Churchill prepared the British people for a long and difficult war.

Three days after taking office, he stood before the House of Commons and said, "We are in the preliminary stage of one of the greatest battles in history. . . . I have nothing to offer but blood, toil, tears, and sweat. We have before us an ordeal of the most grievous kind. We have before us many, many long months of struggle and suffering. . . . You ask, what is our aim? I can answer in one word: Victory. Victory at all costs—victory in spite of terror—victory, however long and hard the road may be, for without victory there is no survival."[1]

Winston Churchill was a great leader in large part because he was a great motivator. Leaders are people who accomplish great things by motivating their followers to work hard, sacrifice, and achieve great goals. Solomon said, "A good leader motivates, doesn't mislead, doesn't exploit" (Proverbs 16:10, *The Message*). Wise leaders do not lie, manipulate, or take advantage of the people they lead. Rather, they inspire their followers to work together to achieve grand visionary goals.

We may define *motivation* as the activation of goal-oriented behavior in either an individual or a group. There are two essential forms of motivation: extrinsic motivation and intrinsic motivation. Extrinsic motivation is triggered by external rewards—such as the desire for money, the desire for recognition, the desire for pleasure, and the fear of punishment.

But Winston Churchill's speech above includes no extrinsic motivation, no promise of reward. Rather, he summoned the intrinsic motivation of his hearers—motivation rooted in character, values, and the qualities of the soul. He appealed to the intrinsic qualities of the British people—to their love of country, their courage, and their moral outrage toward Adolf Hitler. Instead of offering money, recognition, or pleasure, Churchill offered hardship and toil—and the people responded. Though outnumbered and outgunned, the British people stood firm throughout the Battle of Britain. And they won.

‖ MOTIVATION VERSUS MANIPULATION ‖

The people of Israel were *unanimous* in their amazement over the wisdom of their leader Solomon. After the death of King David, the people had wondered if young Solomon would be a good and just king like his father. But due to Solomon's wise ruling, all their doubts about him vanished.

That was a crucial moment in the life of Israel—and in the

leadership career of Solomon. He envisioned an economic boom, a time of expansion of trade routes across land and sea, which would produce unparalleled prosperity. To do this, Solomon knew he would need to increase Israel's military preparedness. He needed to energize and motivate the people of Israel to launch an ambitious program of construction, trade, and military production. He needed a motivated workforce to put all these plans into action.

He also knew the difference between motivation and manipulation. He said, "A good leader motivates, doesn't mislead, doesn't exploit." Author and speaker Zig Ziglar explains the difference between motivation and manipulation this way: "The word *motivation* is often confused with *manipulation*. Motivation occurs when you persuade others to take an action in their own best interests. . . . Manipulation is persuading others to take an action that is primarily for your benefit. . . . Leadership occurs when you persuade a person to take an action that is in your mutual best interests" (emphasis added).[2]

‖ THE FIRE WITHIN ‖

The best way to motivate people is to get to know them as individuals. Find out who they are, where they come from, what they care about, what their values are, what they believe in, what they hope to achieve in their lives. As you get to know your followers, you will quickly discover that no two people are alike. What motivates one person may not motivate another. Your goal is to find out what makes people tick, so that what benefits you and the organization also benefits each follower individually.

Bob Nelson, PhD, is an expert on employee motivation and the author of *1001 Ways to Reward Employees*. He writes, "You get the best effort from others not by lighting a fire beneath them, but by building a fire within them."[3]

It's all about how to reach the inner core of an individual and ignite his or her intrinsic motivation. While extrinsic factors—money, awards, recognition—can motivate people, the most powerful motivators of all are deep inside people. We all want our lives to have meaning and purpose. We all want to be part of a cause that is larger than ourselves. We all want to be personally connected to a community that does good works. That is the intrinsic motivation leaders must tap into.

A leader's *vision* can be a powerful intrinsic motivator. Solomon inspired his people with his vision of a great temple in Jerusalem—and his vision connected with the deep religious reverence of every Israelite. Solomon's vision motivated the people to persevere for seven years in the construction of that temple. Give your followers an inspiring vision that will help them see how their efforts are valuable and meaningful. When people know *why* they are doing something, they will be motivated to do it well.

A leader's *cause* can also be a powerful motivator. Solomon inspired his people by constantly reminding them that they served a great cause—the cause of God himself. As you lead your team or organization, make sure your people understand that the work they do has meaning, that their efforts will impact lives. If you coach a basketball team, your players are not merely trying to win games—they are putting on an exciting show for the fans and making people happy. If you are the CEO of a retail chain, your people are not just stocking shelves and running cash registers—they are providing products and services that improve the lives of people in the community. If you are a director of nurses at a hospital, your subordinates are not just dispensing meds, taking temperatures, and emptying bedpans—they are ministering to the health needs of the sick and injured.

There is no honest work in this world that doesn't serve some noble cause. Would you want to live in a world without janitors and trash collectors? When people see their work as part of a larger and more meaningful cause, they will be motivated to do it well and with all their energy.

Finally, a leader's *actions* can be a powerful motivator. Leadership consultant John Baldoni explains: "Motivation is purely and simply a leadership behavior. It stems from wanting to do what is right for people as well as for the organization. If we consider leadership to be an action, motivation, too, is an active process. And if you go deep enough, motivation itself is driven by a series of actions grouped under three headings: energize, encourage, and exhort."[4]

Baldoni goes on to say that, as leaders, we *energize* our followers by setting a good example, by continually communicating the vision, and by challenging our followers to unleash their creativity in pursuit of that vision. We *encourage* our followers by empowering them (giving them permission and authority to utilize their talent and decision-making ability), coaching them (teaching them how to achieve personal and organizational goals), and recognizing them (letting them know their contributions are valued). And we *exhort* them by calling them to set aside personal ambition for the sake of the collective goal and by inspiring them with a sense of mission and purpose.

Vince Lombardi was probably the greatest football coach who ever lived—and one of the most effective motivators in any field of endeavor. He found a way to motivate his players, both extrinsically and intrinsically, to achieve greatness. That is how he achieved a miracle in Green Bay, Wisconsin, transforming the perpetually losing Packers into perennial champions. He once said, "Coaches who can outline plays on the blackboard are a dime a dozen. The ones who succeed are those who can get inside their players and motivate them."[5]

Henry Jordan, who played right defensive tackle for Lombardi's Packers from 1959 to 1969, said, "I play for the love of the game, the love of the money—and the fear of Lombardi."[6] Another time Jordan declared, "When he says, 'Sit down,' I don't look for a chair."[7]

A fat NFL paycheck and fear of the coach's wrath are both forms of extrinsic motivation. But Vince Lombardi also knew now to "get inside" his players and motivate them through the love of the game, the joy of competition, the appeal to values and character, and pride in a job performed with skill and excellence.

If you want to truly motivate your followers, heed the example of great leaders like Solomon, Churchill, and Lombardi. Tap into the intrinsic motivation of your people and light the fire within them.

GET WISDOM, GET UNDERSTANDING
QUESTIONS FOR PERSONAL REFLECTION OR GROUP DISCUSSION

1 || Solomon tells us, "A good leader motivates, doesn't mislead, doesn't exploit." How do people respond to your motivational leadership? Tell about a time that you led by motivating your followers.

2 || What gets you fired up and motivated? Extrinsic motivation (external rewards)? Or intrinsic motivation (appealing to your character and your values)? Cite an example from your own personal experience.

3 || How do the results of intrinsic motivation differ from the results of extrinsic motivation?

4 || Tell about a time that you, as a leader, were able to intrinsically motivate your followers in your home, at school, in the workplace, in your church, in the military, or anyplace else you can think of.

5 || Tell about a time when a leader, in trying to motivate you, made you feel manipulated. What was the result of that experience?

6 || How would you go about motivating your followers without manipulating them?

7 || Think of the three followers in your organization you feel closest to. How well do you know them? Do you know what fires them up and what they care most deeply about? Do you know the names of those followers' spouses and

children? Do you know what sports teams they root for? Do you know how they spend their leisure time?

8 || If you know these facts about those followers, how do you think it should help you more effectively motivate them?

FOUR

THE LEADER'S
MORAL FOUNDATION
|| Proverbs 16:12 ||

Dietrich Bonhoeffer was a theologian in Berlin in the 1930s, during the rise of Adolf Hitler and the Nazi party. In 1934, Bonhoeffer and other courageous church leaders founded an informal fellowship called the Confessing Church. Their goal was to oppose Nazism and anti-Semitism in Germany. When the state police closed the Berlin seminary where Bonhoeffer taught, he traveled secretly from town to town, organizing opposition against the Nazis.

Following Germany's invasion of Poland in 1939, Dietrich Bonhoeffer joined Operation Seven, a secret society that smuggled German Jews to Switzerland. After an intense moral struggle, he joined a plot to assassinate Hitler. A devout pacifist, Bonhoeffer's conscience revolted against the thought of taking another man's life—even the life of Adolf Hitler. Yet he became convinced that the death of Hitler would spare millions of innocent lives.

In April 1943, the gestapo arrested Bonhoeffer for his involvement with Operation Seven—but the gestapo had not yet learned of the plot against Hitler. On July 20, 1944, German army colonel Claus von Stauffenberg—a secret member of the resistance—placed a suitcase bomb in a briefing room at Hitler's Wolf's Lair fortress. The bomb exploded, killing four—but Hitler escaped with only minor injuries. Von Stauffenberg was arrested and executed, and Bonhoeffer's role in the plot was discovered.

Bonhoeffer ended up at the Flossenbürg concentration camp, where he was hanged on April 9, 1945, just three weeks before the end of the war in Europe. He was thirty-nine. He lived and died as a role model of moral leadership.

Solomon wrote, "Good leaders abhor wrongdoing of all kinds; sound leadership has a moral foundation" (Proverbs 16:12, *The Message*). The *NIV* calls it a "righteous foundation."

|| A FAILURE OF MORAL LEADERSHIP ||

President Dwight David Eisenhower echoed those words of Solomon when he spoke about the importance of moral leadership. "I believe deeply that every occupant of the White House . . . has one profound duty to the nation: to exert moral leadership. The President of the United States should stand, visible and uncompromising, for what is right and decent—in government, in the business community, in the private lives of the citizens. For decency is one of the main pillars of a sound civilization. An immoral nation invites its own ruin."[1]

Former Secretary of the Navy John H. Dalton once addressed a class of U.S. Naval Academy plebes at the U.S. Holocaust Museum in Washington, D.C. In his speech Dalton pointed out that General Eisenhower, who was Supreme Commander of the Allied Forces in Europe during World War II, provided one of the strongest examples of moral leadership. He ordered every U.S. soldier in theater to tour the concentration camps so that they would realize the moral obligation they have to stand against the horrors that had been committed there.

Dalton went on to point out that the Holocaust itself was the result of a failure of moral leadership. He said, "Hitler and the Nazis came to power over the course of a decade," not overnight. When German military leaders were asked why they allowed the slaughter to take place, they replied, "I was just following orders." That, said Dalton, is not an excuse for any member of the American military.

He concluded, "If your gut is telling you that the people around you, whom you respect, are doing something that is not right, you must have the moral courage to act! To be a moral leader you must at times make lonely, unpopular decisions—you must never compromise absolutes."[2]

A leader must know right from wrong, then commit to doing only what is right. But how can we know what is right? After all, we live in a pluralistic society where the teaching of absolute moral values has been replaced by individual preference and situation ethics. In his book *Burden of Truth*, Charles Colson laments the decline of moral decision making, especially among our youth:

> The result can be summed up in the words of one student, who described an ethics course by saying, "I learned there was no such thing as right or wrong, just good or bad arguments." No wonder surveys show more kids than ever are cheating, lying, and sleeping around. . . . Character education has begun to emerge as a countermovement. This approach to teaching ethics is . . . based on the conviction that virtues exist that children ought to know and ought to practice . . . a basic list: things like honesty, courage, and respect for others.[3]

Even though we live in a pluralistic society, we have to acknowledge that our Western culture was built on a foundation of Judeo-Christian values. Central to those values is an ancient document that not only is part of the Jewish and Christian Scriptures but also is the moral bedrock on which our laws and society are founded: the Ten Commandments.

THE TEN COMMANDMENTS—OR THE TEN OPINIONS?

The Ten Commandments form a basic moral code that will enable any leader to tell right from wrong in almost any situation. Some readers may not believe in God. But we can't look at the source of Solomon's wisdom without clearly outlining this code as *his* code.

If you need a refresher on the Ten Commandments, turn to Exodus 20:1-17. Here are a few takeaways from that passage for moral leaders:

- *Moral leaders understand that God alone is God. He makes the rules and is worthy of respect.*
- *Moral leaders respect their followers' need for rest. It's immoral to exploit your people and work them to the point of exhaustion.*
- *Respect for others begins in the home. If you can't show respect to your own father and mother, then you probably will not respect others either. Respect is a basic moral requirement.*
- *Moral leaders not only refuse to commit murder but also refuse to harm other people in ways such as character assassination.*
- *Moral leaders build clear boundary lines around their lives and behavior and do not place themselves in a compromising position.*
- *Moral leaders do not steal by cutting corners on their taxes, padding expense accounts, or overcharging a client.*
- *Moral leaders deal honestly with employees and don't lie about competitors in order to gain some advantage.*
- *Moral leaders respect the marriage and family relationships of others, as well as their possessions. There is nothing immoral about wanting to advance your career, but moral leaders are content with what they have earned.*

It is possible to use the Ten Commandments as a common foundation for a set of shared moral values, even in a pluralistic society. It makes no sense to pretend that these commandments are no longer relevant simply because there are some people in our culture who do not subscribe to Judaism or Christianity. You do not have to adhere to any particular religion to respect the moral foundation of the Ten Commandments. In fact, if you don't respect the Ten Commandments, you cannot call yourself a moral leader. If what we call the Ten Commandments are nothing more than the Ten Opinions, then moral leadership becomes an impossibility.

|| BUILD ON A FIRM FOUNDATION ||

A moral leader is a role model for everyone in the organization. By your example, you teach your followers how to treat each other, how to treat your customers, and even how to treat you—the leader—with proper respect.

When your people see you "walk the talk," they will be inspired to emulate your moral leadership. They will make better decisions, rooted in moral principles, because they will learn moral decision making from you. Nothing undermines respect for leadership more quickly than a leader's hypocrisy. And nothing cements respect for leadership more firmly than a leader's integrity.

In February 2006, my son Bobby and I attended the NBA All-Star Weekend in Houston. The day before the opening events, we left our hotel to take a jog. On our way back we noticed a crowd of TV reporters in front of an office building on the next block. Reaching the corner, we saw a man and woman emerge from the crowd, heading toward us. I recognized the man.

"Bobby," I said, "that's Ken Lay." It was indeed the infamous former CEO of Enron. He was two weeks into a widely publicized federal trial, having been charged with securities fraud and other crimes. I had read his story, and I knew he was the son of a Baptist minister and claimed to live by Christian moral principles. Yet here he was, caught up in one of the biggest corporate scandals in history.

As the couple stepped onto the curb beside us, I extended my hand and said, "Mr. Lay, I'm Pat Williams with the Orlando Magic."

He shook my hand and introduced his wife, Linda. We chatted briefly, avoiding the topic of his trial. Then I said, "I just want you to know we're praying for you."

He seemed surprised, then said, "I appreciate that."

His wife added proudly, "And I'm standing with him all the way."

Then we parted.

"Dad," Bobby said as we continued on to our hotel, "he's really a nice guy."

And he was. I wondered to myself, *What went wrong?* Was he innocent? Was he guilty? Had he been duped? Did he give in to the arrogance of power and greed?

Ken Lay had been a friend and confidant to presidents. In 2001, he urged his employees to buy Enron stock, while he unloaded much of his. When the company collapsed like a house of cards, billions of dollars in pension funds and investor holdings disappeared overnight. Ken Lay still had his millions—but Enron employees who trusted his advice were wiped out. The evidence against him seemed insurmountable.

I did pray for Ken Lay during his trial. I was rooting for him, hoping he would produce the evidence that would prove himself innocent. That evidence never came. On May 25, the jury found him guilty of defrauding employees and investors. Sentencing was scheduled for October 23, but on July 5, he suffered a fatal heart attack.

I accept the jurors' verdict. I don't know where Ken Lay went wrong, but I do know that, somewhere along the line, he must have abandoned his moral and ethical foundation. And I also know I don't want that to ever happen to me—or to you.

Solomon told us, "Good leaders abhor wrongdoing of all kinds; sound leadership has a moral foundation." Heed the tragic lesson of Ken Lay, and listen to the words of Solomon. Be a leader who stands firmly on a solid moral foundation.

GET WISDOM, GET UNDERSTANDING
QUESTIONS FOR PERSONAL REFLECTION OR GROUP DISCUSSION

1 || Recall a time in your childhood or adolescence or young adulthood when you were pressured to do something you knew was wrong, but it would have cost you a great deal to do the right thing. What decision did you make? Did your decision solidify your character as a leader? Why or why not?

2 || Note a time when you faced a tough moral decision in a leadership role in your adult life. Looking back, do you feel you made a moral and ethical decision? Or do you regret your decision?

3 || What factors influenced the decision you made? Pressure from other people? Financial pressure? Time pressure? Stress and exhaustion? Good advice from other people? A character flaw? Or some other factor?

4 || How did that decision make you feel? What was the effect (for good or ill) of that decision?

5 || Do you agree that the Ten Commandments can serve as a basic moral code for making ethical decisions—regardless of one's religious beliefs or cultural orientation? Explain your answer.

6 || Which of the Ten Commandments (Exodus 20:1-17) has been the most difficult to obey in your leadership roles? Why?

FIVE

TRUTH, INC.

|| Proverbs 16:13 ||

I n *The Leadership Secrets of Colin Powell,* Oren Harari describes a leadership tool that General Colin Powell devised as chairman of the Joint Chiefs of Staff. It was simply called "The Phone." It was a private line that went straight to Powell's office, and only a few trusted advisers—the general's inner circle—had the number. These advisers were scattered across the military establishment, and they became his eyes and ears. They did not have to go through a receptionist to reach him. They could call him at any time, bringing him unedited, undistorted truth.

No one was allowed to answer the phone except General Powell. His aides and secretary were forbidden to touch it. If one of Powell's advisers called in and no one answered after three rings, the adviser was instructed to hang up and call later. By enforcing these rules, the general made sure that no one came between him and the flow of unfiltered information.

General Powell knew that one of the most dangerous and stubborn problems of any high office is that powerful leaders tend to become isolated and insulated from important information. Often a leader's direct subordinates become yes-men, devoted to keeping the boss happy instead of giving him accurate (and sometimes unpleasant) information. Powell did not want to be shielded from the truth, and that's why he installed The Phone.[1]

Throughout his leadership career General Powell demanded candor from his subordinates. He maintained open lines of communication. As Oren Harari remarked, Powell's ultimate goal was "to inspire people in the organization not just to *voice* problems, but also to figure out ways to *solve* problems."[2] That's why General Powell advocated what he called "a noisy system" and "a clash of ideas."[3] This is how an effective leader gets to the truth of any matter.

General Powell said, "The day soldiers stop bringing you their problems is the day you have stopped leading them. They have either lost confidence that you can help them or concluded that you do not care. Either case is a failure of leadership."[4]

Solomon observed, "Good leaders cultivate honest speech; they love advisors who tell them the truth" (Proverbs 16:13, *The Message*).

|| EXPOSING ELEPHANTS ||

Great leaders speak the truth and expect the truth from others. Leaders need clear channels of communication between themselves and their followers. If a leader does not get accurate, high-quality information from the front lines, he cannot make high-quality decisions.

In our turbulent, Internet-speed age, problems arise quickly and demand immediate, unflinching decisions. Leaders in every arena— the business sector, the healthcare sector, the government, the military, education, and religion—face critical challenges every day. They cannot make sound decisions if the information they receive is restricted or distorted.

The more candor and honesty there is in a team or organization, the more healthy and responsive it will be. Unfortunately, many teams and organizations (like many families) are afflicted by a phenomenon called "the elephant in the room."

The "elephant" is any issue that is so big and scary that people (though aware of it) are afraid to speak about it openly. So a leader's job often includes exposing elephants, creating an environment of openness, where everyone can freely express opinions, warn about problems, and disclose potentially unwelcome information without fear of reprisal.

Like families, teams and organizations can become unhealthy and dysfunctional when there are elephants in the room. (And it's rare to find an organization that doesn't have at least one or two of these pachyderms lurking in the shadows.) Let's face it: the truth makes people uncomfortable. Even when you invite your subordinates to speak freely, many hold back. You need to find ways to gain their trust and get them to open up.

When you invite candor and openness from your subordinates, put them at ease. Be aware of your body language and facial expressions. If you say "Speak freely. I really want to hear what you have the say," but your tone of voice is gruff, your arms are folded defensively, and your face is scowling, don't expect much candor.

Some leaders pay lip service to openness and candor, but when push comes to shove, they really don't take bad news very well. Few leaders enjoy hearing "Sir, you made a mistake" or "Ma'am, we have a serious problem." But the most effective leaders are those who welcome bad news as an opportunity to exercise leadership and solve problems. They care more about doing the right thing than they do about looking good. They derive their sense of satisfaction from the success of the entire organization, not from having their egos stroked.

|| TRUTH LEADS TO TRUST ||

In July 2009, the *Sporting News* ranked Pat Summitt, the head women's basketball coach at the University of Tennessee, as one of the fifty greatest coaches of all time in all sports, both collegiate and professional. Not only was she the only woman to make the list; she was ranked eleventh, right after legendary Notre Dame football coach Knute Rockne.

In her 1999 book *Reach for the Summit,* Coach Summitt wrote about the importance of encouraging your followers to speak candidly. She says, "People who say yes to you all the time are, in my opinion, insulting you. They assume you are either too immature or unstable or egotistical to handle the truth. . . . The absolute heart of loyalty is to value those people who tell you the truth, not just those people who tell you what you want to hear. In fact, you should value them most. Because they have paid you the compliment of leveling with you and assuming you can handle it."[5]

How do you build the kind of trusting relationship that will enable your people to tell you the truth? It all begins with you. The leader creates the culture of the organization. You provide an environment of candor and openness when you exemplify truthfulness in your dealings with your followers. When they know that you care enough to level with them, they will level with you.

Mike Holmgren has coached football at every level—high school, college, and the NFL. He won a Super Bowl ring as head coach of the Green Bay Packers and was also the longtime coach of the Seattle Seahawks. In *Winning the NFL Way*, sports agent Bob LaMonte wrote these words about Mike:

> You'll never meet a more straightforward guy. Everyone knows he'll always be truthful with them, and he often says, "Look, if you ask me a question, make sure you want to know the answer." One thing is certain—he will let you know where you stand with him. Sometimes you might not like the answer he gives you, but he'll be honest with you. I've never known him to tell a lie. For instance, if a player says, "Coach, why aren't I starting?" he'll give him specific reasons. If a player asks why he got cut, he'll tell him exactly why. He doesn't mince words. He doesn't do it in a harsh way, and it's not personal. The bottom line is that the players respect him because he will tell the truth.[6]

Holmgren once recruited a wide receiver to play for the Seahawks. Unfortunately, because this player felt his previous coach had lied to him, he also didn't trust Holmgren. Before he would agree to sign with the Seahawks, he wanted to make sure that Holmgren would always level with him.

"We want you here," Holmgren told him. "But you are not going to be a starter. We have two young players that we plan on giving every opportunity to be the starters. Now if one of them gets hurt, or he can't do it, then yes, absolutely, you'll get an opportunity to start.

But I'm not going to tell you what you want to hear so you'll sign." The player was so impressed by Holmgren's candor that he signed on and enjoyed a successful career with the Seahawks.

"My philosophy," Holmgren concluded, "is that honesty has to permeate your entire existence . . . because if you lose trust, you can't teach. You can't communicate. Your people won't listen to you and you'll never be able to get them to do what needs to be done."[7]

Solomon put it even more succinctly: "Good leaders cultivate honest speech; they love advisors who tell them the truth." If you are a CEO, your company should become known as Truth, Inc. If you manage a sports team, the word *TRUTH* should be block-lettered across the front of your jerseys. If you run for office, your campaign slogan should be "Nothing but the truth!"

Truth leads to trust. When your people know that you are candid with them, that you always tell them what they need to know, they will trust you. And when your people trust you as their leader, they will follow wherever you lead.

GET WISDOM, GET UNDERSTANDING
QUESTIONS FOR PERSONAL REFLECTION OR GROUP DISCUSSION

1 || Recall a time when someone's deception or withholding of the truth caused you significant harm. How did you feel when you discovered that you had been either lied to or shielded from the truth? What was the effect of that deception?

2 || Do you think there are ever any times when it is morally right and constructive to lie or withhold the truth? Explain your answer.

3 || General Colin Powell advocates what he calls "a noisy system" and "a clash of ideas." How have you cultivated that kind of system in your organization?

Or have you discouraged people from giving you bad news? Cite specific examples from your leadership experience.

4 || What is currently the biggest "elephant in the room" in your organization? Are you purposely, aggressively exposing elephants? Are you trying to get to the bottom of uncomfortable issues and unspoken problems? Or do you simply ignore problems and hope they'll go away? What steps do you need to take this week to take on the elephants in your organization?

5 || If you want people to be candid with you, you have to exemplify truth telling. Do you think your followers see you as a truth teller or not? Explain your answer. Cite examples.

6 || Do you trust your followers? Do your followers trust you? Why or why not? What can you actively do to improve the level of trust in your organization?

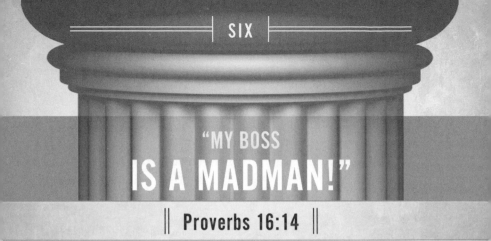

SIX

"MY BOSS IS A MADMAN!"

Proverbs 16:14

The corporate world knew him as Chainsaw Al. In the mid-1990s, Albert J. Dunlap was hired as CEO by the board of directors of the Scott Paper Company. One of his first official acts was to cut eleven thousand employees from the payroll. He engineered a merger between Scott and Kimberly-Clark that left thousands jobless—then collected a $100 million paycheck.

He wrote a book about his corporate exploits called *Mean Business: How I Save Bad Companies and Make Good Companies Great*. Dunlap's technique for saving companies was simple: he shut down factories, put people out of work, and saved the companies tons of money. In his book he proudly proclaimed himself "a superstar in my field" and contrasted himself against other corporate executives whom he considered "weak" and "addle-brained."[1]

Soon after *Mean Business* was published, Chainsaw Al accepted a position as CEO of Sunbeam, a home appliance manufacturer. The announcement of his hiring sent Sunbeam stock up sharply. Factories closed. Employees got the ax.

But when Al Dunlap tried to find a buyer for Sunbeam, as he had for Scott, he could find no takers. It quickly became clear that while he knew how to downsize a company, he didn't know how to run one. Over the next two years, he ran the company into the ground. At that point auditors discovered that Sunbeam had used fraudulent accounting practices to overstate its net income by $60 million. As the company filed for bankruptcy protection, the Securities and Exchange Commission filed suit against Dunlap and Sunbeam. So did the stockholders. Chainsaw Al settled with the plaintiffs and was disallowed from ever again serving as a director or officer of any publicly held company.[2]

Portfolio.com and CNBC.com named Dunlap one of the "Worst American CEOs of All Time." In Jean Lipman-Blumen's book *The Allure of Toxic Leaders,* she defined "toxic leaders" such as Chainsaw Al as those who "engage in numerous *destructive behaviors* and who exhibit certain *dysfunctional personal characteristics* . . . [which] inflict some reasonably serious and enduring harm on their followers and their organizations."[3]

This is precisely the sort of leader Solomon spoke of in Proverbs 16:14: "An intemperate leader wreaks havoc in lives; you're smart to stay clear of someone like that" (*The Message*). Here Solomon spoke from the perspective of the follower, not the leader. He addressed the question of toxic bosses and what to do about them.

|| FUNCTIONAL LEADERS VS. DYSFUNCTIONAL BOSSES ||

To be intemperate is to be excessive and unrestrained in one's passions, emotions, and selfish desires. The *NIV* renders Proverbs 16:14 this way: "A king's wrath is a messenger of death, but a wise man will appease it."

Toxic bosses certainly can be wrathful, and their poisonous passions can bring "death" to a career or to an entire organization. The most wrathful and intemperate leaders in modern history include men like Adolf Hitler, Josef Stalin, and Idi Amin. Their toxic leadership resulted in death on a genocidal scale.

Perhaps the best way to understand the kind of toxic leadership Solomon warns against is to contrast toxic, dysfunctional leadership with healthy, functional leadership. Great leaders are honest, candid, ethical, visionary, competent, confident, and skilled. They show more concern for the welfare of their followers and the organization than for their own egos.

Toxic or dysfunctional bosses are the opposite. They frequently act deceitfully and secretively, cut ethical corners, shift the blame to others to cover up for their own incompetence, and bully others to compensate for their own insecurities. They rarely have a grand vision for the organization, other than using its people to satisfy their self-centered egotism and greed. They have no compassion for people, but use and discard people as if they were things.

If you are suffering under the dysfunctional behavior of a toxic boss, you may be thinking, *My boss is a madman!* But there is a self-centered method to his or her madness. It is all about the toxic boss's ego and selfish wants. Toxic leaders are frequently narcissistic, vain, and intimidating. But many toxic leaders are actually charming and charismatic—and they use their personal charisma as a way of manipulating people and getting what they want. Some toxic leaders are very good at faking sincerity, yet their pattern of deception and manipulation eventually catches up to them.

Healthy, functional leaders encourage their followers to become leaders in their own right. Effective leadership empowers followers to unleash their own creativity and leadership skills. Toxic bosses are threatened by the creativity and abilities of others, so they tend to repress their subordinates. A toxic boss wants an army of robots to carry out orders and will usually punish those who think for themselves.

Toxic leadership has wrecked many American companies—Enron, Adelphia Communications, Tyco International, Fannie Mae, Freddie Mac, AIG—and brought enormous harm to employees, stockholders, and the economy as a whole. When we elect toxic leadership to the White House, the resulting political scandals (such as Watergate and the Lewinsky affair) can shake the foundations of our constitutional republic. Any organization with a toxic boss is an organization in peril. It may seem healthy on the outside, but there's a deadly cancer growing within.

Toxic bosses produce poisonous and dysfunctional environments. They practice deception and don't want to hear the truth. As a result, the flow of information is restricted. Problems proliferate—and no one has the courage to speak openly about them. Eventually, the dysfunctional atmosphere takes its toll on productivity, creativity, and morale. Talented people move away. Those who remain are dispirited and unhappy. The organization is crippled and begins to crumble from within.

‖ DEALING WITH A TOXIC BOSS ‖

Gerri Willis, a contributing columnist for CNN and *Money* magazine, offers five tips for dealing with toxic bosses.[4]

1. Identify the behavior.

Does your toxic boss insult you and berate you, either privately or in front of your coworkers? Does your boss engage in intimidation or sexual harassment? Does your boss unreasonably control you and try to thwart your advancement? Did you discover that your boss has been secretly sabotaging you or undermining your reputation? Is your boss frequently angry and out of control?

Be clear about the specific nature of the toxic boss's behavior and how that behavior directly affects you. Once you have clearly identified that behavior, you can articulate the problem—and you can take intelligent action.

2. Don't take it lying down.

No one has the right to treat you in an abusive way. "You can respond," Gerri Willis says. "Just remember to stay professional." For example, you can respectfully point out to your boss that calling you an idiot does not help you improve your performance.

If you find out that your boss is undermining your reputation with higher-ups in the company, you should gather the evidence, then present that evidence in a professional manner to the higher-ups. "If someone screams at you," Willis says, "don't be a doormat. If you've made a mistake, acknowledge it. But let your boss know that [he or she is] creating a difficult work environment."

Avoid complaining to coworkers about the problem. Adopt a positive attitude and professional behavior. Don't give your toxic boss an excuse to harm your career.

3. Take notes.

Document the destructive behavior of your toxic boss. Write down dates and times. Save e-mails and voice mails and other evidence of destructive behavior. Individually, this or that incident may seem like no big deal. But over time these incidents add up to a pattern. At some point your documentation of the problem may be the key to solving the problem, saving your career, and even saving the organization from destruction or scandal.

4. Know when it's too much.

Is your boss's behavior taking an unacceptable toll on your mind and body? Is your work environment so hostile and stressful that you are experiencing such symptoms as depression, high blood pressure, stomach ulcers, or nausea? Has your old sense of optimism and self-confidence been replaced by dread and anxiety?

No job is worth your stomach lining or a stroke. If you cannot resolve the problem of a toxic boss and the behavior of your boss is having a destructive impact on your life, then it may be time to get out. Remember the advice of Solomon: "You're smart to stay clear of someone like that."

5. Control your destiny.

If you leave the organization because of a toxic leader, be aware that you may have to explain to others why you left. When interviewing for a new job, do not bad-mouth your old boss. That prospective employer will likely view *you* as the troublemaker, and your chances of getting the job will be next to nil. Don't list your toxic boss as a reference; if possible, leave him completely off your résumé.

Above all, no matter what your toxic boss may do, make sure that all your behavior is ethical and above reproach. As Melissa Korn writes in *Fast Company,* "While dealing with your toxic boss, you have to make sure not to become a toxic employee."[5]

|| CAPTAIN OF THE *TITANIC* ||

After nearly ten years at Enron, Sherron Watkins became aware that she was working for a dysfunctional company. As vice president of corporate development, Sherron discovered that Enron had been transformed from an energy company into a massive Ponzi scheme, destined to collapse like a house of cards. So in August 2001, she wrote a seven-page memo, detailing everything she knew, and she sent that memo to her boss, CEO Kenneth Lay.

"I am incredibly nervous that we will implode in a wave of accounting scandals," she warned. She also confided her concerns to a friend at Arthur Andersen, Enron's accounting firm.[6] Sherron Watkins's warnings to Ken Lay went unheeded. She expected him to launch an investigation into the accounting irregularities, but nothing happened.

In fact, Ken Lay discussed Watkins's memo with other executives in the company, and their response was that they wanted to fire Sherron! They decided not to—but only because they feared she would file a lawsuit.

Three months after Watkins wrote that memo, her dire prediction came true. Enron did, in fact, implode in a wave of accounting scandals. By the time the dust settled, a number of top Enron executives either pleaded guilty or were convicted of crimes. Enron shareholders lost billions, and thousands of Enron employees lost their jobs and their pensions. The Arthur Andersen accounting firm was disgraced and closed its doors, with a resulting loss of eighty-five thousand jobs. The Enron debacle sent shockwaves through the economy.[7]

Michael Useem, management professor at Wharton Business School at the University of Pennsylvania, recalls hearing Sherron Watkins speak at a leadership seminar. She likened Ken Lay to the captain of the doomed luxury liner *Titanic*: "The ship has taken a hit in the bow and water is gushing in. The captain knows something is wrong, but he makes sure the band is still playing and the cocktail glasses are still full while his ship is going down."[8]

That is the epitaph of all intemperate, toxic bosses. Don't be a toxic leader. And if your boss is wreaking havoc in your life, take Solomon's advice and stay clear.

GET WISDOM, GET UNDERSTANDING
QUESTIONS FOR PERSONAL REFLECTION OR GROUP DISCUSSION

1 || Think of the meanest, most toxic boss (coach, drill sergeant, instructor, manager) you've ever had. You don't have to name that person, but explain how that boss affected your emotions. How did that boss affect your motivation and performance? your career?

2 || Do you see any toxic behavior in your own leadership style? What tendencies do you need to be aware of?

3 || What changes could you make to become a more temperate and constructive leader to your followers?

4 || In Proverbs 16:14, Solomon wrote from the point of view of a follower or subordinate. On a scale of 1 to 10, how good are you at empathizing with the point of view of your followers? Do you think you understand their feelings and thinking? Or would it be more accurate to say that you really don't care what they think and feel? Why or why not?

5 || What steps have you taken in your organization to encourage followers to become leaders in their own right?

6 || Do you have a toxic boss right now? How are you responding to that individual's distracted behavior? What steps have you already taken to respond to your toxic boss? Which of the five tips shared for dealing with a toxic boss (p. 67) will you act on this week?

SEVEN

"MY BOSS IS A PRINCE!"

‖ Proverbs 16:15 ‖

I n the summer of 1963, after playing two seasons of minor league baseball for the Philadelphia Phillies farm club in Miami, Florida, I prepared to drive to Indiana University to complete my masters in physical education. Before leaving I phoned my mother in Delaware and told her I would stop for a visit on the way.

Mom suggested a different plan. "Why don't you meet me in Washington, D.C.?"

"D.C.? Why there?"

"Have you heard about the March on Washington? Dr. Martin Luther King Jr. is giving a speech at the Lincoln Memorial."

My parents had been involved in social causes as far back as I can remember, and the civil rights movement was dear to Mom's heart. She had been a big fan of Dr. King's ever since the bus boycott in Montgomery, Alabama, eight years earlier.

So I met my mother and sister in D.C. As a young man in my twenties, I was far more interested in sports than in social justice. But I will always be grateful that my mother arranged for me to be present on that hot, humid, historic day when Dr. King addressed the vast crowd on the National Mall.

With my own ears, I heard him say, "I have a dream that one day this nation will rise up and live out the true meaning of its creed: 'We hold these truths to be self-evident, that all men are created equal.'"

I didn't fully appreciate the significance of that moment, that I was a witness to history. I was there when a truly great American leader shared his far-reaching vision with us all.

In Proverbs 16:15, Solomon described leaders who are authentic, positive, and visionary. He wrote, "Good-tempered leaders invigorate lives; they're like spring rain and sunshine" (*The Message*). He was describing leaders who inspire, energize, elevate, and motivate their followers. Lead like that and your followers will think you're a prince (or princess)!

|| THE SEVEN SIDES OF LEADERSHIP ||

On page 18 we looked at what I call the Seven Sides of Leadership. Let's examine these in more detail.

1. Vision

Dr. Jay Strack, founder of Student Leadership University, once defined leadership for me in this way: "A leader sees the invisible. Great leaders are always forward thinking—they look further down the road than anyone else. And leaders have wide-angle vision. They see the big picture." Leaders who envision the invisible inspire their followers to achieve the impossible.

King Solomon saw what Israel could become—a nation at peace, engaged in international commerce by land and sea, strong and prosperous. He envisioned a great temple in Jerusalem, the most beautiful structure ever designed, dedicated to the worship of God.

Throughout the Scriptures, leaders of vision (prophets) called the nation of Israel to transformation, reformation, and repentance. The prophets Ezekiel, Isaiah, and Jeremiah literally *saw visions* from God. These prophets announced their visions to the nation, called the people to turn back to God, and assured them of God's faithfulness.

2. Communication skills

What good is a vision if the leader cannot communicate it to his followers? Solomon communicated his vision to the people. *His* vision became *their* vision. Under his direction and leadership, the people of Israel turned Solomon's vision into a reality.

Another Old Testament figure, the prophet Habakkuk, received a vision from God—and God told him how to announce his vision to the people. In Habakkuk 2:2 God said, "Write this. Write what you see. Write it out in big block letters so that it can be read on the run" (*The Message*).

Announce your vision on a theater marquee or on the Goodyear blimp. Proclaim it with such clarity that even people rushing by can't miss it. Communicate your vision with impact—and your followers will catch your vision and make it come true.

3. People skills

A leader is a person who achieves goals and objectives through other people. In order to lead people, you must have people skills: the ability to listen, empathize, inspire, motivate, manage conflict, and build teams.

In 597 BC the Israelites were defeated by the Babylonians, exiled from their own land, and forced to serve the Babylonian Empire. After the Babylonians were defeated by King Cyrus of Persia in 538 BC, the Israelites were allowed to return to Jerusalem. They found their city in ruins, its walls destroyed. But Israel had two great leaders with people skills, Ezra and Nehemiah, who worked together to restore Jerusalem and revitalize the people.

Ezra took charge of the spiritual rebuilding of the people. He taught them the law of God and led the people in renewing their commitment to God's commandments. Nehemiah took the lead in the physical reconstruction of the city walls and the temple. He surveyed the ruined city by night and carefully planned each detail of its restoration. He organized the government and motivated people to begin rebuilding. These were tense times, and many conflicts broke out—yet Nehemiah repeatedly amazed his followers with his people skills. As a result, they responded, "We're with you. Let's get started" (Nehemiah 2:18, *The Message*).

Nehemiah broke the complex rebuilding project into manageable chunks, organized the people into family groups, and assigned tasks to each group. He put armed guards in place to protect the workers. He broke down barriers of class distinction so that the wealthy and the common people cooperated together. He set an example of personal sacrifice, taking far less than his share of the food and other goods. When people saw that Nehemiah was willing to share what little he had with them, they worked all the harder to complete the project on schedule. As a result, a project that could have taken years to complete was finished in only fifty-two days (Nehemiah 6:15). The swift completion of the project is a tribute to Nehemiah's people skills.

A few years ago, I had a conversation with Howard Schultz, the founder of the Starbucks Coffee empire. While owning three coffeehouses in 1987, Schultz purchased the Starbucks operation in Seattle and eventually expanded the chain to an empire of more than sixteen thousand stores in forty-nine countries. I asked him, "In a company of that size, where do leaders come from? How do you spot leadership talent in your organization?"

His answer was immediate: "People skills! In order to be a leader at Starbucks, you've got to have people skills. That's what our business is all about." Anyone with a strong will and a loud voice can be a boss. But it takes people skills to be a leader.

4. Good character

The first book of the Bible, Genesis, devotes more space to the story of Jacob's son Joseph than to any other person. The life of Joseph is a portrait of great leadership and excellent character. It's the story of how a young man rose to leadership on a world stage.

Joseph's jealous brothers sold him into slavery when he was seventeen. From then on, his life story reads like a series of character tests. The slave traders took him to Egypt and sold him to Potiphar, the captain of the guard of Pharaoh's court. Potiphar was so impressed with Joseph's integrity and business acumen that he promoted Joseph and placed him in charge of his household.

But Joseph found his character tested by sexual temptation. The wife of Joseph's employer repeatedly tried to seduce him. The account tells us, "And though she spoke to Joseph day after day, he refused to go to bed with her or even be with her" (Genesis 39:10). Finally, Potiphar's wife lied about Joseph and accused him of attempted rape—and Potiphar sent Joseph to prison for a crime he didn't commit.

In prison Joseph's character was tested again, but he continued to conduct himself as a leader. He endured mistreatment as a prisoner without complaint for thirteen years. He suffered incredible injustice, yet he never surrendered his character.

In the end Joseph's character was recognized by Pharaoh. The ruler of Egypt took Joseph out of prison and made him the second most powerful leader in the land—second only to Pharaoh himself.

5. Competence

Solomon's father, King David, was a soldier and statesman. When he was just a teenager who spent his days caring for sheep, David was anointed by the prophet Samuel as the future king of Israel, in a private ceremony at Bethlehem (1 Samuel 16:13). David did not actually ascend to the throne until years later, when King Saul died in battle and David was thirty years old (2 Samuel 5:3, 4). However, it is likely that his experiences as a shepherd—defending his sheep against predators, leading his sheep to the freshest watering holes and greenest pastures—helped prepare him to lead Israel.

I once had author and educator Allan Taylor as a guest on my Orlando radio show. During our interview, Allan said something about leadership that really struck me: "Shepherds ought to smell like sheep." In other words, you've got to lead up close, not from a distance. I believe that's one of the leadership lessons David learned as a young shepherd.

David also served an apprenticeship to King Saul. He was Saul's personal musician and poet, and Saul gave David a high rank in the army of Israel (1 Samuel 18:5). So David gained knowledge of the king's court while also gaining firsthand military knowledge. He demonstrated courage and strategic genius as a military leader, defeating the Philistines in a series of battles.

Only after David spent this lengthy apprenticeship, learning the ways of statesmanship and warfare, did he assume the mantle of leadership. Before David was ready to lead, he had to prove his competence to lead. When King Saul went insane with paranoid jealousy and tried to kill David, the young man went into exile as the leader of a band of outlaws. This too was a time of preparation and growth as David learned how to lead men in the wilderness.

Those who would lead must undergo training and firsthand experience to increase their leadership competence. Dr. J. Richard Chase, former president of Biola University, said, "If a leader demonstrates competency, genuine concern for others, and admirable character, people will follow him."[1]

6. Boldness

When the Israelites suffered as slaves in Egypt, Moses overcame his sense of personal inadequacy and stood boldly before Pharaoh. He repeatedly confronted the powerful ruler of Egypt and demanded that he set the Israelite people free. After God demonstrated his mighty power through multiple plagues, Pharaoh yielded to the demands of Moses.

At God's direction Moses boldly led his people out of Egypt. When Moses and the Israelites reached a seeming dead end, with the Red Sea before them and Pharaoh's pursuing army behind, Moses called on God to perform a miracle. The sea parted, and Moses boldly led his people across the dry seabed (Exodus 14).

Boldness is essential to leadership. Recently retired Florida State head football coach Bobby Bowden once told me, "The Bible teaches us to 'fear not.' That's a good starting point for any aspiring leader."

7. Servanthood

King Nebuchadnezzar of Babylon conquered Israel and plundered the temple in Jerusalem. The Babylonians took the best and brightest of Israel captive—"young men without any physical defect, handsome, showing aptitude for every kind of learning, well informed, quick to understand, and qualified to serve in the king's palace" (Daniel 1:4). One of these young men was Daniel.

Daniel was a defeated man from a defeated nation, forced to serve the king who had ransacked the temple of God. Yet Daniel was determined to live according to his principles, no matter what the circumstances might be. And his values required him to be a faithful servant to his master, even if his master was a tyrant and the conqueror of his own people.

When Nebuchadnezzar was troubled by disturbing dreams, Daniel served the king by interpreting those dreams. After Nebuchadnezzar died, Daniel was brought in to interpret the handwriting on the wall for King Belshazzar. He then served the Persian ruler Darius, who conquered Babylon. Darius appointed Daniel to be his own adviser.

Daniel served the Persian conqueror just as he had served his Babylonian masters—with fearless, honest integrity. Darius didn't always appreciate it; one day he became enraged with Daniel and threw him into a den of lions. The next morning, Darius found Daniel alive and unharmed, still giving honor to the God of Israel—and still willing to serve the king of Persia (6:19-28).

Few people today, whether in the business world, the sports arena, the religious sector, or the government, have had as many bad bosses as Daniel endured. Odds are, you've never had to contend with a boss who destroyed your country, ransacked your house of worship, or threw you to the lions. But Daniel did—and he remained faithful in service to his masters.

Daniel was a servant leader, a very different kind of leader from the tyrants and despots he had served. He is a role model for all who find themselves in a hostile work environment. And because Daniel was willing to be a servant, he rose to a position of great authority and leadership in the Persian Empire. The people must have said of him, "My boss is a prince!"

|| LEADERSHIP IS INFLUENCE ||

A leader is a person who achieves great goals through people. Some leaders may think they run a financial business, a retail store, or a widget factory; but in reality they are in the people business, whether they like it or not. The people you lead are watching you. They are taking their cues from you. They are observing your behavior, your attitude, and your character. If they are sold on you as a person of competence, confidence, and strong character, they will buy into your leadership. They will go through walls for you, just as the people of Israel were willing to do for their leader, King Solomon.

That is true leadership. Some leaders are remembered for building profitable corporations. Some leaders are remembered for building winning teams. Some leaders are remembered for building great nations. But the greatest leaders of all are remembered for their influence on others.

━━━━━━━

You will earn the right to be a leader by demonstrating the Seven Sides of Leadership. The good news is that each of the seven qualities is a learnable skill. We can actively practice our visionary skills, we can grow and improve in our communication skills and ability to work with people, we can commit ourselves to continual character growth, we can build our confidence and boldness through accepting challenges and new experiences, and we can daily choose an attitude of humble servanthood.

The leader who exemplifies the Seven Sides of Leadership in an ever-increasing way is destined to become an influential "prince" of a leader like Solomon describes in Proverbs 16:15—a leader who invigorates lives and whose very presence is "like spring rain and sunshine."

GET WISDOM, GET UNDERSTANDING
QUESTIONS FOR PERSONAL REFLECTION OR GROUP DISCUSSION

1 || Name a leader in your life who best fits the description found in Proverbs 16:15. How has that leader affected you? List specific aspects of your life that have been changed as a result of following that leader.

2 || The Seven Sides of Leadership are: vision, communication skills, people skills, good character, competence, boldness, and servanthood. Which two Sides of Leadership are your greatest leadership strengths? Why do you say that?

3 || Which two are your greatest weaknesses? Why? What steps can you take this week to improve in those two areas?

4 || Think about the two Sides of Leadership in which you need improvement. Name a leader (someone you know personally or someone famous) who strongly exemplifies those qualities. What lessons can you learn from that leader about how to become stronger and more effective in those two areas?

5 || Which of the biblical leaders named in this chapter would you most like to emulate—Solomon, Ezekiel, Isaiah, Jeremiah, Habakkuk, Ezra, Nehemiah, Joseph, David, Moses, or Daniel? Explain your answer. Which of their traits most stand out to you?

6 || How will it help you as a leader to be conscious of the fact that you're "in the people business"?

EIGHT

THE COMMUNICATOR
IN CHIEF

|| Proverbs 17:7 ||

I have given literally thousands of speeches and media interviews throughout my adult life. So it amazes me to recall the terror I felt, standing before Miss Bullard's ninth grade English class, delivering a three-minute speech. I was sick to my stomach, my knees knocked, and my voice quavered. Miss Bullard allowed us only an index card for our notes, so I wrote my entire speech out, word for word, in lettering so small I couldn't read it. It was one of the most humiliating experiences of my life. To this day I can't explain how I ever got up the nerve to stand in front of an audience again.

For some unknown reason, I came out of my shell at the beginning of my junior year at Wake Forest University. I had always admired radio sports announcers, and I imagined that broadcasting would come easily to me. So I asked the manager of the campus radio station, Dr. Julian Burroughs, to give me a turn behind the mic. He agreed and assigned me to broadcast freshman basketball games and conduct my own sports interview show. I got to interview some famous athletes, including Ted Williams, Roger Maris, Harmon Killebrew, and Arnold Palmer.

The radio show boosted my confidence as a public speaker and helped launch me into the career I have today. I currently host three weekly radio shows in Orlando—and the ability to communicate before an audience has been a major part of every leadership job I've ever held. In fact, I'm convinced that the ability to communicate was the number one factor in my personal transformation into a leader.

Solomon observed, "We don't expect eloquence from fools" (Proverbs 17:7, *The Message*). Leaders must be communicators or they cannot lead effectively.

SPEAK TO INSPIRE AND MOTIVATE

The great leaders of nations were all known for their communicating ability: Abraham Lincoln, Benjamin Disraeli, Theodore Roosevelt, Winston Churchill, Franklin Delano Roosevelt, John F. Kennedy, Ronald Reagan, and Margaret Thatcher, to name a few. Great social leaders launched major movements with the power of words alone: Edmund Burke, Patrick Henry, Susan B. Anthony, Eleanor Roosevelt, Martin Luther King Jr., Barbara Jordan, Elie Wiesel, and Lech Walesa.

The great sports leaders are also great communicators: Knute Rockne, Lou Holtz, Vince Lombardi, George Allen, Bear Bryant, Tommy Lasorda, John Madden, and Mike Krzyzewski. Great business leaders have multiplied the productivity and profitability of their companies with their powerful words as well: Walt Disney, Lee Iacocca, Steve Jobs, Rich DeVos, Charles R. Schwab, and Meg Whitman. And the world has been changed for the better by the words of great spiritual leaders: Moses, John Wesley, George Whitfield, Billy Sunday, Pope John Paul II, Bill Bright, and Billy Graham.

Great leaders speak to inspire and motivate, to instruct and encourage, to convey hope and optimism. They communicate their vision of the future to the minds and hearts of their followers. Here are four practical suggestions for becoming a more effective communicator—and a more inspiring leader.

1. Practice good listening habits.

Many people in leadership positions are so focused on what they have to say that they are not naturally good at listening. People can tell when you are listening with only half an ear, when you are merely waiting for them to stop talking so you can unload what *you* have to say. Effective leaders have learned the art of listening. They know that communicating is a two-way process, involving receiving as well as broadcasting.

In late 2009, I had a conversation with Al LeBoeuf, who is a long-time coach in professional baseball. We spent some time reminiscing about our mutual friend, Paul Owens, who ran the Philadelphia Phillies for years, and who passed away in late 2003. One thing Al said about Paul really stuck in my mind: "When Paul Owens was running the Phillies, he taught me the best lesson about running a ball club. Paul told me, 'Hire the best people you can. Then listen to them. *Really* listen.'"

Give people the gift of your full attention, with good eye contact and frequent verbal feedback. ("Uh-huh . . . Exactly! . . . I agree!") Let people know that you have heard and understood what they are saying to you by repeating back their key points in your own words. ("In other words, you're telling me . . .")

2. Keep it simple and focused.

Avoid big words, bureaucratese, and techno-speak. Jargon creates confusion, not understanding. It doesn't enhance communication; it stops communication in its tracks.

The Orlando Magic got to the NBA Finals in 2009, where they faced Kobe Bryant and the Los Angeles Lakers. The TV coverage often included live shots of both teams' huddles during timeouts. I remember one timeout when the network camera was in the Lakers huddle, and head coach Phil Jackson stood in front of his players for about a minute, not saying a word. Then as the huddle broke up, he said, "Move the ball. Make shots." That was all he said—and all he needed to say. Unfortunately for the Magic, Kobe Bryant listened and applied Phil's simple advice very effectively.

Commentator and former political speechwriter Peggy Noonan once said, "Every big idea that works is marked by simplicity, by clarity. You can understand it when you hear it, and you can explain it to people."[1]

Since the goal of communication is clarity and understanding, you should always have a clear purpose in mind when you speak. Be clear in your own mind what you want your followers to do. Give them specific action steps you want carried out. After you have finished speaking, your followers should know *exactly* what to do and how to do it.

3. Whenever possible, communicate face-to-face.

As a society we have come to rely far too much on impersonal modes of communication. E-mail and texting are fine for transmitting data such as "Meet u at Strbcks at 11." But if you want to solve problems or inspire the troops, you've got to communicate face-to-face. Your followers need more than just your words glowing on a computer screen. They need to see the passion in your eyes and the intensity in your gestures and body language.

When you speak before an audience, don't read a speech from a sheet of paper. Step out from behind the lectern and move about the stage—or even come down off the stage and get close to your audience. Make sure your voice and face are animated and expressive. Use big arm gestures to underscore your most important points. Make eye contact with various people in your audience.

Don't merely talk *at* your audience. Have a genuine *conversation* with them. Call on people and interact with them. Draw from the energy of your listeners. Tell plenty of stories. Whenever I see the attention of my audience begin to fade, all I have to do is say, "Let me tell you a story . . ." It's amazing how everyone perks up.

4. Communicate to encourage and empower.

When Nazi Germany launched the Battle of Britain during the summer of 1940, Great Britain seemed destined for defeat. Poland, France, Belgium, and the Netherlands had already fallen. German bombers rained death on London and other English cities. The Britons expected the Germans to cross the channel and invade at any time.

Throughout those dark days, British prime minister Winston Churchill made a point of going out among the people, immediately after each bombing raid, to encourage them and lift their spirits. When President John F. Kennedy conferred American citizenship upon Winston Churchill in 1963, he said that Churchill "mobilized the English language and sent it into battle."[2]

After one massive bombing raid over the London docks in September 1940, Churchill visited an air-raid shelter that had taken a direct hit. Forty people were killed in the blast. When he arrived, the fires were still burning and a crowd of survivors stood outside the shelter entrance. When the people saw him, they surged toward him, shouting, "Good old Winnie! We thought you'd come and see us. We can take it. Give it 'em back!" Churchill stood with them, talked to them, and wept openly and unabashedly with them.

"You see, he really cares!" one elderly woman exclaimed.[3]

Churchill rallied the British people and filled them with optimism. Though their cause seemed lost by all rational measures, the people of Great Britain were so inspired by Churchill's words that *they didn't know they had lost.* So they kept fighting—and they won.

Encouragement and empowerment are just as important in the world of business or religion or sports. Former Tampa Bay Buccaneers head coach Jon Gruden tells a story from his days as a graduate assistant coach at the University of Tennessee, where he was mentored by head coach Johnny Majors and offensive coordinator Walt Harris. During a game against Auburn in Knoxville, Gruden saw that Auburn's free safety was playing shallow. He was sure that Tennessee's fastest wide receiver, Terence Cleveland, could outrace the Auburn defender, so he sent a note to Harris: "DP8 Go? Check the post" (meaning "Draw-Pass 8 Go and look for the post route").

Harris liked Gruden's idea and called the play. Just as Gruden predicted, Terence Cleveland beat the safety and made the catch for big yardage.

The next day, Gruden was watching film of the game along with the other coaches. Soon Gruden's big pass play came on the screen. Johnny Majors, not realizing that the idea had come from Gruden, praised Walt Harris. "That's a good call, Walt," he said.

Gruden didn't particularly care who got the credit. He was just happy the play worked. But then Walt Harris spoke up and said, "Jon called that."

Coach Majors gave Gruden a pat on the back and said, "Attaboy!"

"That was a highlight of my career," Jon Gruden later recalled. "That was one of the greatest days of my life."[4]

Effective leaders communicate to encourage and empower their followers. That's how good organizations become great. That's how followers gain the confidence to become leaders in their own right.

‖ ALWAYS TELL THE TRUTH ‖

Earlier we quoted Proverbs 17:7 where Solomon says, "We don't expect eloquence from fools" (*The Message*). That was only part of the verse. The rest of it says, "Nor do we expect lies from our leaders." Leaders must speak the truth. Anyone who deceives his followers is not truly a leader but a demagogue, a manipulator who will lead his followers down a false path.

Whitey Herzog is a retired Major League Baseball manager, general manager, coach, and farm system director. He knows the game—and he knows leadership. In his book *You're Missin' a Great Game,* he said, "Every word you speak has to be honest. If there's one rule you should never violate, it's Always Tell The Truth. . . . You'd be surprised how many managers lie to their players. . . . I never once had a player resent me for telling him the truth."[5]

Make sure you are a truth teller in your organization. Speaking the truth takes courage. Sometimes the truth makes people angry or causes hurt feelings. Sometimes it penetrates denial and forces long-suppressed issues out into the open.

In the words of Alexander Solzhenitsyn, the Russian dissident who spoke the truth against the tyranny of Soviet Communism, "One word of truth outweighs the whole world."[6] Communicate truthfully and be a leader.

GET WISDOM, GET UNDERSTANDING
QUESTIONS FOR PERSONAL REFLECTION OR GROUP DISCUSSION

1 || On a scale of 1 to 10, rate your ability as a public speaker. Next, rate your *confidence* as a public speaker.

2 || Citing specific examples, explain why you gave yourself those ratings. Recall any experiences that either damaged or boosted your confidence as a communicator.

3 || Who are two or three of your leadership heroes? What do you admire most about your heroes?

4 || How much are you influenced by your heroes' ability to inspire you with the way they communicate? Are there any leaders you admire who are *not* effective communicators?

5 || What practical steps can you take in the coming week and throughout the coming year to become a more confident, competent, effective communicator? (Ask someone—a mentor, friend, or colleague—to hold you accountable for taking those steps.)

6 || Do you think you are a good listener? Why or why not? What specific things can you do this week to develop or practice better listening skills?

7 || Do you rely too heavily on impersonal forms of communication, such as e-mails and text messages? What can you do to become a more effective and face-to-face communicator?

8 || How would you rate yourself as an encourager, as a leader who uses praise and affirmation to energize your followers? Do you give people recognition and a pat on the back when they do a good job? If not, why not?

9 || Would your followers say that you show up even more during the "dark days," or do you retreat to the safety of your bunker? What can you do about changing that impression—if it's a negative one? What intentional steps can you take this week to become a more effective encourager of your followers?

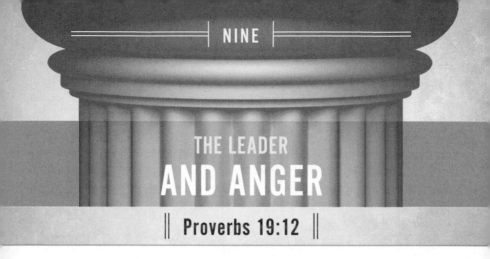

NINE

THE LEADER AND ANGER

‖ Proverbs 19:12 ‖

I n 1973, when I was general manager of the Chicago Bulls, we were scheduled to go into the first round of the playoffs against either the Milwaukee Bucks or the Los Angeles Lakers—whichever team had the best record. As it turned out, the Bucks and Lakers finished the season with identical records. A coin toss determined that we were to play the Lakers in Los Angeles—and the commissioner's office decided that the Bulls had to be in LA for game one the following night.

"You've got to be kidding!" I told the commissioner's representative over the phone. "You can't expect the Bulls to play on the West Coast on one day's notice! We need time to travel, to rest up, and to practice! This isn't just unfair . . . it's insane! How are we supposed to be in any shape to play? Tell the commissioner that we refuse to play under such conditions."

"If you choose not to play," the representative replied, "you forfeit the game."

I was furious. I hung up, then called head coach Dick Motta and told him the news.

"This is nuts!" Dick shouted in my ear. "While they're at it, the league might as well tie our shoelaces together! Pat, why didn't you refuse?"

"I *did* refuse! They said it was play or forfeit!"

"You shoulda been tougher! You shouldn't let them push you around!"

I could understand Coach Motta's emotion, because I shared it—but I didn't appreciate being criticized for not being tough enough. So now I was mad at the commissioner's office *and* our coach—and he with me. I let Dick vent for a while; then I wished him well and hung up.

The team went to LA, and our public relations director, Ben Bentley, tried to keep Coach Motta away from the media—to no avail. He complained loudly about the "spineless management" in Chicago (that would be me) that permitted the team to go into the playoffs at a disadvantage.

The Bulls played as you would expect a jet-lagged team to play without rest or practice. We lost the first game in LA, but ultimately pushed the series to a full seven games. The last game ended with the Lakers coming from behind to beat us in a heart-stopping (and heartbreaking) finish. If the deck hadn't been stacked against us, who knows how history might have changed?

A few weeks later, one of the owners called me into his office. "What would you think of giving up player negotiations," he said, "to concentrate on promotions?"

"Who would handle negotiations?" I knew the answer but had to ask.

"Well, we naturally thought Dick Motta—"

"That's a terrible idea! You can't send a ballplayer out to play for a guy he's haggled with over money. How can Dick maintain rapport with the team?"

"I see your point," the owner said. "Well, I wanted your views. I'll think it over and get back to you."

A few weeks passed. Then I received word through an intermediary that I was to make an announcement to the press that the Bulls head coach was taking over as director of player personnel. I would remain in charge of promotion and ticket sales. I was shocked—and angry. I was sure Coach Motta had engineered this move.

I went before the reporters and announced my reassignment without comment. Inside, however, I felt crushed. The sportswriters quizzed me, asking how I felt about the change. I pretended it didn't bother me—but it was obvious to all that I'd been demoted. It was humiliating, and I was bitter about it.

I called some of my mentors for advice. I wrestled intensely with my anger. I even considered resigning—but I knew better than to make a decision in the heat of anger. I went through weeks of soul-searching and praying, "God, why is this happening?"

Finally, it hit me: Why *shouldn't* I go through some tough times in my career? The professional sports business is a tough business. I had enjoyed three very satisfying years with the Chicago Bulls. Now I had hit a rough patch. So what? There are plenty of people in the world who were in far worse circumstances than mine—people who were out of work, had lost a loved one, or were facing a serious medical diagnosis. God had been good to me, and it was time to quit feeling sorry for myself . . .

And that's when I quit being angry.

Looking back, I realize it was good for me to go through that experience. I learned an important lesson in how to deal with opposition and setbacks—and how to deal with anger.

Within a few days I was offered opportunities to become general manager of the Baltimore Orioles and the Atlanta Hawks. Although the baseball offer was tempting, I elected to take the Hawks job because I wanted to continue my NBA career.

I realize now that one of the worst things a leader can do is to hold on to anger. Leaders who remain stuck in their anger run the risk of letting anger turn into bitterness, and bitterness into a mean-tempered personality.

Wise King Solomon said, "Mean-tempered leaders are like mad dogs; the good-natured are like fresh morning dew" (Proverbs 19:12, *The Message*). A leader who has not learned to manage his anger cannot inspire others to follow. He may intimidate and terrify his followers—and that may get results for a while. But people won't follow a mad dog for long.

‖ DEALING WITH ANGER ‖

You can't help getting angry from time to time. Anger is a feeling, and feelings aren't right or wrong. They are simply responses to things that happen to us. If someone threatens you, strikes you, insults you, or frustrates you in some way, you're going to feel angry. That's normal.

But once you experience a feeling of anger, you have a choice to make: Will you respond in a constructive or destructive way? Will you control your response to your angry feelings—or will your anger control *you*?

Leaders have to be in control of themselves at all times, and self-control is never more important than when you feel like you're about to *lose* control. Leaders have to set a positive example, think clearly, and make good decisions—even in emotionally charged situations.

Have you ever been arguing angrily with your spouse or your kids—and suddenly the phone rang? You answered the phone and forced yourself to be pleasant to the caller, but as soon as the call ended, you let the hostilities resume! While you were on the phone, you controlled your responses and your behavior. You *proved* that you can be self-controlled when you want to be. You can't control your feelings, but you can control your responses and your behavior. Solomon said in Proverbs 25:28, "A person without self-control is like a house with its doors and windows knocked out" (*The Message*).

Here are four tips to help you learn to deal with anger in a controlled and healthy way.

1. Acknowledge your anger.

Don't deny your emotions or pretend they don't exist. Be honest with yourself about your anger. It's a lot easier to maintain self-control if you simply admit, *OK, I'm mad. This is how I feel. Now I can deal with it.*

If you fall into an icy river, you'll feel cold. When you climb out of the water, you'll shiver and your teeth will chatter. You wouldn't tell yourself, *I shouldn't feel cold. It's wrong to feel this way. I must be a bad person to feel cold right now.*

Don't beat yourself up for feeling angry. Accept your feelings; then seek a way to resolve the situation that makes you feel angry.

2. Take time to gain a healthy and realistic perspective on your anger.

There's wisdom in the adage "When angry, count to ten." When a situation provokes you to anger, pull back and clear your thoughts. Strong emotions can distort your thinking. If you pause and reflect, you can regain a clear perspective. Avoid making major decisions in the heat of the moment. Above all, don't say anything that you can't take back.

Solomon's father, King David, wrote in Psalm 4:4, "In your anger do not sin; when you are on your beds, search your hearts and be silent." David acknowledged that we can be angry and still be morally righteous and emotionally healthy. The key is to take time and reflect, regaining a realistic perspective on our emotions. We should search our hearts and ask, *What am I angry about? How is my anger affecting others and me? How should I respond to this situation?*

3. Refuse to let anger take control.

It's OK to feel what you feel. It's not OK to lash out and hurt other people. It's foolish and immature to allow our emotions to control our actions.

Many people in leadership positions seem to feel justified in lashing out at subordinates when they are angry. Their attitude is, *I'm the boss! I run this place! I sign the paychecks! And if anybody here objects to my ranting and raving, he is free to walk out that door and find himself another boss to work for.*

That's the attitude of a tyrant, not a leader. Authentic leaders exemplify good character and healthy workplace behavior—and above all, they model clear thinking and emotional control in times of stress.

4. Resolve your anger quickly.

Deal with the problem openly, honestly, and as calmly as possible. Communicate with the people who triggered your feelings of anger. Avoid blaming and finger-pointing; focus on resolving misunderstandings. If necessary, involve a wise mediator who can help all participants hear each other clearly.

Unresolved anger tends to fester over days, months, and years. It gradually turns into bitterness. Bitter, unhappy people seem angry all the time. Everything they say and do is poisoned by anger. They've never resolved anger from the past, so it clings to them today. They are like mad dogs.

Momentary anger is normal; holding on to grudges is not. If you fail to resolve your anger while it is fresh, that anger will affect your actions, your relationships with others, the decisions that you make, your leadership role, and your entire future. It will control you.

Let's say you have an angry incident with a subordinate in your organization. Instead of resolving that anger, you hold it in. You stew in your own juices. Finally, at the end of the day, you come home and kick the dog or scream at your family for no reason. Why? You aren't angry at the dog or your family. You're angry over a completely unrelated situation. But anger has a way of causing collateral damage.

Unresolved anger can build up in our lives to the point where it becomes increasingly hard to deal realistically with our feelings. An unrealistic perspective prevents us from making sound, clearheaded decisions. If we cannot lead effectively, then we let down our entire organization and all the followers and people in the community who depend on our leadership.

‖ RIGHTEOUS ANGER ‖

One of the most influential leaders in my life was R. E. Littlejohn, the owner of the Spartanburg (South Carolina) Phillies, where I worked as a minor league baseball executive in the mid-1960s. He was a wealthy and influential businessman with an impressive personality, yet he was amazingly humble and soft-spoken. I never saw him behave in an arrogant or vengeful way, and I only saw him angry once.

The radio announcer for our games was John Gordon. After our 1965 season, the radio station that broadcast our games fired Gordon. Why they fired him is a mystery; John was an excellent young broadcaster with a very bright future.

After the firing Mr. Littlejohn demanded a meeting with the station manager, and I went with him to the meeting. There I saw something I had never seen before. I saw Mr. Littlejohn—this soft-spoken, gentle man—launch like a ballistic missile! He made sure the station manager knew that his treatment of John Gordon was unacceptable.

Mr. Littlejohn's anger was *righteous anger*. He would never lose his temper to defend himself. But if he saw someone being unfairly treated, he could be as fierce as a grizzly bear. At the end of that meeting, Mr. Littlejohn informed the station manager that he was pulling the Phillies games off his station and taking them to another station—and John Gordon would be back in the booth, broadcasting our games. That station manager may have thought he had a mad dog in his office that day—but to John Gordon, and to me, Mr. Littlejohn's *anger* was, as Solomon said, "like fresh morning dew"!

That incident was a turning point for John and may well have saved his career. He has been a Major League broadcaster for thirty-five years and has been the radio voice of the Minnesota Twins since 1987.

———

Lead like Solomon. You can't help being angry from time to time, so go ahead and be angry. Just don't lash out at other people. Whatever your feelings may be, maintain control. Resolve your anger quickly. Always set a good example for the people who follow your lead.

GET WISDOM, GET UNDERSTANDING
QUESTIONS FOR PERSONAL REFLECTION OR GROUP DISCUSSION

1 | What attitudes were you raised with regarding anger? Were you taught to believe that anger is a sin? Did your family of origin exemplify healthy or dysfunctional attitudes toward anger?

2 | How have those attitudes, which you may have absorbed as a child, affected your adult perspective on anger?

3 || Recall a time when your anger interfered with your leadership life or turned you into a mean-tempered leader behaving like a mad dog. How could you have handled the situation differently? How did you deal with the damage caused by your anger?

4 || Now recall a time when you felt angry but were able to maintain control over your behavior and respond in a responsible way. What was the key to your ability to maintain control? Were there inward or outward factors that enabled you to keep from flying off the handle? (prayer, your conscience, a wise saying, a passage of Scripture, a technique such as counting to ten, the presence of a friend)

5 || On a scale of 1 to 10, rate your ability to control the way you respond to feelings of anger (1 equals a complete lack of control). Explain your answer.

6 || How would you define *righteous anger?* Do you believe it is possible to express righteous anger? Explain your answer.

7 || How do you make sure that righteous anger doesn't turn into unrighteous rage?

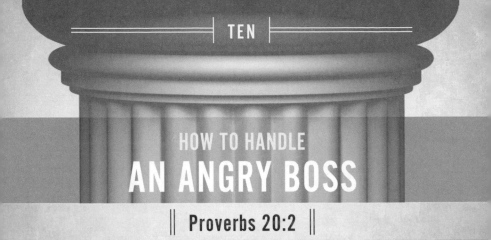

TEN

HOW TO HANDLE
AN ANGRY BOSS
|| Proverbs 20:2 ||

saw this advertisement for computer software being sold over the Internet:

> I HATE MY BOSS
> Hate Boss lets you execute hateful photos. It may be a picture of your boss or somebody who makes you crazy.[1]

What does this kind of software tell us about both leadership and followership in our culture today? For one thing, it says that a lot of subordinates out there don't think much of their bosses. They don't view the boss as a leader, they don't respect the boss, and they are not inspired by the boss to work hard to achieve the organizational vision. Whose fault is this—the leader's fault or the followers' fault?

Clearly, there are many people in today's workforce who simply cannot be motivated to work hard and show respect to leadership. A slacker mentality definitely infects our culture. Some in the workforce are spoiled and consider it beneath them to actually put forth effort in exchange for their paycheck. Others feel entitled to be entertained 24/7, so they spend their on-the-job hours finding ways to avoid work—texting, Web surfing, Internet gaming, and so forth.

But there are also many in the workforce who have been turned off by bad bosses who are not authentic leaders. Bad bosses make life miserable for their subordinates. They assign impossible tasks ("I want that fifty-page report on my desk by noon or else!"), and they explode in rage when their impossible demands are not met. They take credit for the work of others and shift blame for their own mistakes.

Some bosses think the only way to get results out of subordinates is by threats and intimidation. They don't know how to inspire loyalty, so they inspire fear instead. The problem is that when you rule by fear, you generate resentment. And resentful employees will never be motivated to achieve your goals. They will only be motivated to undermine and sabotage you at any opportune moment. They will use software like Hate Boss to ridicule you and escape your scrutiny.

Solomon wrote, "Quick-tempered leaders are like mad dogs—cross them and they bite your head off" (Proverbs 20:2, *The Message*). Even if you have subordinates under your command, you may have to answer to someone higher up the chain of command. So while you are trying to be an inspiring leader to your followers, you may be dealing with a "mad dog" boss who is continually biting your head off. How do you handle a situation like that?

‖ HOW TO RESPOND TO YOUR QUICK-TEMPERED BOSS ‖

Great leaders inspire their troops to buy into the leader's vision. They bring out the best in their followers—qualities of diligence, perseverance, enthusiasm, integrity, and loyalty. The greatest leaders of all can turn even slackers into followers. That's the *ideal* leader.

Unfortunately, that may not be the leader *you* are required to answer to. Some bosses are insulting and abusive toward their subordinates because they lack empathy. They have no sensitivity to other peoples' feelings.

Other bosses use anger as a defense mechanism. They bluster and rage and insult their subordinates to hide their insecurities. As long as they can keep subordinates off balance, no one will uncover the secret of their own lack of competence and confidence.

Whatever prompts the bad behavior of a quick-tempered boss, you need to find a way to survive in that environment. How, then, should you respond if you have a mean-tempered boss? Here are a few suggestions.

1. Maintain your professionalism.

Don't allow your emotions to overrule your good judgment. Don't engage in backstabbing or sabotaging your boss. Don't engage in gossip with coworkers or people outside the organization. Your boss may be wrong, but your wrong behavior won't make it right.

2. Don't give your boss cause to reprimand you.

Diligently devote yourself fully to your duties. Be conscientious. Deliver excellent service to the organization. You may ask, "Why should I knock myself out for an abusive boss?" No one says you should. Instead, focus on being the best subordinate you can be—and do it for the sake of your own self-respect. Do it out of service to God. No matter what kind of boss you may have, live according to your own code of ethics, values, character, and faith.

3. If you are wrong, apologize.

Don't make excuses or defend yourself. Just say, "You're right. I blew it. It won't happen again." Usually, if you admit your mistakes, even a bad boss will stop yelling. There's not much more he can say if you have already taken responsibility for your error. Some bosses may continue to berate you even after you have apologized. If so, just wait until your boss has spent his anger, then calmly repeat the apology.

Learning the art of saying "I was wrong" and "I'm sorry" is good training for leadership. All leaders should know how to apologize and mean it. Management guru Tom Peters refers to the skill of apologizing as "strategic competence." He quotes Marshall Goldsmith, author of *What Got You Here Won't Get You There*: "I regard apologizing as the most magical, healing, restorative gesture human beings can make. It is the centerpiece of my work with executives who want to get better."[2]

4. Remain calm and respectful.

When a mean-tempered boss loses control, make sure *you* maintain control. When you respond to a boss's tirade in a calm and respectful manner, you will likely see your boss back away from his anger. People feel foolish and conspicuous when they are yelling at someone who responds calmly and reasonably.

5. Disagree agreeably.

If you disagree with anything your boss says, state your disagreement respectfully and calmly. If your boss criticizes you in generalities ("You're doing a lousy job!"), ask for specific examples and clarification. If you think your boss might be receptive, you could say, "I welcome your feedback on my work, but I'd appreciate it if you wouldn't insult me or swear at me."

6. Document everything.

If your boss gives you instructions, write them down and include the time and date. Let your boss see that you are conscientiously taking notes on everything he tells you. Later, if your boss accuses you of not doing what you are told, you can produce proof that you carried out his instructions to the letter.

If you are subjected to abusive behavior, keep a journal of those occurrences. Record the facts as objectively as you can, leaving out any insulting or derogatory remarks about your boss. You may need a contemporaneous record of events to defend yourself at some future date.

7. Think twice about reporting your boss to superiors.

Higher-ups often view people with complaints as troublemakers, and you may end up sabotaging your own career. In general, it's not a good idea to go over your boss's head to lodge a complaint.

8. Find a mentor or a support group.

Select one wise and trusted friend, or a group of trusted friends, with whom you can speak openly and confidentially, and who will give you an honest reality check. Ideally, these people should be outside your organization. Invite them to set you straight whenever your perspective is skewed.

9. In extreme cases, consider transferring or finding a new job.

Don't think for a moment that you can change a bad boss. Most mad-dog bosses have decades-old emotional issues that have made them what they are today. Don't waste years of your life in a stressful, dysfunctional workplace. Put your résumé back in circulation and chart a new course for your life.

YOU MAY BE WRONG ABOUT YOUR "MAD DOG"

My writing partner, Jim Denney, worked with Green Bay Packers defensive lineman Reggie White on his autobiography, *In the Trenches*. Reggie told Jim that one of the best coaches he ever played for was Buddy Ryan, who was head coach of the Philadelphia Eagles.

Reggie told Jim about attending the Eagles training camp in August 1986, when Buddy Ryan took over as head coach. Camp was held at West Chester University, near Philadelphia. It was a torrid, humid summer with temperatures in the nineties, and Coach Ryan put his players through a series of murderous drills.

"It was like Buddy was mad at us," Reggie said. "He was screaming at us and pushing us in that heat, making us run sprints and laps. Guys would drop from dehydration, but he'd yell at us to get up and do it again. I thought he was going to kill us!

"One day, I was taking a break and wondering why Buddy hated us. He came over to me and said, 'Reggie, I just want to tell you that you are the best defensive lineman I've ever seen. You do things I've never seen guys do before.'

"Those words challenged me. I wanted to be worthy of the praise he'd given me, so I worked harder for Buddy Ryan than for any other coach I had played for. That was my second year in the NFL, and I got eighteen sacks that season.

"Why did Buddy push us so hard? I think he wanted training camp to be tough in order to weed out guys who weren't committed. A lot of guys quit because Buddy was so tough on us. But I figured out that he was cutting the team down to a core of committed guys who'd be loyal to him.

"I respect tough coaches, and Buddy was one of the toughest I ever played for. He was tough but fair. We all loved him and wanted to work hard for him."

Bottom line: before you judge your leader too harshly, before you think he is just a mad dog biting your head off, get a reality check. You may find out that there really is a method to his madness. You may find out that he's tough but fair.

You may even learn to love him.

GET WISDOM, GET UNDERSTANDING
QUESTIONS FOR PERSONAL REFLECTION OR GROUP DISCUSSION

1 || Think of a time when a quick-tempered leader or boss unleashed his or her anger like a mad dog. How did that person's anger make you feel? How did it affect your performance as a subordinate? Explain your answer.

2 || Recall a time when you responded to an angry boss in a healthy and successful way. What was the attitude or action you took that turned out to be the key to an effective resolution of the angry situation?

3 || Do you find it easy, or difficult, to apologize when you make a mistake? Why? Do you feel you need to defend yourself when others are angry with you? Why or why not?

4 || If you are dealing with an angry boss right now (or if you have dealt with one in the past), do you have (or did you have) a mentor or support group to help you gain a healthy perspective on the situation? If you answered yes, how has that mentor or support group helped you? Provide specific examples. If you answered no, how do you imagine such a mentor or support group might help you to deal more effectively with such a situation?

5 || Did you ever have a boss or leader who *seemed* like a quick-tempered mad dog—but turned out to have a method to his "madness"? Looking back, do you see how some of the bosses or leaders who were hard on you have actually had a positive impact on your life? Explain your answer.

ELEVEN

QUALITY AND EXCELLENCE

‖ Proverbs 20:8 ‖

I live in Orlando, Florida, the quality capital of the world. Walt Disney World sets the mark for quality, and everyone else must strive for that same standard. Whether you build a theme park, hotel, restaurant, convention center, or sports organization, you'd better strive for absolute quality and excellence—or you cannot compete.

In 1986, Orlando businessman Jimmy Hewitt brought me down to work with him on building an NBA expansion team in central Florida. I knew that Orlando sports fans would have high expectations, and we'd have to build our organization to Disney standards of excellence.

Great leaders demand quality and excellence, both from their followers and from themselves. Solomon understood this when he penned, "Leaders who know their business and care keep a sharp eye out for the shoddy and cheap" (Proverbs 20:8, *The Message*). Or as the great NFL coach Vince Lombardi put it, "The quality of a person's life is in direct proportion to their commitment to excellence, regardless of their chosen field of endeavor."[1]

‖ A FANATIC ABOUT EXCELLENCE ‖

In August 1989, three months before the Magic opened its first season, I attended a reception and dinner at one of the Disney hotels in Orlando. I was seated next to Dick Nunis, who had joined the

Disney organization after graduating from USC in the 1950s. He had worked alongside Walt Disney for many years and rose to the position of chairman of Walt Disney Attractions. I was fascinated by the legendary Walt Disney, and I asked Dick, "What were the traits of Walt Disney that made him so successful?"

As Dick spoke, I grabbed a paper napkin and scribbled down everything he said. "You can chalk up Walt Disney's success to nine character traits," he began. "One, integrity—you could absolutely trust the man. Two, creativity—he was a true visionary. Three, administrative ability—he knew how to get the best out of people. Four, motivational ability—he was not easy to work for, but he could inspire you to perform at a higher level than you ever thought possible. Five, he was willing to gamble—he wasn't reckless, but he took bold, calculated risks. Six, he was a good listener—he was willing to learn from anyone. Seven, he wanted people to challenge him. Eight, he did his homework—he looked at decisions from all angles."

"And nine?" I asked.

"That's the most important trait: Walt was fanatically committed to excellence. He was a stickler for getting every detail exactly right. Everything he did had his name on it, and it all had to be top quality."

Then Dick told me a story to illustrate Walt Disney's intense commitment to quality and excellence. Dick was a training supervisor in 1955 when Disneyland opened in California. He was in charge of training the people who operated the attractions, such as the boat operators on the Jungle Cruise attraction in Adventureland.

One day Walt showed up at the Jungle Cruise and boarded one of the boats with the other passengers. Then Walt took off on his cruise. When the boat returned to the dock, Dick was waiting anxiously—and he could see that Walt was not happy. Stepping onto the dock, Walt asked, "How long is that cruise supposed to take?"

"Seven minutes, Walt."

"That trip took just over four minutes. We shot through there so fast, I couldn't tell the hippos from the elephants!"

So Dick retrained each of his boat operators. He rode in each boat, timing each operator with a stopwatch, making sure that every cruise lasted a full seven minutes. A few weeks later, Walt showed up for another surprise inspection—and he rode with every operator of every boat. Each cruise lasted exactly seven minutes. Walt was pleased.

"That," Dick Nunis concluded, "is how committed Walt was to quality. He demanded excellence from every member of the organization. Not one detail ever escaped his notice."

In September 2009, I received an invitation from Walt Disney's family to attend the grand opening of the Walt Disney Family Museum in San Francisco, which was built to honor his incredible life. A Walt Disney quotation was prominently displayed at the museum. It read, "We can lick them all with quality." That was the hallmark of everything Disney did throughout his long and successful career.

|| TEN KEYS TO QUALITY ||

"It costs a lot to build bad products," says Norman Augustine, former CEO of Martin Marietta and the author of *Augustine's Laws.*[2] The best is always a bargain—and the cheapest is often the most expensive. If you sell inferior products or services, you will lose your customers, your reputation, and your livelihood. Don't be too quick to undercut your competitors' prices; instead, deliver better quality and better service. People will notice, and your business will thrive. Let me suggest ten principles of quality and excellence that will set your organization apart.

1. Maintain a quality attitude.

Excellence is a state of mind. "Good enough" is never good enough. In his book *Letters of a Businessman to His Son*, businessman G. Kingsley Ward said, "The road to business success is paved by those who continually strive to produce better products or service. It does not have to be a great technological product like television. Ray Kroc of McDonald's fame did it with a simple hamburger."[3]

2. Build a quality team.

This means that you, the leader, must encourage a culture of quality. You must set an example of excellence in everything you do. Business consultant Chris Widener says, "In everything [great teams] do, their goal is to achieve at the highest level. And this commitment is held throughout the team and at every level."[4]

3. Make every individual responsible for excellence.

No one is allowed to say, "That's not my job." Anyone in the organization who notices a substandard product or unsatisfactory service is expected to do what it takes to make it right. Teach everyone in the organization, "You are personally responsible for our reputation for excellence. If a customer is unhappy with the quality of our product, you are personally empowered and expected to do what it takes to make it right. If you see a paper clip on the floor, you are expected to pick it up, not step over it. Quality is everybody's job."

4. Inspire a passion for quality.

Everyone in the organization should be enthusiastic about excellence. Everyone should derive satisfaction and pride from the quality of his or her performance. And it's your job to inspire that kind of passion in your troops.

5. Motivate your people to work hard.

Reward those who go the extra mile to deliver those extra touches that add up to excellence. Set an example of hard work for your followers. When Jon Gruden was head coach of the Tampa Bay Buccaneers—and shortly before he led the Bucs to victory in Super Bowl XXXVII—he told sportswriter Mike Freeman, "I know there are some people, even coaches, who might think the way I do things is over-the-top. I feel like I have to work harder to be the best."[5]

6. Welcome competition.

If you are committed to excellence, you don't fear competition; you welcome it. You know that competition forces you and your organization to improve. Be thankful for your competitors, because they push you toward excellence.

7. Maintain consistency.

The only way to truly produce quality is to achieve the same high standard every time.

If you produce a hundred pizzas per day, and you get the order right on ninety-nine of them, you have not achieved excellence. In fact, there's a good chance that you will lose a customer that day. Consistency is an essential ingredient in quality.

8. Speed is a component of quality.

A commitment to quality requires you to deliver your product or service at warp speed—and without shortchanging excellence. The most delectable, aromatic pizza in the world will not please the customer if it arrives three hours late. Speedy delivery is as much an ingredient of a great pizza as the crust, sauce, cheese, and toppings.

In an operating room scene in the TV series *M*A*S*H,* the newly arrived Major Winchester was having trouble keeping pace with his fellow surgeons. In annoyance, Colonel Potter asked, "Winchester, is that still your first patient? I've done three since you started!"

Winchester responded, "Do you want it good, Colonel, or do you want it fast?"

Colonel Potter replied, "Good and fast!"

In a competitive world, you can't settle for one or the other. You must deliver both quality and speed.

9. Pay attention to detail.

Great achievements are made up of thousands of small details. In his book *A Passion to Lead,* Jim Calhoun, men's basketball coach at the University of Connecticut, explained why leaders must focus on the details: "[A basketball game is] really a long series of little battles played out over forty minutes, hundreds of momentary skirmishes—battles for loose balls and rebounds, one-on-one matchups between a guy who, with the shot clock running down, is going to shoot the ball and a defender who must keep him from putting it in the basket. Win enough of those little fights and you win the game. By doing lots of little things well, you've accomplished a very big goal."[6]

If you maintain a high standard of excellence in the little things, you'll never have to worry about the big things.

10. Make it fun!

Many leaders and organizations use negative reinforcement, attempting to motivate their people to strive for quality. If someone makes a mistake, he suffers criticism or a reprimand. You won't inspire an attitude of quality by instilling fear. Instead, make quality fun!

Paul Kahn is president of Goldcon Enterprises LLC, a finance and marketing consulting company. From 1989 to 1993 he was president of AT&T Universal Card Services. He described how AT&T UCS maintained a positive, *fun* emphasis on quality:

> We actually stole an idea from the FBI. . . . Every department at UCS had a 10 Most Wanted List [of quality defects] that it put up on a wall. Teams were assigned to work on each item on the list, and when they corrected one of those defects, we would have town meetings with every employee, and we would bring the teams up and applaud them and give all of them ceremonial plaques. . . . When one improvement project was retired, the next one went up on the list. It was a continuous process.[7]

Before Walt Disney, King Solomon set the bar for quality and excellence. He built the temple in Jerusalem from stones that were so precisely measured and cut that no hammer, chisel, or other iron tool was heard at the temple site during construction (1 Kings 6:7). The interior of the temple was paneled in rich, aromatic cedar and ornamented with beautifully detailed sculptures. The inner sanctuary and altar were overlaid with pure gold. The doors to the temple were intricately carved and overlaid with gold (vv. 15-35). The temple of Solomon was probably the most breathtakingly beautiful structure ever built. It was Solomon's tangible expression of honor to God, and nothing less than absolute excellence would do.

Solomon was committed to quality and excellence, and he advises us to unswervingly make that same commitment: "Keep a sharp eye out for the shoddy and cheap."

Doesn't God deserve your best effort?

1 || Recall a time when you received a poor-quality product or service from a company you had always trusted. How did you feel about that company as a result of that experience? Did you ever use that product or service again?

2 || Do you agree or disagree with this statement: "The best is always a bargain—and the cheapest is often the most expensive"? Why?

3 || What organizations come to mind that thrive by delivering a shoddy product or service for a low price? What do you think of their products/services?

4 || What two or three actions can you take this week to inspire a quality attitude in your organization? Be as specific as possible.

5 || Do you resent your competitors—or do you welcome competition as a motivator for improvement? Who is the toughest competitor you face? Name one lesson you can learn from that competitor to improve the quality of your own organization.

6 || A leader is responsible for the big picture, the organizational vision. How can you maintain a focus on the big picture while simultaneously remaining aware of the details? Explain your answer using specific examples.

7 || List one or two changes you can implement to make quality a fun experience in your workplace or organization.

TWELVE

THE LEADER AND HIS TEAM

|| Proverbs 20:26 ||

Marvin Lewis is head coach of the Cincinnati Bengals. When he assumed the helm in 2003, the Bengals had a 2–14 record the previous year and had not had a winning season in thirteen years. Just two years later, he coached the Bengals to an 11–5 record and an AFC North division title. Before he coached in the NFL, Marvin Lewis coached linebackers at the college level. It was there that he learned the importance of recruiting players with good character traits.

One year during the recruiting season, Marvin heard about a highly talented junior college linebacker who had been heavily recruited by several universities. Marvin asked the other coaches and scouts why no one had suggested recruiting this player. Without exception they said that this young man was a bad apple. Sure, he was loaded with talent—but he was arrogant, disrespectful, and not coachable. "Steer clear of this guy," they said.

As Marvin told me the story, he admitted, "I didn't listen. I recruited the guy because of talent alone. Once he was on the team, he was nothing but trouble. Even worse, his bad character and bad attitude infected two other promising players, including a talented freshman. That was a rough year. I learned then and there that, though talent is important, character is essential."

That's the same lesson taught by Solomon in Proverbs 20:26: "After careful scrutiny, a wise leader makes a clean sweep of rebels and dolts" (*The Message*).

A great leader knows his people well. He knows their talents, abilities, attitude, and character. He knows how they fit together and complement one another as a team. He knows which ones are team players—and which ones are rebels and slackers, incapable of being taught. A few bad apples really do spoil the whole barrel, and a few bad hires can cripple your organization.

|| ASSEMBLING YOUR TEAM ||

Pat Summitt, head basketball coach of the University of Tennessee's Lady Volunteers, has collected eight NCAA titles, second only to John Wooden's ten NCAA championships at UCLA. In *Reach for the Summit,* she describes the challenge of building a team: "A lot of coaches or managers try to force personnel into a system or framework that doesn't suit them. They have a certain way they think things should be done. What they don't understand, out of stubbornness or ego, is that it may not be the most intelligent use of talent. . . . When you force somebody into a slot, you're inviting disaster."[1]

Knute Rockne of Notre Dame was "American football's most-renowned coach," according to his biography at the College Football Hall of Fame in South Bend, Indiana. He changed the game of football by popularizing the use of the forward pass. Though he majored in chemistry as a college student, his genius as a football coach was *team chemistry.* He knew how to put together just the right combination of talent and ability to produce consistently great teams. Rockne once said, "The secret of winning football games is working as a team. I play not my eleven best, but my best eleven."[2]

A great team is a well-orchestrated, carefully balanced assemblage of individuals whose talents, personalities, and character traits mesh together to maximum effect. Sometimes two people with a lot of talent—and even good character traits—simply don't fit well together or work well together. To build an effective organization, you must take a collection of individuals and match their skills, abilities, and personalities to the needs of your team. Once you've assembled your team, you must coach them and inspire them to work together as a unit. Remember Coach Rockne's advice, and play your "best eleven."

THREE KEYS TO A WELL-BALANCED ORGANIZATION

Let me suggest three keys to assembling an organization that is well-balanced—a team in which the talents and personality traits of your players harmonize and complement each other.

1. Maintain a balance of talent and good character traits.

Whether you are the leader of a nonprofit organization, the CEO of a corporation, the pastor of a church, or the coach of a sports team, it's important to assemble a well-rounded mixture of abilities and temperaments. You need some natural leaders and some willing followers. You need to balance bold, flashy risk-takers with modest, unassuming journeymen. My friend, Hall of Fame baseball manager Sparky Anderson, often said, "Every great team needs at least one guy who enjoys picking up the trash."

Recruiting the right person for your organization can be expensive. But it's much more expensive to recruit the *wrong* person. According to Atlas Advancement, a Virginia-based executive search firm, it can cost up to 265 percent of a terminated employee's annual salary to recruit a replacement. That includes recruiting costs, interview costs, travel and relocation expenses, advertising, training costs, missed deadlines, lost productivity—as well as reduced organizational efficiency, morale, and customer goodwill. When the stakes are that high, it's essential to accurately assess every individual recruit.

As an NBA executive since 1968, I have worked with some of the legendary coaches of the game—Jack Ramsay, Dick Motta, Gene Shue, Billy Cunningham, Matt Guokas, Brian Hill, Doc Rivers, Stan Van Gundy, and more. Each of these leaders approached the game in his own unique way. Yet at one time or another, I've heard each of these coaches ask the same questions when recruiting new players: "Can I coach him? Will he listen to me?"

If being coachable is so important in the NBA, at the highest level of the game, then it's certainly important in every leadership arena. The people in your organization must be eager to listen, to learn, and to grow. They must respect your leadership and respond to your coaching.

2. Don't avoid conflict; manage it.

Conflict in an organization is not necessarily an unhealthy sign. Conflict often means that talented, committed personalities are contending for their beliefs and their vision of success. If you manage conflict well, you will often see creative solutions emerge.

In *The Five Dysfunctions of a Team,* leadership expert Patrick Lencioni presents a conversation to illustrate how the *fear* of conflict, not conflict itself, produces dysfunction in an organization. This conversation takes place between three fictional characters: Kathryn, CEO of a company called DecisionTech, and two of her subordinates, Nick and Carlos. Kathryn speaks first:

> "If we don't trust one another, then we aren't going to engage in open, constructive, ideological conflict. And we'll just continue to preserve a sense of artificial harmony."
>
> Nick challenged, "But we seem to have plenty of conflict. And not a lot of harmony, I might add."
>
> Kathryn shook her head. "No. You have tension. But there is almost no constructive conflict. Passive, sarcastic comments are not the kind of conflict I'm talking about."
>
> Carlos weighed in. "But why is harmony a problem?"
>
> "It's the lack of conflict that's a problem. Harmony itself is good, I suppose, if it comes as a result of working through issues constantly and cycling through conflict. But if it comes only as a result of people holding back their opinions and honest concerns, then it's a bad thing. I'd trade that false kind of harmony any day for a team's willingness to argue effectively about an issue and then walk away with no collateral damage."[3]

As the leader, you have a responsibility to bring different points of view out into the open, where they can be discussed rationally and constructively. When people feel free to share their views, you unleash the creativity of your organization. New ideas will bubble to the surface faster than you can write them down. Teach your people how to exchange viewpoints without exchanging insults.

Of course, not all conflict is constructive. Sometimes conflict is a result of discordant personalities, ego rivalries, and political turf battles. When people lack the maturity and character to get along with others, then you have to remove the bad apples that are spoiling your barrel.

3. Get rid of bad apples.

I have made personnel mistakes in the past, and I'm sure you have too. It's the height of foolishness not to correct a mistake once you recognize it. If you find out that you have recruited some "bad apples"—the kind of people Solomon calls "rebels and dolts"—then do something about it. If some of your people are spoiling your team chemistry and keeping you from your goals, then it's time to prune your team, just as an arborist prunes a fruit tree to make it more productive.

Remove those who demonstrate a poor work ethic, who are rebellious and not teachable, who show disrespect for authority, who are a bad influence, or who display a halfhearted commitment to the team and its vision. It doesn't matter how talented they are; treat them as you would your least-talented benchwarmer. If a member of the team breaks the rules, he suffers the consequences, period.

‖ "HAVE YOU SIGNED ANY GOOD PLAYERS?" ‖

Rollie Massimino coaches men's basketball at Northwood University in West Palm Beach, Florida. Back in the 1970s, Rollie learned the ropes of coaching while assisting Chuck Daly at the University of Pennsylvania. When Rollie took the position at Northwood in 2006, Chuck was his biggest booster, attending every home game.

In March 2009, Chuck Daly was diagnosed with pancreatic cancer. During Chuck's hospitalization, Rollie came to visit him every day. Even though Chuck was growing weaker by the day, he always had enough strength to needle his former assistant.

"Rollie," he'd say, "have you signed any good players? Remember, we want to be happy after the games."

Rollie knew exactly what his friend and mentor was saying: the way to be happy after a game is to *win*. To win, you need a good, well-balanced, well-meshed team—a team with good talent, good character, good chemistry, and no "rebels and dolts." Even in the closing days of his life, Chuck Daly was reminding Rollie Massimino of the wisdom of Solomon: Know your people—fit them together like pieces of a puzzle so that they all mesh together. Make a clean sweep of rebels and dolts. These things are vital to being an effective leader of a great team.

GET WISDOM, GET UNDERSTANDING
QUESTIONS FOR PERSONAL REFLECTION OR GROUP DISCUSSION

1 || Have you ever recruited someone who turned out to be a mismatch for your team? How did that person adversely affect your organization? What led you to hire or recruit that individual? Were you misled? Did you fail to properly research and investigate that person? Did you fail to listen to your intuition about the person? Or was there some other factor that caused you to make a costly mistake?

2 || Once you had made a hiring mistake, what steps did you take to correct the situation? How successful were you?

3 || "A great team is a well-orchestrated, carefully balanced assemblage of individuals whose talents, personalities, and character traits mesh together to maximum effect." Name two or three qualities you should look for when hiring or recruiting that you have overlooked in the past.

4 || When you interview people for a position in your organization, they are trying to impress you. It's difficult to tell in a single interview whether an individual has poor character traits, a rebellious attitude, or other traits that might make that person a mismatch for your organization. What are some ways you could go beyond mere issues of talent and performance and learn more about a person's character and attitudes?

5 || How well do you manage conflict in your organization? Name one specific action you could undertake in times of conflict to manage that conflict more effectively.

THIRTEEN

LEADING
THROUGH LOVE

‖ Proverbs 20:28 ‖

My friend Jay Strack is a renowned speaker, author, and president of Student Leadership University, an organization that equips and empowers young people to become leaders. Jay has spoken at many chapels for pro sports teams. Years ago, when the NFL's Tampa Bay Buccaneers were coached by Tony Dungy, Jay accepted an invitation to conduct a pregame chapel for the Bucs. Arriving early, Jay found the room where the chapel would be held. The room was empty except for a man setting up chairs.

"Excuse me," Jay said, walking into the room. "I'm Jay Strack."

The man looked up and said, "Hi, Jay. I'm Tony."

Jay extended his hand. "Coach Dungy?"

"Yes, I'm Tony Dungy. Thanks for coming. I'm just setting up the room for you."

Jay was amazed that the head coach was setting up chairs. "Let me help you," he offered.

"No thanks," Dungy said. "I like to do this myself. I know where each man sits. I know what each one's going through and where he's hurting. I pray over each man's chair as I set it up."

When Jay shared that story with me, I thought, *That says a lot about Tony Dungy*. I've heard many stories about Coach Dungy—how his players look up to him as a mentor and father figure, how he motivates them without screaming or cursing at them, how his players love him, and how he loves them. Tony Dungy amassed a career record of 139–69–0 (.668) and a victory in Super Bowl XLI. He was successful not merely because he is a master football strategist but because his players were motivated to go above and beyond for him. They were motivated by love for the leader who loved and cared about them.

Solomon wrote, "Love and truth form a good leader; sound leadership is founded on loving integrity" (Proverbs 20:28, *The Message*). Great leaders demonstrate love for their followers.

LOVE AND LEADERSHIP

Retired NFL tight end Chad Lewis played for the St. Louis Rams and the Philadelphia Eagles. Though he played only half a season with the Rams, he has high regard for his coach at that time, Dick Vermeil.[1]

"I developed great respect for Coach Vermeil that season," Lewis recalls. "He cares so much about his players. He has every player to his house for dinner in the offseason and he cooks for them— 8–10 players at a time with their wives or girlfriends. . . . He just cares about every person who plays for him. . . . Players love Dick Vermeil."

Lewis recalls the day Coach Vermeil summoned him to give him the news that he was being cut from the team. "When I went in his office, he was crying. He had to walk to the corner of his office to compose himself. . . . He told me, 'I did not want to do this. I love having you around. I know we're going to win the Super Bowl and I wanted to put you on the injured reserve for that, but the more I thought about that it wasn't fair to you. I know you're going to do great things. I want you to have that opportunity. I'm going to do what I can to get you a job.'"

The next day, Coach Vermeil called Chad's wife, told her how sorry he was, and asked if there was anything he could do to help the family. "Chad's going to be fine," he reassured her.

Lewis concluded, "No one does that! . . . And it wasn't just me; [Coach Vermeil] was like that with his players."

One of the most important qualities a leader can have is genuine love for his people. You can't fake love, at least not for long. The way we care about other people and reach out to them when they are hurting defines the kind of leaders we are—and it determines how our followers will remember us after we're gone.

Many leaders are uncomfortable with the word *love*. They seem to think that talking about love is at odds with the requirements of leadership. Nothing could be further from the truth. In my study of NFL teams, I'm amazed at how often that word *love* comes up. Vince Lombardi's biographer, David Maraniss, observed that Coach Lombardi "had a strong sense of team as family. He was not afraid to use the word *love,* and he used it a lot."[2]

As this book was nearing completion, I had former Packers offensive tackle Forrest Gregg on my radio show. Gregg, an NFL Hall of Famer, played for Green Bay from 1956 to 1970, and Coach Lombardi called him the "best player I ever coached."[3] I asked Gregg if David Maraniss was right about the sense of family and love on the old Lombardi Packers team.

"Oh yes," he said, "it's real. It was true then, and it's still true today. We're all in touch with each other, and we care about each other. I bought a home in Colorado Springs, and my old teammate Willie Davis bought a home in the same neighborhood. We hang out together. All of us old Packers from the Lombardi days still get together. Bart Starr, Paul Hornung, Jimmy Taylor, Boyd Dowler, Carroll Dale—we're all in touch with each other. Our families get together all the time. Coach Lombardi built the team on love, and the love goes on. Nothing will ever stop that."

In the context of leadership, *love* can be defined as "a heartfelt concern for the well-being of others." A leader loves his followers by caring about their personal, emotional, spiritual, and financial needs; their career advancement; their character growth; their health; and their families. A genuine leader does not view his subordinates as cogs in an organizational machine but as real people with feelings, personal goals, and family responsibilities.

To love your people does not mean that you won't have to make difficult, painful choices that affect them, as in the case of Dick Vermeil and Chad Lewis. It doesn't mean that you will necessarily resolve their financial crises by writing a check, nor does it mean that you will overlook their failures or neglect to hold them accountable for their actions. In fact, genuine love sometimes requires that you discipline them for the sake of their own growth and maturity.

Lisa McLeod, a principal of the consulting firm McLeod & More, Inc., and the author of *The Triangle of Truth: The Surprisingly Simple Secret to Resolving Conflicts Large and Small*, writes:

> Love is one of the most effective and efficient business strategies that ever existed. And infusing love into an organization delivers a better ROI than any other single investment you can make. . . .
>
> The truth is, love has been the cornerstone of every successful venture since the dawn of time. From the American Revolution to Apple Computer, the great ones are always fueled by love— by people who love what they do and who love the people they do it with.
>
> Our reluctance to embrace love as a business strategy is rooted in three common misperceptions: feelings don't belong in the office; love is mushy and therefore unmeasurable; and loving your employees means letting them off the hook. . . .
>
> Infusing love into your organization is just as challenging as infusing love into your family or any other relationship. And you don't really master the art of love until you stop thinking of it as a noun and start practicing it as an active verb.[4]

|| YOUR SOLDIERS, YOUR CHILDREN ||

General Tommy Franks (U.S. Army, retired), the former head of the United States Central Command, was responsible for combined military operations throughout the Middle East during the early stages of the war on terror. After his retirement I interviewed General Franks by phone. I told him that my son David was a marine and saw combat during the 2003 invasion of Iraq.

I heard the general's voice quaver with emotion as he said, "Well, you tell your son that someone else loves him besides you." Soon afterward, I proudly passed General Franks's message along to my son.

I have another son, Peter, who is also a Marine Corps veteran. "Every day in the Corps was a lesson in leadership," he once told me. "I believe every leadership lesson I've learned in the Corps is transferable to civilian life." I would add that the Marine Corps is the most intense leadership environment in the world. Both of my leatherneck sons are exemplary leaders.

Required reading for every marine, the *Guidebook for Marines,* includes eleven Principles of Leadership. Though the word *love* doesn't appear in the list, it's clear that Marine Corps leaders are taught to love their subordinates. The eleven Principles of Leadership are:

> *1. Take responsibility for your actions and the actions of your Marines. Use responsibility with judgment, tact, and initiative. Be loyal, be dependable.*
>
> *2. Know yourself and seek self-improvement. Evaluate yourself. Be honest with yourself about yourself.*
>
> *3. Set the example.*
>
> *4. Develop your subordinates.*
>
> *5. Ensure that a job is understood, then supervise it and carry it through to completion.*
>
> *6. Know your men and look after their welfare. Share problems but don't pry.*
>
> *7. Every man should be kept informed.*
>
> *8. Set goals you can reach.*
>
> *9. Make sound and timely decisions.*
>
> *10. Know your job.*
>
> *11. Teamwork.*[5]

Those eleven principles show marine leaders and marine subordinates how to love each other, support each other, and work together as one. The Marine Corps motto—*Semper fidelis!* Always faithful!—is a statement of faithfulness and love. It reflects love of country, the Corps, and one's fellow marines.

In the classic book of counsel on leadership and the military arts, *The Art of War,* Chinese philosopher Sun Tzu wrote, "Look upon your soldiers as you do infants, and they willingly go into deep valleys with you; look upon your soldiers as beloved children, and they willingly die with you."[6] Those words are as timely today as they were when they were written 2,500 years ago—and they agree with the words of Solomon.

On July 4, 1996, I had a speaking engagement in Kansas City, Missouri. As I always do, I took some time to get out of the hotel and run. In a small park at the corner of 40th and Main, I came upon a simple stone marker with a bronze plaque. I'm fascinated with monuments and plaques, so I read the inscription while jogging in place. The monument was dedicated to a Kansas City native, Major Murray Davis, who died in World War I. He was killed in action in the village of Exermont, France, on September 28, 1918. A second bronze plaque on the side of the monument read:

A KINDLY, JUST, AND BELOVED
OFFICER, WISE IN COUNSEL,
RESOLUTE IN ACTION,
COURAGEOUS UNTO DEATH.

And a third bronze plaque on the other side read:

SERIOUSLY WOUNDED, HE
REFUSED TO RELINQUISH HIS
COMMAND UNTIL, MORTALLY
WOUNDED, HE FELL, LEADING
HIS COMRADES TO VICTORY.
HIS LAST WORDS WERE,
"TAKE CARE OF MY MEN."

In September 2009, I returned to Kansas City for another speaking engagement. I again visited the now polished up and refurbished monument. Later, I went to the recently opened National World War I Museum at Liberty Memorial. I asked one of the guides there, a retired military man, if he had ever heard of Major Murray Davis.

"Oh yes," he said. Using his flashlight as a pointer, he indicated the picture of a military officer on a mural. "That's Major Davis right there. We all know about him." The man has been gone for ninety-plus years, but people never forget a leader.

What love Major Davis had for his men! His dying words were of leadership and love. Great leaders love their followers, even unto death.

GET WISDOM, GET UNDERSTANDING
QUESTIONS FOR PERSONAL REFLECTION OR GROUP DISCUSSION

1 || Does it surprise you to hear that love is a necessary component of leadership? Explain your answer.

2 || Do you find it easy or difficult to verbally express love to your followers and subordinates? Why?

3 || Think back over your childhood or young adulthood. Can you point to a person or an experience that shaped your attitude and feelings about love for others—and that makes it either easy or difficult for you to express love to others?

4 || Describe a time when someone (especially a leader) demonstrated a heartfelt concern for your well-being. How did that impact your life and make you a more effective member of the organization?

5 || On a scale of 1 to 10, rate your ability to lead your organization through love. What specific action could you take this week to improve that rating?

6 | How would your organization be impacted if you could more freely express love to your followers and subordinates?

7 | In every organization or team, you must maintain discipline and consequences for bad behavior. How do you express love to your followers while still maintaining team discipline? Explain your answer with a specific example.

8 | Which one or two Principles of Leadership from the *Guidebook for Marines* (p. 120) do you especially need to build into your leadership life?

FOURTEEN

THE SPIRITUAL DIMENSION
OF LEADERSHIP

|| Proverbs 21:1 ||

I n the late 1800s, a great crowd filled Faneuil Hall in Boston to hear a former slave, Frederick Douglass, speak about civil rights in America. In his deep and powerful voice, Douglass said, "The Negro has no hope of justice from the whites, no possible hope save in his own right arm. It must come to blood. The Negroes must fight for themselves."

Another former slave was in the hall that day. Her name was Sojourner Truth. She stood and asked Douglass a question: "Frederick, is God dead?" In other words, did African-Americans have no hope except through bloodshed? Or was there another path to equality, sanctioned by God?

No one could blame Frederick Douglass for believing "it must come to blood." There had been plenty of blood shed already—the blood of enslaved men, women, and children; the blood of Union and Confederate soldiers in the Civil War; the blood of blacks lynched throughout the South by the Ku Klux Klan. So much blood, so much suffering, and still there was no equality. But Sojourner Truth believed that if God lived, there was hope for equality without bloodshed.

Another civil rights leader of the late 1800s was Booker T. Washington. Like Sojourner Truth, he believed that authentic leadership must have a spiritual dimension. Washington's daughter Portia recalled that her father began and closed each day with prayer. "He prayed all the time," she said.

Booker T. Washington was impatient with churches that preached only a sentimentalized form of religion, who taught about a future Heaven but avoided the fight for equality here and now. His goal was not merely to change the circumstances of black people, but to change the hearts and minds of white people. He blazed a trail for future leaders, such as Martin Luther King Jr. (who attended Booker T. Washington High School in Atlanta).

Washington did not want sympathy for African-Americans. He wanted simple justice. His leadership wisdom was rooted in the spiritual principles of the Bible. He taught that the way to achieve justice was by honoring God, working hard, and "building a good school and church, by letting your wife be partners in all you do, by keeping out of debt, by cultivating friendly relations with your neighbors both white and black."[1]

I grew up in Wilmington, Delaware, and I remember witnessing several shocking incidents of racism in my youth. My father cofounded the Delaware High School All-Star Football Game, which benefited the state's mentally retarded children. The game pitted high schools from north Delaware against high schools from south Delaware.

One year, two of the best players in the north were a pair of African-American athletes from Wilmington's predominantly black school, Howard High. All the players from the north trained for the big game at Sanford Prep. But Sanford's headmaster was nervous about having black students on his campus. The headmaster insisted that the two black players, Joe Peters and Alvin Hall, be housed off-campus at night.

I remember my father's anger at seeing those fine young men insulted merely because of the color of their skin. When the headmaster refused to budge, Dad invited Joe and Alvin to stay at our house. I had just gotten my driver's license, so I drove them to the prep school every morning for practice. I remember being amazed at the stupidity of some segments of white society.

After I graduated from Wake Forest University and began playing minor league baseball in Florida, I was again struck by the foolishness of racist attitudes. The African-American players on our team couldn't stay at the same motels with the rest of us. They couldn't eat at the same restaurants. At the end of one season, I offered a ride home to one of our black players, Fred Mason. We drove from Fort Lauderdale to Jacksonville and stopped for gas. While the attendant filled the tank, I went to the vending machine.

I had no sooner uncapped the Seven-Up bottle when I heard the attendant shouting curses and racial slurs. Fred had gotten out of the car to go to the restroom, but the attendant had grabbed a huge monkey wrench and wielded it like a club. My friend just wanted to use the restroom, and this idiot looked like he was ready to commit murder. Fred jumped back into the car. I paid for the gas and we took off.

Segregation and Jim Crow laws died hard in America. Racist attitudes died even harder and are still with us today. Hosea Williams—one of the voting rights marchers who braved police bull whips and tear gas at the Edmund Pettus Bridge in Selma, Alabama, in 1965—visited the scene thirty-five years later and said, "We're not where we used to be but we're not where we ought to be, either."[2]

We have a long way to go. But the major reason we have come as far as we have is because we've had leaders like Booker T. Washington, Sojourner Truth, and Dr. Martin Luther King Jr., who have recognized the spiritual dimension of leadership. They have led the fight for equality as a battle for truth and love and righteousness. That's the kind of leadership Solomon spoke of in Proverbs 21:1: "Good leadership is a channel of water controlled by God; he directs it to whatever ends he chooses" (*The Message*).

Norm Sonju, longtime president and general manager of the Dallas Mavericks, has been a mentor to me since the earliest stages of my career. When I joined the Chicago Bulls organization as general manager, Norm was living in Chicago and working for ServiceMaster. During those years, I was dealing with a headstrong coach and struggling with some strong-minded, powerful owners.

Whenever I felt discouraged or overwhelmed, I would turn to Norm for counsel, and he usually referred me to Proverbs 21:1. In the *King James Version*, it reads, "The king's heart is in the hand of the LORD, as the rivers of water: he turneth it whithersoever he will."

Norm would remind me that my coach's heart and the owners' hearts were in God's hands. The Lord can turn a human heart any which way he wants. Forty years later, I still cling to that truth.

|| MORAL RELATIVISM AND LEADERSHIP ||

You might think, *I'm not a religious person. I don't believe in God—and I don't need to believe in God in order to be an effective leader.*

This book is about Solomon's leadership wisdom, and his teachings in Proverbs 21:1 are essential to his view of leadership. So whether you consider yourself religious or not, whether you believe in God or not, let's explore this wise leader's statement and see what Solomon has to say to us today.

Solomon emphasizes the connection between faith and character. An effective leader exemplifies deeply ingrained traits of good character—things like honesty, integrity, courage, diligence, dependability, fairness, compassion, generosity, humility, loyalty, perseverance, and so forth. These traits are built on a strong moral and ethical foundation.

Can atheists and agnostics have these same traits? Yes. And it is certainly possible for people who *claim* to be religious to lack these traits. But faith in God, by its very nature, places a demand on the believer's life. People of faith believe that God expects them to live moral and ethical lives. They seek to obey the Ten Commandments and the Golden Rule and to serve others—not merely because they believe they will one day have to account to God but also because the more they follow God's ways, the more they see that he knows what he's doing.

Many atheists, agnostics, and humanists will tell you that they live moral, ethical lives as well. That's true to an extent. But people who believe in God and derive their moral principles from the Judeo-Christian Scriptures all have a common moral frame of reference. Those who do not believe do not necessarily share that same frame of reference. As belief in God has declined in our society, there has been a growing acceptance of the concept called moral relativism, the belief that there is no fixed, objective standard of morality.

A moral relativist would say, "What is right for you might not necessarily be right for me. It depends on the situation and the context." A leader who is a moral relativist is a potentially dangerous leader, because he has no fixed moral frame of reference. He might lie or cheat or even kill if he thought such actions best suited his needs. Leaders who are moral relativists are more likely to be manipulators, demagogues, or even tyrants.

Solomon pictures good leadership as a channel of water controlled by God, directed wherever God chooses. By contrast, then, bad leadership is a flash flood, water that is uncontrolled and overflowing its banks. Bad leadership is unpredictable, ungovernable, and potentially destructive because it is unchanneled, undirected, and unrestrained.

‖ DANGEROUS LEADERSHIP ‖

The *New Yorker* has called Peter Singer "the most influential living philosopher" in America.[3] He is the DeCamp Professor of Bioethics at Princeton University's Center for Human Values and an opinion leader in the world of ethical thinking. He's an atheist and a moral relativist. Because he has positioned himself as an ethicist—a leader in the field of ethical thinking—he is, in my opinion, doing enormous harm in our society.

Singer is the author of *Animal Liberation* (1975), considered the "bible" of the animal rights movement. He has also written other books that argue against a traditional moral view of ethics and the value of human life. Having rejected any fixed morality rooted in Judeo-Christian beliefs, he advocates a secular, pragmatic, and utilitarian approach to ethics. According to Singer's belief system, animals have rights—but human children may not. In 1993, he stated that newborn babies should not be considered legal "persons" until thirty days after birth. In his view it should be legal to "abort" newborn infants for any reason in the first month of life. Some newborns with disabilities, he said, should be euthanized immediately upon delivery.[4]

In his book *Practical Ethics,* Singer writes:

A week-old baby is not a rational and self-conscious being, and there are many nonhuman animals whose rationality, self-consciousness, awareness, capacity to feel, and so on, exceed that of a human baby a week or a month old. If the fetus does not have the same claim to live as a person, it appears that the newborn baby does not either, and the life of a newborn baby is of less value to it than the life of a pig, a dog, or a chimpanzee is to the nonhuman animal. . . . Infants appeal to us because they are small and helpless, and there are no doubt very good evolutionary reasons why we should instinctively feel protective towards them. . . . None of this shows, however, that the killing of an infant is as bad as the killing of an (innocent) adult.[5]

Singer has been on a lifelong quest to deconstruct traditional morality. If Peter Singer's views sound disturbingly similar to the eugenics arguments of the Nazis, it's because they *are* disturbingly similar.

Ronald Bailey, who interviewed Singer for *Reason* magazine, noted that Singer's ethical theories were tested by a harsh reality: "Singer's mother suffers from severe Alzheimer's disease, and so she no longer qualifies as a person by his own standards, yet he spends considerable sums on her care. This apparent contradiction of his principles has not gone unnoticed by the media."[6]

Peter Singer is a leader, but his leadership is not controlled by God. He instructs young minds at Princeton University in his so-called "ethics." He writes books, gives speeches, and seeks to shape our society. He has severed all connection to the moral and ethical principles that have anchored our society for centuries and has set himself and his followers adrift on a moral and ethical sea. Such results are why Solomon urges us to place God in control of our leadership lives.

1 || Do you agree or disagree with the assertion that there is a spiritual dimension to leadership? Explain your answer.

2 || Do you believe progress toward racial justice and racial harmony could have been made in America *without* spiritual leadership—that is, through secular leadership alone? Explain your answer.

3 || Do you agree with the assertion that while atheists can have character and people of faith can lack character, people of faith are generally more likely to be people of character? Explain your answer.

4 || What kinds of dangers does moral relativism pose to society and to your organization? Explain your answer, citing specific examples.

5 || Are faith and moral relativism compatible or incompatible concepts? In other words, is spiritual leadership opposed to moral relativism? Explain your answer.

6 || In your role as a leader, have you seen yourself as "a channel of water controlled by God"? List two or three actions you can take this week to become a more effective spiritual leader.

FIFTEEN

HOW TO REACH THE HEART
OF A LEADER
|| Proverbs 22:11 ||

During my second year operating the Spartanburg (South Carolina) Phillies in the mid-1960s, we won a championship, set new attendance records, and I became a minor local celebrity around town. After the Spartanburg Jaycees named me Outstanding Young Man of the Year and the league named me Executive of the Year, my head expanded by three full hat sizes.

The Philadelphia Phillies brass took note of what I had accomplished. In September 1966, owner Bob Carpenter (who was a longtime friend of my father) phoned me.

"Pat," he said, "we're going to start a new double-A farm club in Reading, Pennsylvania. We want you to run it. I'd like you to come to Philadelphia to talk it over."

I should have felt honored. Instead, I was disappointed. I was so full of myself, I thought I was ready for the big leagues after a mere two seasons in the minors. Mr. Carpenter was offering me the chance to build a team from scratch—proof that he had big plans for my future. But I didn't see it that way. I agreed to meet with Mr. Carpenter and his staff—but I had already decided to turn down their offer.

Arriving in Philadelphia, I sauntered into the Phillies executive offices. Everyone was there: Bob Carpenter, his son Ruly (my boyhood friend from Wilmington), farm director Paul Owens, general manager John Quinn, and other assorted executives.

Mr. Carpenter greeted me warmly, shaking my hand: "We're all very impressed with what you've accomplished in Spartanburg." Then he proceeded to lay out his plans for the new ball club in Reading.

When it was my turn to speak, I let my youthful arrogance do the talking. "I don't see why I should jeopardize my career by getting myself mixed up in that town," I said. "How do I know it's really a baseball town? I'd be risking everything I've built up in Spartanburg, with no guarantee of success."

I spread it on thick. To this day, I cringe when I recall that moment. There would have been nothing wrong with a cordial "thanks but no thanks." I could have told them I had made a commitment to the owners in Spartanburg. I could have thanked Mr. Carpenter for his faith in me. I could have responded graciously.

But I had to play the big shot and toss Bob Carpenter's offer back in his face. Even while I was speaking, I could see the smiles in that room turn to scowls. I saw the glare of anger in Mr. Carpenter's eyes.

Not much more was said after I finished talking. I had turned the job down flat, and the meeting was over. I had just ended any chance of advancing in the Phillies organization. It was a painful lesson, and I've carried it throughout my career.

Years later I discovered that Solomon once wrote about this very issue: "GOD loves the pure-hearted and well-spoken; good leaders also delight in their friendship" (Proverbs 22:11, *The Message*). The *NIV* renders it, "He who loves a pure heart and whose speech is gracious will have the king for his friend."

When I walked into Mr. Carpenter's office with an arrogant heart and arrogant speech, I lost the friendship of a true "king," a powerful and generous man who had already opened many doors for me. It was a foolish, self-defeating act and an outrageous demonstration of ingratitude on my part.

On my local radio show, I once interviewed Dr. Sheila Murray Bethel, author of *A New Breed of Leader*. She told of sitting at a luncheon next to Katharine Graham, the longtime publisher of the *Washington Post*. Graham was a political and social force to be reckoned with in those days. Leaders came from around the world to stop at her office or attend one of her parties and pay their respects to Katharine

Graham. Dr. Bethel asked Katharine Graham if there was one trait she admired in all the great world leaders she had met.

"Yes," Graham replied without hesitation. "Absence of arrogance."

Shortly after my conversation with Dr. Bethel, I read a quote in the *New York Times* by Senator Tom Coburn of Oklahoma: "Judgment gets impaired by arrogance."[1]

Solomon's counsel in this passage is directed not at leaders, but at followers and subordinates who seek to rise in the leadership world. This is good advice for leaders-in-training, for people in the early stages of their careers. Solomon wants us to know how to reach the heart of a leader.

HOW TO BEFRIEND A "KING"

Where are you on the ladder of your career? Near the bottom rung but climbing? Halfway up? What are you doing to advance toward your goals? Have you sought out a mentor who can help you, instruct you, make you wise, and open doors for you? Have you sought out a leader—a "king"—to be your friend? I have had "kings" as friends and mentors. One of those was Mr. Carpenter—until the day I damaged our friendship with my foolish behavior.

To fulfill your leadership potential, you must demonstrate the qualities that leaders and "kings" value: sincerity, integrity, a strong work ethic, respect for authority, gratitude, and gracious communication. Here are seven practical suggestions for befriending "kings."

1. Be assertive.

Don't be afraid to approach a leader and ask, "Would you consider mentoring me?" You may think, *This leader is too busy. I don't want to annoy this person.* But look at it this way: What's the worst that can happen? That leader may say no—and you'll be no worse off than if you hadn't asked. Explain that you admire his or her accomplishments and leadership traits, and you want to learn to become that kind of leader yourself.

2. Be persistent.

If your request is turned down by one leader, seek out another. Don't be discouraged. Continue moving forward toward your goals, keep seeking mentors, persist in working hard to be a friend to "kings." Success is a ladder, not an express elevator. You've got to keep climbing, rung by rung, in order to reach your goals.

3. Demonstrate a willingness to pay your dues.

Many newly hatched college grads think they are ready to run the world. Though they often don't have the patience to start in the mailroom, they want to be the CEO! But a leadership position isn't an entitlement. You have to *earn* it. You need to start at the bottom, work your way up, and prove you've got what it takes to be a leader.

You can't short-circuit the process of learning, growing, and maturing. You have to crawl before you can walk, and walk before you can run. Above all, you have to follow before you can lead. Harold Geneen was founder and CEO of MCI Communications. He once said, "In the business world, everyone is paid in two coins: cash and experience. Take the experience first; the cash will come later."[2]

4. Demonstrate humility.

As a leader who has hired literally hundreds of people over the years, one of the first qualities I look for is humility. If I detect an attitude that says "This job is beneath me," the job interview is over. I'm looking for people who are willing to do whatever it takes to make the organization successful.

Don't expect your entry-level job to be fulfilling. If your job involves making coffee or setting up chairs or cleaning restrooms, then do your job cheerfully. If you want the friendship of "kings," show them you are a team player—and one day your big break will come.

In 1964, I officially started my front-office career with the Miami Marlins. The general manager, Bill Durney, assigned me many tasks, including making a pot of coffee every morning. I had never made coffee before in my life! Needless to say, the concoction I brewed was more reminiscent of industrial-strength solvent than anything you could order at Starbucks. And frankly, I haven't made coffee since. But for the 1964 baseball season, I was the Miami Marlins' official barista. It was all part of my leadership training. So whatever task you are given to do, do it cheerfully.

5. Speak well of everyone.

Be positive all the time, in everything you say and do. Never bad-mouth your fellow employees—and above all, never bad-mouth the boss. Any negativity you spread in a casual conversation or an e-mail could come back to haunt you. Solomon challenges us to have a pure heart and gracious speech. A pure heart is a positive heart. Gracious speech is positive speech. Violate this principle and you just might shoot your leadership career in the foot.

6. Express gratitude.

When a leader offers you an opportunity, convey sincere thanks. In addition to your verbal thanks, send a handwritten thank-you note. And no, an e-mail is not the same. A handwritten note demonstrates thoughtfulness and the willingness to take the time to purchase a card, write a personalized note, put a stamp on it, and mail it. Handwritten notes are an increasingly rare act of grace and gratitude in our culture. If you take the time to demonstrate that level of thoughtfulness, the "king" will notice and appreciate it.

7. Be sincere.

Those first six suggestions will be worthless without sincerity. Leaders can spot insincerity in a heartbeat. Make sure you are not simply trying to exploit a friendship with that leader. Your goal should not be merely to impress but to demonstrate the genuineness of your character and leadership ability. Your sincerity is crucial to reaching the leader's heart.

|| "I DIDN'T RECOGNIZE YOU" ||

Here's a postscript to the story of my foolish behavior in Philadelphia. Three months after that meeting with the Phillies brass, I was home in Wilmington, visiting my mother, when Mr. Carpenter called and asked me to come see him at his home. I could feel the tension in the phone line.

I had known this man since I was seven years old, had gone to school with his son, had been a guest in his house many times. As a boy, I had practically been a member of the Carpenter family. Bob Carpenter had paved the way for me to play minor league baseball in

Florida, then got me the job in Spartanburg. But as we sat together in his study, there was a coldness in the room. Mr. Carpenter got right down to business.

"Pat," he said, "what have they been feeding you down there in Spartanburg?"

"Excuse me, sir?"

"You were always a decent, well-mannered young man. You've changed, and not for the better. That arrogant big shot I met in Philly—Pat, was that really you? I didn't recognize you that day. What happened to you?"

"Mr. Carpenter," I said, "I know I made a fool of myself. I don't know what got into me. All I can say is—I'm sorry and it won't happen again."

Bob Carpenter accepted my apology. His forgiveness helped assuage the embarrassment and humiliation I felt. But his forgiveness couldn't undo the damage I had done. I had ruined my chances of advancing in the Phillies organization.

I ended up leaving professional baseball and taking a position in the front office of a different Philadelphia sports franchise, the Philadelphia 76ers of the NBA. I've had an exciting career as a pro basketball executive, and I wouldn't have missed a moment of it. But I can't help wondering how my life would have turned out if I hadn't so thoughtlessly abused the friendship of a true "king" in my life, Bob Carpenter.

My friend, keep your heart pure. Keep your speech positive and gracious. Be a friend to "kings." And do it all with sincerity. There's no substitute for sincerity for anyone wishing to rise in the leadership world.

GET WISDOM, GET UNDERSTANDING
QUESTIONS FOR PERSONAL REFLECTION OR GROUP DISCUSSION

1 || Give details of a time when you suffered the consequences of an arrogant attitude.

2 || Drawing on your own experience or from situations you've heard about, explain how arrogance impairs good judgment.

3 || On a scale of 1 to 10, rate yourself as a person who is "pure-hearted and well-spoken." Consider how people who know you might rate you. Do you think others perceive you differently than you perceive yourself? Explain your answer.

4 || Do you have a "king" as a friend? Have you sought out a mentor who gives you insight and instruction and helps to open doors for you? If you do not have a mentor or "king," what specific steps could you take this week to seek out such a person to help you in your leadership career?

5 || Who serves as your role model of leadership humility? Describe that person's admirable qualities, especially the qualities you wish to emulate. What specific steps could you take to become more like that leader?

6 || Is there someone to whom you should express gratitude? Perhaps that individual did something to advance your leadership career last week, last year, or even decades ago. It's probably not too late to go back and say thank you. What can you do this week to express gratitude to that person?

SIXTEEN

RESPECT—PAVING THE WAY
TO YOUR FUTURE

Proverbs 24:21, 22

Max McGee was a wide receiver for the Green Bay Packers from 1954 to 1967. He earned a special place in football history during Super Bowl I, the Packers versus the Kansas City Chiefs. McGee was a backup to starting wide receiver Boyd Dowler and didn't expect to play in that game. In fact, he didn't even bring his helmet out of the locker room. So early in the first quarter, when Dowler was knocked out of the game with an injury, McGee borrowed a helmet from a teammate and went onto the field.

A few plays later, Packers quarterback Bart Starr lofted a deep pass. McGee made a spectacular one-handed reception, then sped thirty-seven yards to score the first touchdown in Super Bowl history. He went on to deliver one of the best performances of his career, making seven catches for 138 yards and two touchdowns. The Packers won the first Super Bowl, 35–10.

In *What It Takes to Be #1: Vince Lombardi on Leadership,* Vince Lombardi Jr., son of the legendary Packers head coach, called Max McGee "one of my father's favorite players"[1] and told a story about the role of respect in a leader-follower relationship.

Vince Lombardi used to run a drill in training camp that the players hated. The more they hated it, the more Lombardi enjoyed inflicting it. The drill pitted an offensive player and a running back against a defensive player, positioned between a pair of tackling dummies.

The offensive player's job was to push the defender off the line and open a hole for the running back. This drill produced ground-shaking collisions between players—and occasional injuries.

McGee was built for speed, not bruising collisions. He knew that as a wide receiver, he would never have to make this kind of block in a game. So he went to Lombardi and asked to be excused from the drill. Lombardi replied that he couldn't let any player out of the drill, but if McGee could find a way to stay out of the rotation without being noticed, Lombardi would keep his mouth shut.

Amazingly, McGee pulled it off. He played for Coach Lombardi for nine years and always managed to be tying his shoes or getting his ankles taped while his teammates were bashing each other silly in the drill. True to his word, Lombardi kept silent—and McGee's fellow players never noticed.[2]

Lombardi appreciated that McGee respected him enough to approach him directly with his concerns about the drill. And Max McGee was grateful that Coach Lombardi respected him enough to suggest a way around the drill without sacrificing team discipline. Lombardi's players didn't always agree with him or even like him, but they always respected him—and he respected them.

Vince Jr. observed that, like most leaders, his famous father "had a few people who rebelled against his way of leadership. They went somewhere else, and he stayed. The interesting thing is that almost every one of his players, even the ones who left, still respected him."[3] Vince Jr. went on to recite one of his father's rules of leadership:

Win respect; affection may follow.
Respect motivates. Win their respect first.[4]

Leaders don't have to be liked, but they *must* be respected or they cannot lead. Offensive guard Ray Schoenke, who played one season for Lombardi with the Washington Redskins, put it this way: "As much as I hated the guy, and I did—I *hated* him!—I had tremendous respect for him. Tremendous. I played some of my best football of my life under him."[5] Coach Lombardi's relationship with his players was always paradoxical. He could be harsh and abrasive, berating and insulting his players on the practice field—then he'd go inside the locker room and affirm them, telling them what a great future they had in the NFL. And when his players showed him respect, he repaid their respect with loyalty and kindness. Vince Jr. recalled:

> He was at times a spontaneously warm, genuine, and compassionate individual who privately took steps to help his players through troubled times. When a player's son broke his leg, Lombardi called the hospital to check on the boy's progress. When a player's mother died in an auto accident, Lombardi arranged to fly that player home and have a wreath of flowers sent. There were countless incidents like these, most of which went unnoticed by anyone except those directly involved. He laughed and cried openly with his players. He lived their lives with them, and that, for many, was enormously motivating.[6]

Respect paves the way to your future as a leader. Solomon said, "Fear GOD, dear child—respect your leaders; don't be defiant or mutinous. Without warning your life can turn upside down, and who knows how or when it might happen?" (Proverbs 24:21, 22, *The Message*). Here Solomon addresses his leadership wisdom to followers and subordinates. He is saying, in effect, "Life is uncertain. You never know when disaster might strike out of nowhere. So it's wise to be on good terms with people in leadership positions. Respect your leaders and their authority. Don't defy them—because a time may come when you will need a leader's help."

Let me suggest two principles of respect from these two verses.

‖ BUILD BRIDGES OF RESPECTFUL RELATIONSHIPS; DON'T BURN THEM ‖

Make a conscious effort to build a network of mutually beneficial relationships with other people—and especially with those who have the power to affect your future. Show respect to people in authority, even to people you dislike. You may think they are unfair; respect them anyway. You may disagree with their leadership style; respect them anyway. You may think they have mistreated you; respect them anyway.

Is there a leader who has been tough on you or has even made your life miserable? Perhaps you have fantasized about marching right up to him and telling him off to his face. Don't. No matter how he behaves, no matter how overbearing or unfair he seems, be respectful. Work hard. Earn your paycheck. Put any mutinous thoughts out of your mind. You may think that the satisfaction of telling off your boss is worth whatever consequences might ensue—but the consequences may be far worse than you have imagined.

In his 2009 mystery novel *Still Waters,* Nigel McCrery relates a fictional conversation between two women, Eunice and Daisy. Eunice is the sole proprietor of a failing art gallery. She admits that her art gallery is on its last legs because she has no business skills. "I can't do advertising," she says. "I don't know how people think. No head for business. Accounts just leave me cold. Don't understand cash flow; don't understand the lingo."

Daisy is sympathetic. "You need someone to help you out."

Eunice shrugs. "I used to have someone to do that, but they left. I have a tendency to speak my mind, you know. Some people respond badly to that. Good riddance to them, I say. Problem is, I seem to have burned my bridges. Nobody here wants to help out anymore."[7]

That's what happens to people who simply have to speak whatever is on their minds. They burn their bridges behind them—and when times get tough, there is no one around to bail them out.

‖ MAKE RESPECT FOR OTHERS A CORNERSTONE OF YOUR LIFE ‖

Treat *everyone* with respect: your leaders, your peers, your subordinates, and strangers on the street. If you ingratiate yourself with leaders but treat everyone else with disrespect, then you're simply a manipulator. There are names for people who show insincere "respect" only to people who can do something for them in return: apple polisher, bootlicker, sycophant, yes-man.

Insincere respect is easy to spot. Savvy leaders know when subordinates are just trying to get on their good side. Choose to become a person who *genuinely* respects everyone. Treat the server at the restaurant with respect. Treat the panhandler on the street corner with respect. If you cultivate a habit of showing respect to everyone, then respecting your leaders will come naturally and easily.

In 1996, the Magic played the Bulls in the Eastern Conference Finals of the NBA Playoffs. We were quickly dispatched in four games. Michael Jordan had returned from his baseball odyssey, and he was very focused. Before game three in the Orlando Arena, I was standing outside the Bulls locker room. Dr. John Heffernon was there—he was the Bulls' team physician throughout the Jordan era. I asked him, "Twenty years from now, what are you going to remember most about Michael Jordan?"

He said, "Aside from the fact that he is the most competitive human being ever to walk the face of the earth and has absolutely no fear of failure, what I'm most going to remember is that he respected everybody the same. It didn't matter if you were the president or the ball boy, the pope or the equipment manager, he treated everybody with respect."

Coach Mike Krzyzewski told me of the time when he served on the 1992 Olympic Dream Team as assistant to head coach Chuck Daly. He recalled that Michael Jordan, who was at the peak of his stardom, always addressed him with the utmost respect: "Coach, would you please help me with my shooting? Thank you, Coach. Thank you very much." Jordan always said please and thank you and addressed his coaches as Coach. To this day, Mike Krzyzewski is amazed that the great Michael Jordan treated him, a college coach, with such respect.

John Wooden tells this story from his basketball coaching experience at UCLA that illustrates the importance of showing respect to others:

> I once interviewed a very talented young man who wanted to attend UCLA on a basketball scholarship. I was even prepared to offer him a scholarship during our meeting. His mother was there, and at one point she politely asked me a question. Her son immediately looked over at her and snapped, "How can you be so ignorant? Just keep your mouth shut and listen to

what the coach says." I assured her the question was fine and answered it.

The young man, however, had revealed an aspect of himself that wasn't fine. In fact, it was unacceptable to me: disrespect for his mother. If he couldn't respect her, how could he possibly respect me when things got tough? I politely ended the meeting and excused myself. The scholarship was never offered.[8]

That young man's mother was the first leader and authority figure in his life—and he had treated her with disrespect. A player who will disrespect one leader will eventually disrespect others. There's no room on anybody's team for defiance or disrespect.

———|————|———

Are you building bridges—or burning them? Do you respect everyone you meet—or only those who can do you a favor? Make respect for others an absolute and unbending rule for your life. Heed Solomon's wise advice: "Fear GOD, dear child—respect your leaders."

GET WISDOM, GET UNDERSTANDING
QUESTIONS FOR PERSONAL REFLECTION OR GROUP DISCUSSION

1 || Has there been a time when you rebelled against leadership? Describe the consequences of that rebellion. If you had it to do over again, would you handle things differently? Why or why not?

2 || Explain the difference between being *liked* and being *respected*. If possible, cite examples.

3 || Have you ever had a leader whom you disliked but still respected? Explain, from your own experience, how it is possible to respect someone you dislike.

4 || Are there any relationship bridges you have "burned" in the past? What actions can you take this week to repair those bridges?

5 || On a scale of 1 to 10, how would you rate yourself at showing respect for others—not only leaders but also subordinates, followers, and strangers? How well do you show respect even for people who cannot help you, such as panhandlers on the street?

6 || Twenty years from now, what do you think people will remember most about you? What would you *like* for them to remember most about you?

7 || How does that question affect the way you intend to live this coming week and beyond?

SEVENTEEN

THE BREADTH AND DEPTH
OF A GREAT LEADER

Proverbs 25:3

L eadership authority John C. Maxwell formulated a principle he calls the Law of Process. He says that if you make a diligent, daily effort to grow in leadership skills, you will undergo a lifelong process of becoming increasingly more competent as a leader.

Maxwell tells about a time he spoke at a leadership seminar in Denver. During the seminar he noticed a nineteen-year-old attendee named Brian. During the first couple of days, he observed that Brian was a sponge for knowledge. The young man took copious notes, interacted with fellow attendees, and asked Maxwell question after question.

On the third day of the seminar, Maxwell talked to the group about the Law of Process, and asked Brian to stand up.

"Brian," he said, "I've been watching you here, and I'm very impressed with how hungry you are to learn and glean and grow. I want to tell you a secret that will change your life."

The moment he said that, everyone in the room leaned forward. Maxwell continued:

In about twenty years, you can be a *great* leader. I want to encourage you to make yourself a lifelong learner of leadership. Read books, listen to tapes regularly, and keep attending seminars. And whenever you come across a golden nugget of truth or a significant quote, file it away for the future. . . . And in twenty years, when you're only thirty-nine years old, if you've continued to learn and grow, others will likely start asking you to teach them about leadership. And some will be amazed. They'll look at each other and say, "How did he suddenly become so wise?"[1]

An authentic leader is a lifelong learner. He can never afford to settle for the narrow and the shallow. Solomon said, "Like the horizons for breadth and the ocean for depth, the understanding of a good leader is broad and deep" (Proverbs 25:3, *The Message*). We must continually widen the breadth of our knowledge and deepen the oceans of our understanding.

|| THE BREADTH OF A GREAT LEADER ||

Theodore Roosevelt was a kind leader of great breadth and depth. His mind was like the horizon—wide and all-inclusive. He was curious about everything. His reading list was eclectic, ranging from history to biography to science to sports to the arts and literature. As committed to building up his body as he was to building his mind, he was an avid weightlifter, hiker, hunter, boxer, and horseman.

Roosevelt was elected vice president of the United States in 1901 and became president later that year after the assassination of President McKinley. At forty-two, he was the youngest president in U.S. history. He was later reelected by a large majority. Under his two-term leadership, America emerged as a major power, constructed a world-class navy, dug the Panama Canal, and brokered peace between Russia and Japan—a feat that won him the Nobel Peace Prize.

As soon as he was out of office in 1909, he headed a scientific expedition to Africa under the auspices of the Smithsonian Institution. Four years later, he led a mapping expedition up the previously unexplored River of Doubt in Brazil. His curiosity was boundless and energized by childlike wonder and curiosity. He described the Brazil expedition, undertaken when he was fifty-five years old, as "my last chance to be a boy."[2]

Theodore Roosevelt had an insatiable hunger for knowledge that lasted literally until his dying day. He died in his sleep of a heart attack on January 6, 1919. When the coroner came to remove Roosevelt's body, he found something hidden under the late president's pillow—a book.[3] I would love to know the author and title of the last book Teddy Roosevelt ever read. Unfortunately, that bit of information was not preserved for us.

Great leaders have always been avid readers. Charles Stewart Given, in his 1905 book *A Fleece of Gold,* discussed the many leaders in history whose lives have been shaped by books. He wrote:

> We see Lincoln reading his favorite volumes by the dim light of a pineknot blaze . . . or [U.S. president James] Garfield gazing intently at the pages while riding a mule on the banks of a canal. [Preacher John] Wesley likewise diligently searched the scriptures while riding horseback over the country . . . and we are told that Alexander the Great, each night on retiring, would place his favorite book, the *Iliad,* under his pillow and during his waking moments would peruse its pages.[4]

As a leader, you *must* cultivate a taste for good books of all kinds—a wide-ranging curiosity about many subjects. Most of us tend to confine our reading to a limited spectrum of favorite books. But if you cultivate a curiosity about a broad horizon of subjects and read great books on each of those subjects, you will discover a whole world of knowledge—and insights and ideas that you can apply to your leadership life—that you never could have found any other way.

Explore every facet, every principle, every insight you can learn about leadership. John C. Maxwell put it this way: "When . . . [people] ask me what I do for a living, some of them are intrigued when I say I write books and speak. And they often ask what I write about. When I say leadership, the response that makes me chuckle most goes something like this: 'Oh. Well, when I become a leader, I'll read some of your books!' What I don't say (but want to) is: 'If you'd read some of my books, maybe you'd become a leader.'"[5]

‖ THE DEPTH OF A GREAT LEADER ‖

A leader teaches, mentors, coaches, counsels, and empowers. Leaders inspire and influence others. They exemplify character. They are the living embodiment of the vision and values of the organization. Anyone with a loud voice can give orders, but it takes an authentic leader to impart knowledge and wisdom to his followers.

John F. Kennedy once said, "Learning and leadership are indispensable to each other."[6]

In order to teach, you must be intensely committed to continual learning. You must understand that learning is not a process that ended years ago when you graduated. Authentic leaders are committed to *lifelong learning*—and to *learning in depth.*

The breadth of a leader is his wide-ranging curiosity about a vast array of subjects and issues. The depth of a leader is his willingness to dig deeply into every issue, to master many fields of knowledge, to plumb the uttermost reaches of each subject.

Years ago, I attended a seminar in Orlando conducted by management guru Tom Peters. Tom was roaming around the room, speaking extemporaneously and straight from the heart. All the attendees were spellbound. I remember vividly one statement he made: "Look in the mirror! If the chief isn't curious, the troops aren't likely to be."

My wife, Ruth, and I share a fanatical zeal for learning. She and I have both earned masters degrees, and Ruth is enrolled in Walden University pursuing her PhD in organizational leadership. Most people can't wait to get out of school so they don't have to spend so much time thinking and reading and learning. Ruth and I feel like we've never left school—and never want to. Learning is fascinating. Nothing makes you feel quite so alive as daily, continually making new discoveries and gaining new insights into the world.

Success and leadership authority Brian Tracy once told me that if I were to read just one hour a day, I would read a book a week. I could schedule my hour of reading anyway I liked—one sixty-minute session, two thirty-minute sessions, or sixty one-minute sessions. If I just committed myself to reading one hour per day, I would read 52 books per year—or 520 books per decade. Then Brian said something that really hit home: "Pat, if you read just 5 books on a specific subject, you can consider yourself a world-class expert on that subject." By reading those 5 books, I could become a *leader* on that subject! I could become an *authority*!

Brian Tracy's formula for leadership success inspired me so much that today I never spend just one little hour of reading per day. Fact is, I read 3 or 4 books a week, between 150 and 200 books a year. My favorite subjects are the Bible, American history (especially the Civil War), the lives of great leaders, biographies of sports heroes, and principles of management and business leadership.

I could probably give an hour-long impromptu speech on any one of those fields of study—on a moment's notice. Why? Because Brian Tracy is right! Having read so many books, I am an authority on many subjects. Not only do I have breadth as a reader, I have a depth of knowledge. I have plunged into the ocean of knowledge, and I would gladly drown myself in those depths and never come up for air.

The older I get, the more devoted I am to my reading. I've found that as I have trained myself to read, year by year, my brain has become more discerning. I can scan pages and tell very quickly whether or not there are useful ideas and information there. My eyes glide down the page very quickly. As soon as I spot a profound idea, a fascinating story, or some useful information, I slow down, I savor, I highlight and scribble notes in the margins.

With practice I've been able to read faster and retain more of the truly essential ideas in every book I read. My mind has become like a gold miner's pan. All the worthless sand and pebbles are sluiced away, leaving behind the flecks and nuggets of pure, precious gold.

———

Best-selling author Rick Warren challenged me recently when he said, "How do I have time for all the books I read? I don't watch television. Nothing you watch on TV will matter five years from now. It's not that it's bad; it's just not necessary. You trade your life for a TV show."[7]

Dr. Sheila Murray Bethel, an expert on leadership and organizational change and in great demand as a keynote speaker, is the author of *A New Breed of Leader*. In that book she writes, "Make lifelong learning a way of life, and in so doing, nourish a spirit of curiosity and develop a desire for intellectual growth. Use whatever experiences life provides to follow your passions, to aim high, and to remain committed to excellence."[8]

Let your mind span the broad horizon of knowledge. Let your soul plumb the ocean depths of understanding. Effective leadership is the reward of continuous learning.

GET WISDOM, GET UNDERSTANDING
QUESTIONS FOR PERSONAL REFLECTION OR GROUP DISCUSSION

1 || On a scale of 1 to 10, how would you rate the breadth of your leadership understanding? Do you have a broad knowledge of a lot of leadership subjects and issues? Explain your answer. Which areas do you consider your greatest strengths?

2 || On a scale of 1 to 10, how would you rate the depth of your leadership understanding? Do you have deep insight and great depths of knowledge of those leadership issues? Explain your answer.

3 || How many books would you say you read in an average month? Could you call yourself a broadly and deeply read individual? If yes, explain how you came to be motivated to read on a regular basis. If no, what are the factors that keep you from reading? What specific steps can you take this week to become a broader, deeper reader?

4 || What kinds of books or periodicals do you generally read? What are the gaps in your leadership knowledge base that you should fill by reading books in those areas?

5 || What steps could you take this week to cultivate a greater curiosity about a broad horizon of subjects?

6 || How much television do you watch in an average day? What kinds of shows do you watch—shows that inform, enlighten, and engage your mind or mindless television merely to stop thinking for a while?

7 || What changes could you make in your entertainment and leisure habits in order to spend more time learning and growing, and less time zoned out in front of the TV?

EIGHTEEN

WHEN LEADERS
GO BAD

‖ Proverbs 25:4, 5 ‖

Jim Jones was a natural leader with a charismatic personality. A committed Marxist, he was troubled by the anti-Communist fervor that swept the country in the 1950s. He once told an interviewer, "I decided, how can I demonstrate my Marxism? The thought was, infiltrate the church."[1] So Jim Jones became a student pastor at a Methodist church in Indianapolis. Later, after attending a healing service at a Seventh Day Baptist Church, he decided that he could use religion to attract a crowd—and make a lot of money.[2]

So Jim Jones founded his own church in Indianapolis, which he called the Peoples Temple. At the same time, he became a political activist and community organizer. In 1961, the mayor appointed him executive director of the Indianapolis Human Rights Commission.[3]

As a leader, Jones did many good things. He pressured Indianapolis hospitals to desegregate their wards. He and his wife adopted several non-Caucasian children, and he called his family a "rainbow family." He encouraged other Temple members to adopt children of other races.[4] In the mid-1960s, Jones moved the Peoples Temple to northern California and began preaching a "gospel" he called "apostolic socialism." His stated goal was to create a socialist "Eden" on earth. Though he ridiculed traditional religion, he used religious language to attract followers and donations,[5] while privately confiding that he was actually an atheist.[6]

Jim Jones openly claimed to be the reincarnation of Jesus, Buddha, Gandhi, and other political and religious leaders of the past. One former Peoples Temple member, Hue Fortson Jr., told interviewers that Jones would say, "If you see me as your friend, I'll be your friend. If you see me as your father, I'll be your father. . . . If you see me as your savior, I'll be your savior. If you see me as your God, I'll be your God."[7]

In 1975, Jones moved the Peoples Temple headquarters to San Francisco. There he again became deeply involved in local politics, urging his people to get out to vote for George Moscone as mayor. It was a close election, and Jim Jones's support was decisive in getting Moscone elected. In return, Moscone appointed Jones chairman of the San Francisco Housing Authority Commission. As in Indianapolis, Jones gained prominence as a religious leader, a community organizer, and a political kingpin.[8] His prominence enabled him to befriend such leading personalities as First Lady Rosalynn Carter, Vice President Walter Mondale, California governor Jerry Brown, and political boss Willie Brown.[9]

|| "DIE WITH SOME DIGNITY" ||

While the Peoples Temple flourished in San Francisco, Jones began building his ultimate "socialist paradise" in the remote jungles of Guyana, South America, where he hoped to escape the scrutiny of the U.S. government and the media. He called it Jonestown. Once Peoples Temple members moved to Jonestown, they were not allowed to leave.

In November 1978, Congressman Leo Ryan conducted a fact-finding mission to Jonestown, investigating charges that Peoples Temple members were being held against their will. Congressman Ryan visited the site, spoke with Peoples Temple members, and agreed to take several of them back to the States. At the airstrip, Ryan was preparing to board his plane when members of the cult opened fire, killing Ryan and four other members of his delegation (including three journalists).[10]

Later that day, 909 Peoples Temple members, including 276

children, died in Jonestown, most of them by self-ingested cyanide poisoning. Jim Jones himself died of a gunshot wound to the head. A tape recorder made an audio record of the last minutes of the people of Jonestown. Jones is heard on the tape, speaking over the sound of screaming women and wailing children: "Lay down your life with dignity. . . . This is not the way for people who are socialists or communists to die. No way for us to die. We must die with some dignity. . . . Look children, it's just something to put you to rest. . . . I don't care how many screams you hear, I don't care how many anguished cries, death is a million times preferable to ten more days of this life."[11]

Jim Jones exemplifies the most dangerous sort of leader—one who is charismatic and charming, a persuasive speaker, and a ruthless manipulator. He easily made friends in high places, and they helped him to build his reputation and increase his power. No one challenged him. No one tried to stop him. As a result, nearly a thousand of his followers died in the jungle.

The leadership world is filled with example after example of bad leaders who lead for the wrong reasons—and who lead their followers into destruction. These bad leaders are not guided by ethical principles or a desire to serve others, but by their own greed, lust, and narcissistic ambition. Ever see any of those traits crop up in *your* life? Beware. A bad leader can drive a company into bankruptcy, take a nation into a costly war or financial collapse, or leave a church divided and dying.

Solomon wisely warned us against bad leaders when he said, "Remove impurities from the silver and the silversmith can craft a fine chalice; remove the wicked from leadership and authority will be credible and God-honoring" (Proverbs 25:4, 5, *The Message*). We need to take the hint not to *become* bad leaders. Corrupt leaders are like gross impurities embedded in precious metal. The finest, most skilled silversmith in the world cannot make a beautiful silver chalice from metal that is defiled by impurities. And a great nation, a great organization, a great team, or a great church cannot survive being led by a corrupt leader.

When a leader goes bad, his corruption must be exposed and removed. Otherwise, everything he touches will be ruined. Bad leadership almost always produces death—the death of the team, the death of the dream, the death of an organization. And sometimes bad leaders—like Jim Jones, Hitler, Stalin, Mao—produce *literal* death on a massive scale.

THE TRAGIC LESSON OF SOLOMON'S FATHER

Solomon knew about the dangerous side of leadership. His father was King David. In 2 Samuel 11:1-5, we read of a time when King David did indeed go bad. It was the time of year when kings go off to war—yet King David didn't go to war. Instead, he sent his nephew Joab, the general in command of the army, out to the battlefield, and he remained behind. During David's reign, Israel's borders were continually under attack from various tribes. David had certain duties as a leader, including overseeing the national security and defense of Israel. But he was derelict in that duty this time. He sent Joab out and remained behind in Jerusalem. He let down his guard as the leader of the nation.

Next, David let down his guard as a man of integrity. From his palace roof he saw a beautiful woman bathing. He engaged in voyeurism—the ancient version of Internet porn. He probably thought, *What's the harm in looking?* But of course, it didn't end there. The mental image of this woman stayed with him and haunted him. He couldn't stop thinking about her and fantasizing about her. He had already surrendered his integrity by not attending to his duties as king. He surrendered a bit more by lusting after this beautiful woman.

Then David took the deconstruction of his integrity one step further: "David sent to ask about her, and was told, 'Isn't this Bathsheba, daughter of Eliam and wife of Uriah the Hittite?' David sent his agents to get her. After she arrived, he went to bed with her. . . . Then she returned home. Before long she realized she was pregnant" (2 Samuel 11:4, 5, *The Message*).

David knew that Bathsheba was married to Uriah, one of David's most loyal, conscientious, and decorated soldiers. Yet David chose to commit adultery with Bathsheba, betraying this man.

And it got worse. When David learned that Bathsheba was

pregnant, he tried to cover up his sin. He called Uriah home from the battlefield and urged the man to spend the night with his wife. This way, David's baby would appear to be the child of Uriah—and no one would be any the wiser. But Uriah was such a principled and upright man that he refused the rightful pleasures of his own marriage bed as long as his men were undergoing hardship on the battlefield.

When David's cover-up plot failed, he resorted to murder. He sent Uriah back to the front lines and ordered Joab to withdraw his men and allow Uriah to be killed by the enemy. Faithful Uriah was murdered because of his own king's scheme—and David married Bathsheba.

But God sent the prophet Nathan to confront David and call him to repentance. Nathan showed David that he was a leader-gone-bad. In a flash, David saw how far he had fallen, and he repented. God forgave and restored David—but the son he and Bathsheba had together died. David's life was never the same after that. The consequences of David's sin would haunt him until his death.

Later, David and Bathsheba had another son—Solomon. So the story of David's sin with Bathsheba is an integral part of Solomon's own family history. David chose Solomon to be his successor, so we can be sure that he invested a great deal of time teaching Solomon what he would need to know to lead the nation. He mentored Solomon and taught him all about statecraft, diplomacy, economics, commerce, the military arts, and more.

I imagine that, in the course of those conversations, David sat down with Solomon and had the most painful conversation a man could ever have with his son. I believe David told young Solomon about his failure to be a leader to his army, about his sin of adultery, his crime of murder, his cowardly act of covering up his actions. Perhaps the reason Solomon was so wise at such an early age was that David had been brutally honest with him concerning his own moral failures.

I can picture King David, with tears streaming down his cheeks, confessing what he had done—then pleading with Solomon, "My son, don't do what I did. I murdered a man who was loyal to me. Don't let lust drive you to abuse your power. Learn from my failure. Be wise. Guard your integrity."

And for most of Solomon's tenure as king of Israel, he ruled wisely. He was the greatest national leader the world had ever seen and was renowned and respected throughout the world. He did not abuse his power, he did not compromise his integrity . . . until the final years of his reign. Then, the Old Testament grimly reminds us, "Even he was led into sin by foreign women" (Nehemiah 13:26).

‖ THOSE WHO CORRUPT POWER ‖

The abuse of power is an ever-present temptation in leadership. Authentic leadership is the effective and ethical use of power—the power of position, the power of persuasion, and in some situations, the power of coercion. There are many so-called leaders who abuse their power in order to inflate their own egos, to fill their bank accounts, to get sex, or to control the lives of others. You find corrupt leaders at every level of the social order, from the aisles of the local retail store to the hallways of the university to the corridors of power in New York and Washington, D.C.

English historian Lord Acton (1834–1902) said, "Power tends to corrupt, and absolute power corrupts absolutely." I disagree. I don't think power corrupts people. Rather, people corrupt power—and they do so whenever they *abuse* power. Power cannot corrupt anyone. It only *reveals* the corruption and lack of integrity that is *already* within some people. There are many ways a leader may go bad by abusing power. Here are a few examples:

- *Nepotism—abusing power by dispensing unmerited favors to family members*
- *Plagiarism—abusing power by stealing the ideas of or taking credit for the work of others*
- *Cruelty—abusing power through harmful or humiliating behavior toward subordinates*
- *Intimidation—abusing power by controlling subordinates with threats or fear*
- *Self-deification—treating subordinates as servants and demanding that they treat the leader as a master*

- *Sexual exploitation—abusing power to exploit subordinates for sexual favors*
- *Inequity—abusing power by dispensing benefits based on favoritism*
- *Misappropriation—wrongfully enriching oneself at the expense of the organization*

If I asked your followers whether you, their leader, had ever committed any of those abuses of power, what would they say? Confront these issues head-on today. As with David, it may not be too late to repent, to ask forgiveness, to become an exemplary and inspiring leader once more.

But what if you are a subordinate who knows that your leader abuses power? What if your leader exploits you or others? leads by intimidation or cruelty? engages in sexual harassment or financial corruption? orders you to do things that are dishonest or illegal?

You have a choice to make. You have to do what's right, even if you must pay a price to do so. Don't let a bad boss turn you into an accomplice in his corruption. If a bad leader abuses power, you are not obligated to follow him. In fact, you have an obligation *not* to obey any orders that violate your conscience or the law.

Ultimately, leaders only have the power that followers give them. When you see a leader go bad, it may be time for *you* to become a moral leader and set an ethical example. It may well be time for *you* to take a stand and say, "What you want me to do is wrong—and I won't participate in it." That's moral leadership. Sometimes moral leadership is costly. Step up and pay the price.

Henrik Ibsen writes in his play *An Enemy of the People,* "The strongest man in the world is he who stands most alone."[12] Remove the impurities from the silver—and remove corrupt people from leadership. Then leadership will be credible and honorable and a service to God and humanity.

GET WISDOM, GET UNDERSTANDING
QUESTIONS FOR PERSONAL REFLECTION OR GROUP DISCUSSION

1 || Can you recall a time when a leader you trusted in the government, your organization, or some other leadership arena went bad? How did you feel when you discovered that leader was corrupt? How did that leader's actions impact your life?

2 || In the situation you just cited, what happened to that leader? Did he or she stay in power—or was that leader removed from power? Do you think the situation was resolved in a healthy way or a dysfunctional way? What was the long-term result of that situation?

3 || King David, Solomon's father, committed terrible acts of moral failure, including adultery and murder. What specific parallels do you see between King David's moral failure and the failures of any leaders today, including leaders in the arenas of government, business, and religion?

4 || What lessons do you find in David's tragic story?

5 || Which do you believe—that power corrupts people or that people corrupt power? Explain your answer.

6 || Look back at the list of abuses of power on page 157. Have any of those actions by a bad leader adversely affected your life and your leadership career? How so?

7 || How should organizations respond when leaders go bad and commit such acts? Be as specific as possible.

8 || If your leader goes bad, how should you respond? Take into account the advice given in this chapter as well as this observation from chapter 10: "Think twice about reporting your boss to superiors. Higher-ups often view people with complaints as troublemakers, and you may end up sabotaging your own career." How do you reconcile the advice in this chapter with the advice in chapter 10?

9 || What safeguards can you implement that will ensure that you won't become a bad leader yourself?

NINETEEN

LEADERSHIP IN TIMES
OF CRISIS

|| Proverbs 28:2 ||

A t 4:00 AM on October 6, 1973, an operative of the Israeli spy agency Mossad relayed an urgent message to the Israeli high command. The message warned that Egypt and Syria would launch a coordinated surprise attack within hours. It was Yom Kippur, the Day of Atonement, the holiest day on the Jewish calendar.

Prime Minister Golda Meir ordered the Israeli Air Force to full alert and mobilized the reserves. The first soldiers streamed into their bases along the northeastern border with Syria and the southern border with Egypt. They arrived mere minutes before both Arab nations launched their attack.

The Arab offensive began with massive artillery shelling and air attacks along the Sinai frontier. About an hour later, Egyptian tanks and infantry poured across the border. Because the Israelis were caught off guard, they had only 300 tanks in defensive position when the Egyptians crossed the Suez front with an estimated 90,000 soldiers and 850 tanks. The element of surprise tilted the battle heavily in the favor of the Arab attackers, and even the Egyptians were amazed at their early successes.

In the north, some 180 Israeli tanks defended the Golan Heights against the advance of 1,400 Syrian tanks. After a long, fierce battle, the Israeli tanks succeeded in driving the Syrians back—but the counteroffensive was costly in both soldiers and war matériel.

Israel did not gain the initiative until the third day of the war—and even then, Israeli losses were so heavy that Golda Meir and her cabinet met to consider seeking a cease-fire. The Israeli Air Force had lost many planes and could not replace them, because the U.S. government inexplicably refused to ship replacements. Meanwhile, the Soviet Union was rapidly rearming Syria and Egypt. After a heated discussion, Meir concluded that a cease-fire would constitute an acknowledgment of defeat—and Israel could not afford to admit weakness.

So Golda Meir made the decision: fight on. The Egyptians launched another major offensive on October 14—and the Israelis responded by destroying 250 Egyptian tanks while losing only 25 of their own. The collapse of the Egyptian offensive was the turning point of the southern war. The next day, the Israelis crossed the Suez Canal and encircled the Egyptian 2nd and 3rd Armies.

At that point, the United States belatedly began airlifting military hardware to Israel. By October 22, the Egyptian forces had been so thoroughly devastated that the Soviets urged Egypt to seek an immediate cease-fire. That cease-fire was agreed to on October 24. The Yom Kippur War was over—at a cost of 2,688 Israeli soldiers killed and 7,250 wounded.

The Yom Kippur War was the greatest crisis in the short history of the modern state of Israel. At least nine Arab nations actively aided the Egyptians and Syrians, contributing funding, weapons, and soldiers in an effort to destroy Israel. Had the war gone differently at a few key junctures, Israeli forces might well have been defeated—and the Jewish state would have ceased to exist.[1]

The tipping point in the war was probably the moment Golda Meir made her decision *not* to seek a cease-fire, even though Israel appeared to be losing. At the darkest moment of the crisis, she chose to bet everything on victory. In hindsight, it was clearly the right decision. But in a crisis, such decisions must be made without the benefit of hindsight.

Solomon wrote, "When the country is in chaos, everybody has a plan to fix it—but it takes a leader of real understanding to straighten things out" (Proverbs 28:2, *The Message*).

"ATTENTIVE TO THE PEOPLE'S VOICE"

Who was this woman who led Israel through its most perilous crisis? Golda Meir was born in the Ukraine in 1898. Her family emigrated to the United States when she was eight years old, and she grew up in Wisconsin. In high school, she joined a Zionist group, the Workers of Zion. In 1921, she and her husband moved to British-controlled Palestine and lived in a kibbutz. She learned the ropes of leadership by working her way up the ranks of a trade union and a construction corporation. After Britain terminated its mandate over Palestine in 1948, she helped raise funds to finance Israel's war of independence against its Arab neighbors.

She demonstrated amazing courage when, in 1948, Israel's first prime minister, David Ben-Gurion, sent her on a dangerous mission to Jordan. Disguised as an Arab woman, she went to Amman and secretly met with Jordan's King Abdullah, urging him not to attack the newborn state of Israel. Later that year, she was appointed Israel's ambassador to the Soviet Union. She eventually served in the Israeli legislature, the Knesset. From 1956 to 1966, she was Israel's foreign minister and worked to build strong relations with the United States and Latin America. She became prime minister in 1969, following the death of her predecessor, Levi Eshkol.

After the Yom Kippur War, there was considerable criticism of Golda Meir's leadership. Why had her government missed the warning signs that Egypt and Syria were preparing to attack? Why were the Israeli defense forces caught off guard? Even though her government won reelection, Golda Meir decided that she lacked the full support of the people, and she resigned in 1974 in favor of Yitzhak Rabin.[2]

Golda Meir did not view power and leadership as a personal entitlement but as tools to serve the people. If the people questioned her leadership, then she would willingly relinquish her authority. As Israeli historian Yaakov Hasdai observed, Golda Meir "understood what it means to have leadership that draws its power and trust from the people and was attentive to the people's voice. Therefore, when she sensed she lost the source of her true power, she quit. This was an impressive display of real leadership that we did not appreciate at the time."[3]

Though Golda Meir was forced to fight a war, her goal was always peace. She once said, addressing the Palestinians and other Arabs with whom her nation so often struggled, "I can forgive you for killing my sons, but I cannot forgive you for forcing me to kill your sons."[4] She was a role model to you and me of bold, steady leadership in a time of crisis.

‖ RESPONDING TO A CRISIS ‖

Leaders are tested continually, but the most crucial test of leadership ability comes in times of crisis. A president or prime minister is tested by times of war, terrorist attacks, or natural disaster. A corporate CEO is tested when a downturn in the economy sends profits and stock prices crashing. A coach is tested when his star quarterback is sidelined and he must find a way to win with his untested backup.

Great leaders must cut through the clutter of conflicting advice and calm those who are panicking. They must radiate confidence and lay out a winning strategy. They must make high-quality decisions under high-pressure conditions. And they must find a way to succeed under the worst possible conditions. Here are seven surefire strategies for being a great leader in times of crisis.

1. Be prepared.

It's your job to imagine every conceivable worst-case scenario—then think of ways to keep those scenarios from happening. For every Plan A, you should have a Plan B. For every contingency, you should have a contingency plan. Drill your people periodically in how to respond to various crises. Make sure everyone knows his or her job in an emergency. A crisis may catch you by surprise, but it should never catch you unprepared.

As part of your crisis preparation, read about great leaders who faced major crises. Study the actions of Mayor Rudy Giuliani after the 9/11 terror attacks. Read about Winston Churchill's inspirational leadership during the Battle of Britain. Study Lech Walesa's leadership in the Lenin Shipyard strikes at Gdansk, Poland, in 1980. Examine the leadership style of Antarctic explorer Ernest Shackleton who, despite being shipwrecked for months at the bottom of the world, managed to bring his crew home without a single loss of life.

Study their leadership styles, their approach to decision making, the way they formed their teams, the way they communicated. Learn how the great leaders responded under fire—and when you find yourself in a crisis, you'll have a depth of insight to draw on.

2. Be visible.

Your followers need to know that you are a hands-on leader and that you have the situation under control. When there is a crisis, don't barricade yourself in an office. Don't rely on reports and phone calls from the front. Go to the front yourself. Let your people see you. Ask for their information and ideas. Show them you care about them and express your confidence in them.

Most of the great leaders we admire—George Washington, Abraham Lincoln, Winston Churchill, Dwight Eisenhower, Dr. Martin Luther King Jr.—were beloved because they were out among the people. They were in the trenches with them, not ensconced in ivory towers.

3. Be poised.

Don't let yourself or your organization be panicked or stampeded by a crisis. Help your followers and subordinates to remain calm and confident by maintaining an unruffled demeanor.

On March 30, 1981, a gunman attempted to assassinate President Ronald Reagan, just two months into his presidency. In the first hour following the shooting, there was confusion and disarray at the White House. Then Secretary of State Alexander Haig monitored events from the Situation Room. There were several televisions turned on with network coverage of the crisis. Haig saw the assistant press secretary, Larry Speakes, being questioned by reporters as he returned from the hospital where President Reagan was being treated. Reporters asked Speakes who was running the government—and Speakes answered that he didn't know.

Haig was horrified. The first job of the government in a time of crisis was to reassure the American people. So along with National

Security Adviser Richard Allen, Haig rushed out of the Situation Room, up a series of stairs, and into the pressroom. By the time he arrived, he was perspiring and out of breath—and many observers thought that he looked anxious and stressed. Even Richard Allen, standing at his side, was alarmed when he noticed that Haig's knees wobbled and his voice cracked.

When a reporter asked who was making decisions for the government, Haig stepped forward and replied, "Constitutionally, gentlemen, you have the President, the Vice President and the Secretary of State in that order. . . . As of now, I am in control here in the White House, pending return of the Vice President, and in close touch with him."[5]

Problem: What Haig described was *not* the constitutional order of succession, so it appeared to some that Haig had practically staged a palace coup—and had done so looking nervous and out of breath. It was not a reassuring performance!

The moral of the story: In times of crisis, always take a few moments to catch your breath and compose yourself before you try to reassure your followers. A poised leader can fill a room—or a nation—with confidence. A shaky leader can shake everyone's confidence.

4. Be bold and decisive.

Indecision is fatal to good leadership—especially in a crisis. Critical situations rarely improve while you wait for more information. When a leader puts off a decision, he is really deciding *not* to decide. Former Chrysler CEO Lee Iacocca once said, "I have always found that if I move with 75 percent or more of the facts, I usually never regret it. It's the guys who wait to have everything perfect that drive you crazy."[6]

Leaders must make decisions precisely because the best way forward is *not* always obvious. In a crisis, your followers need a leader to point the way through the fog of chaos and uncertainty. So decide boldly and sell that decision confidently to your followers. If you convince them it's the right decision, they will carry it out with such confidence and optimism that they can't help but succeed.

5. Be principled.

Don't let a crisis stampede you into betraying your principles. In a time of stress, it is easy to make decisions based on panic, fear, or other emotions. Some people, while in the throes of a crisis, say, "This is no time for standing on principle. This is an emergency!" But principles are *especially* important in a crisis.

In November 2009, I had General Richard B. Myers (USAF, retired) as a guest on my radio show. As Chairman of the Joint Chiefs of Staff (2001–2005), General Myers was the chief military adviser to President George W. Bush, the Secretary of Defense, and the National Security Council during the planning and execution of the war in Iraq. He is the author of the 2009 book *Eyes on the Horizon*.

During our interview, I asked about his memories of President Bush. He recalled one specific incident: "After 9/11, I was called to a private meeting at an underground location. President Bush was there with all his key cabinet members. He opened the meeting by telling us, 'We have some tough decisions to make which will be unpopular with the American public. I may end up being just a one-term president. So be it. We have to do what's best to protect our nation, and we'll let the chips fall where they may.'"

Ethical and moral principles are your guide to making wise decisions under stressful conditions. In a time of crisis, listen to your principles.

6. Focus on victory.

In the darkest hours of the Yom Kippur War, as Israel's losses mounted, Golda Meir and her cabinet considered the possibility of a cease-fire. But she wisely understood that *Israel had to win*—or the nation would surely lose everything. By pressing for total victory instead of a negotiated stalemate, Golda Meir led Israel to a decisive victory over the enemy.

In times of crisis, don't focus on curbing your losses—focus on victory. Find the will to win.

7. Learn the lessons of your crisis.

Once the crisis has passed, take time to analyze the situation. Meet with your subordinates. Ask yourselves, "Were we adequately prepared for this crisis? Did we respond effectively to the emergency? What did we do well? What could we have done better?" There are always lessons to be learned from a crisis. Make sure that none of those learning experiences is ever wasted.

When the country, the corporation, or the team is in chaos, everybody has a plan to fix it. Crises have a way of bringing forth all sorts of conflicting plans and ideas. Great leaders quickly sift through the conflicting advice, they remain calm and steady, and they make high-quality decisions amid perilous circumstances. They calm the fears of their followers and point the way to victory. Leaders of real understanding confidently straighten things out.

GET WISDOM, GET UNDERSTANDING
QUESTIONS FOR PERSONAL REFLECTION OR GROUP DISCUSSION

1 || Reflect on a time when your team or organization was thrown into chaos. In that situation did the leader straighten things out? Or was the leader overwhelmed by chaos? Explain your answer. What lessons did you learn from that situation?

2 || Note a time when you were tested by crisis. On a scale of 1 to 10, how would you rate your response to that crisis? Citing examples from that experience, explain how you arrived at that rating. With the benefit of hindsight, how could you have responded more effectively?

3 || Do you feel prepared for your next great leadership crisis? Why or why not? What are some specific actions you can take this week to prepare for a future crisis?

4 || On a scale of 1 to 10, how would you rate yourself as a decision maker? Cite specific examples from your experience to support your answer. What kind of grade would your followers give you as a decision maker?

5 || In times of crisis, do you find that your decisions are prompted primarily by panic, personal feelings, the views and arguments of others, or ethical principles? What specific steps can you take this week to become a more principle-driven decision maker?

TWENTY

AVOIDING
THE FALL

|| Proverbs 28:16 ||

In November 2009, I spoke to a gathering of executives from a company that had recently acquired a portion of Tyco International. A number of people there had come over to this new company from Tyco, and they remembered the most difficult era in that company's history—the Dennis Kozlowski era. At a predinner reception, several people talked to me about the scandal and upheaval. Though nearly a decade had passed, some were still shaking their heads in disbelief as they recalled those days.

As the CEO of Tyco International, Dennis Kozlowski engineered a number of successful mergers and profitable acquisitions. During his tenure, the company's revenue rose by an average of 48.7 percent per year from 1997 through 2001. By 1999, his annual compensation totaled $170 million.

In addition to his lavish compensation, Kozlowski arranged to have Tyco buy him a $30 million apartment, bankroll a $1 million birthday party for his wife on a Mediterranean island, and spend millions on fine art for his apartment (while he evaded $1 million in state sales taxes). In June 2005, he was convicted of misappropriating $400 million from the company.[1]

The Securities and Exchange Commission filing against Kozlowski catalogued a list of items he purchased with company funds, including "$15,000 for a dog-shaped umbrella stand . . . $17,000 for a traveling toilette box, $2,200 for a gold-plated wastebasket, $2,900 on coat hangers, $1,650 for an appointment book, $5,900 for sheets, $445 for a pincushion, and $6,000 on a shower curtain."[2]

Dennis Kozlowski is serving a term of up to twenty-four years in a correctional facility in New York. He was one of the top business leaders in the world, but he took a great fall—from the penthouse to the house of correction. He was one of the highest-paid executives in America, pulling down a generous nine-figure annual paycheck; yet all those millions weren't enough to satisfy him. He felt entitled to take money from his company and lavish it on his already-over-the-top lifestyle.

Who thinks so much of himself that even his *trash* deserves a gold-plated receptacle? Perhaps because he had overseen the company's growth, he felt he had earned every cent Tyco paid him—plus millions more to squander however he chose. But he operated without any ethical or moral restraint. He adopted a mind-set that rationalized unbelievable corruption—and he fell from power.

King Solomon wrote, "Among leaders who lack insight, abuse abounds, but for one who hates corruption, the future is bright" (Proverbs 28:16, *The Message*). If you want to enjoy a long and bright future as a leader, you need to build ethical guardrails around your life—safeguards to help you avoid a fall.

|| THE EXAMPLE YOU SET ||

In July 2002, I contacted the office of Gerald R. Ford, who had served as president of the United States from 1974 to 1977. I was working on a book about my friend Rich DeVos, and I wanted an interview with Mr. Ford because he and Rich were good friends. A few days later, my office phone rang and a woman said, "Are you available to take a call from President Ford?"

I certainly was! Moments later, I heard, "Pat Williams, this is Jerry Ford."

With my yellow legal pad at the ready, I proceeded to interview the former president for about a quarter of an hour. He had many fascinating reminiscences to share.

Mr. Ford was also an avid basketball fan, and he quizzed me about the prospects for the Orlando Magic's coming season. He was well acquainted with our team and the players we were drafting. Though he was a fan of the Denver Nuggets, he wished our team well.

After we ended the call, I sat back and thought to myself in amazement, *I just spoke with a man who was at the center of so much U.S. history—the man who healed the nation after Watergate! Yet he made it seem as if he was honored to talk to me!*

Four and a half years passed. The day after Christmas 2006, I heard the news that President Gerald Ford had died. I listened to the pundits on the news shows and read the columnists in the newspapers. They all summed up President Ford's legacy as one of forgiveness and healing. His decision to pardon Richard Nixon, though controversial at the time, was unanimously praised in hindsight.

And there was another trait of Gerald Ford that was widely praised following his death: his moral and ethical character. Thomas M. De-Frank, Washington Bureau Chief of the *New York Daily News,* covered Gerald Ford while he was in office and interviewed him many times during his retirement years. In a tribute to Ford published in the *Daily News* the day after Ford's death, DeFrank wrote, "After Nixon's divisive reign, Ford's normalcy and personal integrity were potent political assets. Asked at his first press conference if he planned to issue ethical guidelines to avoid another Watergate, he politely replied: 'The code of ethics will be the example I set.' Coming from Ford, no follow-up was required."[3]

Those are profound words. The leader of any organization sets the moral tone and defines the ethical culture of that organization. The life you and I live as leaders is a more powerful ethical teacher than any written code of ethics we might issue.

Leadership guru John C. Maxwell, in his book *There's No Such Thing As Business Ethics,* tells about a business dinner he had in New York with Lawrence J. Kirshbaum, chairman and CEO of the AOL Time Warner Book Group. Kirshbaum asked him, "What would you think about writing a book on business ethics?"

Maxwell replied, "There's no such thing."

Kirshbaum was surprised. "What do you mean?"

"There's no such thing as business ethics," Maxwell explained. "There's only ethics. People try to use one set of ethics for their professional life, another for their spiritual life, and still another at home with their family. That gets them into trouble. Ethics is ethics. If you desire to be ethical, you live it by one standard across the board."[4]

You cannot separate your leadership life from any other aspect of your life. You dare not say, "I am morally and ethically upright in my home and my place of worship, but in my leadership role I have to do whatever it takes to win." Any leader who takes that position is headed for a fall.

‖ YOUR ETHICAL GUARDRAILS ‖

Football coach John McKay was the winningest coach in the history of the University of Southern California, compiling a record of 127–40–8 from 1960 to 1975. Three of his USC Trojan teams went undefeated, and five won Rose Bowl games. Retired NFL coach Don Coryell worked as an assistant under John McKay at USC in 1960. I've met Don a time or two, and I once heard him tell this story about his mentor, John McKay:

> When I was working for him, one of our players found the opposing team's game plan in the locker room. He brought it to me and said, "What should we do with this?"
>
> I said, "We'd better show this to John."
>
> I took the game plan sheet to John and told him what it was. Without even glancing at it, he took it out of my hand, crumpled it into a ball, and threw it away. That's the kind of ethical leader John McKay was. Great coaches want to win honestly—no cheating, no cutting corners. If you have to cheat to win, what have you won? If you can't win without cheating, you shouldn't be coaching, because you're teaching the wrong kind of life lessons to your players.

Don't rationalize away your personal ethics in order to win. Great leaders do what is right, not what is easy. It can be convenient to lie, make false promises, cheat, or cover up a mistake you've made; but when you sacrifice your ethical principles to do what's convenient, you have ceased to lead. You have taken one more step toward creating a climate of corruption in your organization.

Ethics consist of the practical application of our moral philosophy to the everyday decisions we make and actions we take. Ethics must not be determined by our circumstances—they must be as immovable as granite, as upright as the Washington Monument. The decisions we make and the actions we take expose the truth about our ethics and character. We could have the most lofty and idealistic moral principles in the world, but if we continually violated them, we would have poor ethical character. In fact, the continual violation of our professed moral principles would make us hypocrites.

Unethical decisions leave cracks in our character. Every tiny compromise chips away at the foundation of who we are. As the compromises and unethical decisions add up, our character begins to crumble. And so goes our reputation—and our credibility as leaders.

One of the best ways to guard ourselves from moral and ethical decay is to place ourselves in accountable relationships with a few trusted friends and mentors. When you open your life to inspection by others, when you give other people the right to ask you the tough questions—"Have you compromised your integrity this past week? Have you been totally honest in your business dealings? in your bookkeeping and paying your taxes?"—then you put guardrails in place to keep you on the right path.

‖ YOUR BRIGHT FUTURE ‖

In 2007, federal investigators found that roughly 130 American companies had engaged in an illegal practice of backdating executive stock options in order to fatten the compensation packages of corporate executives. In his book *Come Home, America,* William Greider wrote, "A few [companies and executives] were prosecuted; most pleaded innocent error and promised not to do it again. The *Wall Street Journal* suggested that when so many CEOs had made the same 'mistake,' it could hardly be thought of as a crime. Warren Buffett, the billionaire investor, expressed a darker view: "The five most dangerous words in business may be "Everybody else is doing it," Buffett told his Berkshire Hathaway managers."[5]

Raymond V. Gilmartin, a professor at Harvard Business School, was president and CEO of Merck & Co., Inc., from 1994 to 2005. In a June 1999 commencement address at Union College in Schenectady, New York, he said:

> When we were young, I think most of us learned basic ethics: Don't lie, don't cheat, don't steal. Share what you have with others. Treat others with respect.
>
> Unfortunately, as we get older, there is a tendency to view things relatively. Don't cheat too much on your taxes. Don't lie to your friends . . .
>
> Genuine success depends on your values and your ethics. . . . Others may tell you that it's impossible to maintain certain values, because that's not the way it's done. . . . Some say that aggressive marketing means bending the rules; otherwise you can't win. I completely disagree. Not only do I think it's possible to succeed while maintaining ethical standards, I think it's the only way.[6]

Let me suggest that you ask yourself these five questions whenever you face a moral and ethical dilemma:

1. Is this decision permissible and legal? Would this decision violate the Ten Commandments, your personal moral code, company policy, or civil or criminal law?

2. Is it edifying? Will this decision build up people, improve lives, and enhance reputations—or will it tear people down? The goal of leadership should always be to edify and build people up.

3. Is it fair to everyone? Will this decision be equitable and just for all concerned? Or will someone get the short end of the stick?

4. Is this a decision I can be proud of? If news of this decision were published in the newspaper, would you feel good knowing that your friends and family members are reading about it? Any decision that you would feel embarrassed about or ashamed of is an unethical decision.

5. Is it consistent with the Golden Rule? How would you feel if the tables were turned and someone did this very thing to you? If you wouldn't like it, you shouldn't do it, period.

If the answer to even one of those questions is no, then the decision you are pondering is almost certainly unethical and a violation of integrity and good character. So make a habit of screening all your decisions through an ethical filter. The more frequently you analyze each decision from an ethical standpoint, the easier it gets to make wise decisions. Business speaker and author Price Pritchett said, "Your ethical muscle grows stronger every time you choose right over wrong."[7] So flex your ethical muscles.

Seek ethical insight. Hate corruption—avoid it with every fiber of your being. As Solomon promised, if you do these things, your future will be bright.

1 || On a scale of 1 to 10, how are you doing in setting an ethical example by the way you pay your taxes, practice corporate ethics, demonstrate personal honesty and integrity, and treat your followers and subordinates? Explain.

2 || Looking back over your life, who has had the most significant impact on your ethical principles and moral behavior? How did that person make an impression on you?

3 || Do you have a few trusted friends and mentors with whom you can be totally honest and transparent about ethical issues? If yes, how do these people influence your life? If no, why not? What can you do this week to provide this safeguard in your life?

4 || Note a recent decision you made in your leadership role—a decision that involved a difficult ethical dilemma. Now examine that decision in light of these five questions, asking yourself whether that decision passes the test:

  1. Was the decision permissible and legal?
  2. Was the decision edifying?
  3. Was the decision fair to everyone?
  4. Was it a decision you could be proud of?
  5. Was this decision consistent with the Golden Rule?

5 || What changes can you make this week to build stronger ethical guidelines into your leadership life?

TWENTY-ONE

A LEADER OF
GOOD JUDGMENT

Proverbs 29:4

I n 1619, a Dutch warship landed at the English colony of Jamestown, Virginia, and sold twenty Africans to the English colonists as
indentured servants. This was the first documented instance of the
enslavement of black Africans on the North American continent.[1]

Almost two and a half centuries passed before Abraham Lincoln
was elected president of the United States. By that time, there were
more than three million slaves of African descent in America, com-
prising more than a third of the population of the slave-holding states
in the South. The enslavement of human beings was intolerable to
half the American population, yet the other half refused to give up
their slaves.

Some American leaders, including Edward Bates and Henry Clay,
proposed freeing the slaves, compensating the slave owners, and returning the freed slaves to Liberia in Africa. But Lincoln knew that
this plan, though well-intentioned, couldn't work. Slave owners were
dead set against emancipation—and African-Americans wanted freedom, not deportation.

President Lincoln was convinced that the practice of one man owning another had to cease—but slavery couldn't be abolished by laws
alone. In her book *Team of Rivals*, historian Doris Kearns Goodwin
wrote, "Lincoln understood that the greatest challenge for a leader
in a democratic society is to educate public opinion. 'With public
sentiment, nothing can fail; without it nothing can succeed,' he said.

'Consequently he who [molds] public sentiment, goes deeper than he who enacts statutes or pronounces decisions.'"[2]

Lincoln intuitively understood that even after African-Americans were emancipated, they would still face bigotry, discrimination, and segregation. Yet he envisioned a time when there would be not only an end to slavery but also an end to irrational hatred and suspicion between the races.

Doris Kearns Goodwin concluded: "Armies of scholars, meticulously investigating every aspect of [Lincoln's] life, have failed to find a single act of racial bigotry on his part. Even more telling is the observation of [black abolitionist and reformer] Frederick Douglass . . . that of all the men he had met, Lincoln was 'the first great man that I talked with in the United States freely, who in no single instance reminded me of the difference between himself and myself, of the difference of color.'"[3]

Some of the greatest minds of that era could see no solution to the issues of slavery and race other than deporting ex-slaves to Africa. Some of the most compassionate minds could not see beyond the color of a black man's skin. Yet Abraham Lincoln understood that African-Americans were Americans. They were born *here,* not in Africa. Their destiny was freedom and equality, not segregation and discrimination.

Lincoln possessed sound judgment far beyond that of his contemporaries. His judgment gave him a vision for America's future as a nation of free, equal people.

As Gil Troy, professor of history at McGill University in Montreal, observed, "Abraham Lincoln was a great and good man whose genius, like George Washington's, lay in that ineffable quality called judgment. . . . Lincoln's good judgment, common sense, democratic humility, pragmatism, and humanity not only saved the Union; he forged a new center. . . . This united nation began wiping away the moral stain of having enslaved millions."[4]

"A leader of good judgment gives stability; an exploiting leader leaves a trail of waste," Solomon said (Proverbs 29:4, *The Message*). Let's explore what it means to be a leader who brings stability to his organization, a leader of good judgment—like Abraham Lincoln.

|| BEYOND COLD, HARD FACTS ||

Former Secretary of State Colin Powell said, "Experience is helpful, but it is judgment that matters."[5] As we have previously seen, Solomon's wise judgment was demonstrated early in his leadership career (see 1 Kings 3). Because of his wisdom Israel enjoyed four decades of peace and prosperity. He had the good judgment to establish colonial outposts to defend Israel's military and commercial interests. He formed mutually beneficial alliances with King Hiram of Tyre, the Queen of Sheba, and other neighboring rulers.

One of the evidences of Solomon's judgment was his great patience. He had a grand vision for all he wanted to achieve, plans for elaborate palaces and a great temple to honor the God of Israel. Yet he was careful to lay a firm foundation for his future accomplishments. Before he began construction, he made sure that Israel was secure and at peace. Though Solomon was lacking in experience as a young ruler, he was richly endowed with good judgment.

John William Gardner (1912–2002) served as president of the Carnegie Corporation and founded the nonprofit public interest group Common Cause. In his book *On Leadership,* Gardner wrote, "Judgment is the ability to combine hard data, questionable data and intuitive guesses to arrive at a conclusion that events prove to be correct. Judgment-in-action includes effective problem solving, the design of strategies, the setting of priorities and intuitive as well as rational judgments. Most important, perhaps, it includes the capacity to appraise the potentialities of coworkers and opponents."[6]

Judgment must consider the hard facts—but it must do more than merely gather them and arrive at a conclusion like an adding machine. Sound judgment also takes into account what Gardner calls "questionable data and intuitive guesses." Sometimes our data is fuzzy and questionable. Sometimes the facts tell us one thing but that nagging feeling in our gut tells us another. When logic fails, good judgment demands that we act on faith or an instinct we have about a situation or a person.

Management expert Peter F. Drucker put it this way: "A decision is a judgment. It is a choice between alternatives. It is rarely a choice between right and wrong. It is at best a choice between 'almost right' and 'probably wrong'—but much more often a choice between two courses of action neither of which is provably more nearly right than the other."[7]

What do you do when the pros and cons of the situation are evenly matched? Flip a coin? That's not leadership; that's just gambling. When logic and data can't tell you what to do, you must make a *judgment call*. You have to size up the situation as best you can, make a bold decision, and then accept responsibility for the outcome. That's what leaders do.

‖ MAKING JUDGMENT CALLS ‖

In their book *Judgment: How Winning Leaders Make Great Calls,* Noel M. Tichy and Warren G. Bennis write about the importance of taking responsibility for our judgment calls. These decisions, in fact, define us as leaders. Tichy and Bennis explain:

> Throughout our lives, each of us makes thousands of judgment calls. . . . The measure of our success in life is the sum of all of these judgment calls. . . . As we rise to positions of leadership, the importance and consequences of our judgment calls are magnified exponentially by their increasing impact on the lives of others. The cumulative effect of leaders' judgment calls determines the success or failure of their organizations. . . .
>
> Take any leader, any U.S. president, a *Fortune* 500 CEO, a big-league coach, wartime general, you name it. Chances are you remember them for their best or worst judgment call.
>
> Can anyone forget that Harry Truman issued the order to drop an atom bomb? When Nixon comes to mind, so does Watergate. If you are thinking of Bill Clinton, there's the Monica episode. . . . Leadership is, at its marrow, the chronicle of judgment calls; this is the leader's biography. Good leadership requires good judgment.[8]

Good judgment is important when making personnel decisions. Great leaders know how to select the right people for key positions. It takes good judgment to assemble a strong team with good chemistry—one that will perform well in times of stress and crisis. You have to recruit people with the right set of abilities and character traits to complement one another. And you need good judgment to know when to take control and when to let your followers make their own decisions.

In 1 Kings 4 we read that King Solomon began his reign by assembling his team. He considered each person's traits and leadership skills, then selected the right person for each position—priests, secretaries, the royal historian, military commanders, mid-level managers, and so forth. Solomon had the good judgment to restructure the government and recruit top talent to every key position. He created twelve districts with a regional manager over each one.

It takes good judgment to create a sound organizational structure. There are many matters that only the leadership team can decide:

- *Who is responsible for what?*
- *Should the organization have a tightly controlled structure with a lot of rules, or a loose and informal structure with a fair amount of freedom?*
- *What is the vision and purpose of your organization?*
- *What strategy will you and your people follow to achieve that vision and fulfill that purpose?*

Great leadership makes each of those judgment calls boldly and clearly, without hesitation or equivocation. Any leader who dithers and delays over major decisions is failing to lead. A great leader explains his judgment calls so that everyone in the organization understands them.

|| GOOD BRAIN—BUT BAD JUDGMENT ||

In the summer of 1961, after my junior year at Wake Forest, I played in a summer college baseball league on a team that was based in

Huron, South Dakota. Our coach, Don Lund, was a former Major League outfielder and head baseball coach at the University of Michigan. I learned a lot from him. He cautioned us, "Use good judgment, men! Use good judgment!" Almost fifty years later, I can still hear his voice.

Where does good judgment come from? Unfortunately, it does not come from an excellent education, high intelligence, or from depth of experience. Some of the smartest people in the world have terrible judgment.

Robert S. McNamara joined the Ford Motor Company in 1946 after four years with the Army Air Force, serving in the Office of Statistical Control. He had a good mind for statistics and was known as a brilliant systems analyst. McNamara was a key proponent of smaller, less expensive cars, especially the hugely successful Ford Falcon. In 1960, McNamara became president of Ford—the first president of the company who was not a member of the Henry Ford family. Though he held the position for only a year, Ford prospered under his leadership.

In 1961, President John F. Kennedy tapped Robert McNamara for the cabinet position of Secretary of Defense. After the JFK assassination, President Lyndon Johnson retained McNamara in that position. Following the Gulf of Tonkin incident in August 1964, in which two U.S. destroyers engaged three North Vietnamese torpedo boats, McNamara became the principal architect of the Vietnam War—the only war America ever lost.

Robert McNamara left government service in 1968, accepting the post as president of the World Bank, where he served until 1981. He died in 2009 at age 93. After McNamara's death, business writer Tom Davenport of Babson College in Massachusetts wrote an assessment of McNamara's legacy as a leader, entitled "Robert S. McNamara's Good Brain—and Bad Judgment." Davenport wrote:

> Robert S. McNamara . . . was perhaps the first systematic analytical thinker to lead in both the private and public sectors. He had brains, an appetite for evidence and data, and confidence

that rational analysis would win out over emotion and guess-work. . . . McNamara proved the value of these methods in turning around Ford . . . He only reluctantly accepted John F. Kennedy's invitation to lead the Department of Defense. There he attempted to apply the same rigorous, systematic ways of thinking and managing to the war in Vietnam. Needless to say, they didn't work. Metrics and analysis degenerated into mind-less body counts. . . .

Judgment consists not only of applying evidence and ratio-nality to decisions, but also the ability to recognize when they are insufficient for the problem at hand. McNamara had a good brain, but not good judgment.[9]

Wise, effective leadership is more than just number crunching and systems analysis. Leadership requires good judgment. Great leaders examine the facts and take an unflinching look at reality—but they also listen to their hunches, their compassion, their conscience, and their values. They use the whole brain—not just left-brain logic but right-brain intuition as well.

Solomon says that a leader without good judgment leaves a trail of wreckage in his wake. But leaders with good judgment create stable organizations, well-balanced teams, and healthy societies.

GET WISDOM, GET UNDERSTANDING
QUESTIONS FOR PERSONAL REFLECTION OR GROUP DISCUSSION

1 || Think of a time in your leadership career when you were called on to make a Solomonic decision, a seemingly impossible decision. How did you resolve that dilemma? In hindsight, were you correct or mistaken in your decision? What could you have done differently to make a better decision? What does that decision say about your judgment?

2 || When you make judgments and decisions, do you rely primarily on hard data, on intuition, or on some mixture of the two? In your opinion, how does intuition work—and how reliable is it?

3 || Have you ever made a truly major decision by flipping a coin? If so, how did that decision work out? In the future, would you decide an important issue by a coin toss or some other random means? Why or why not?

4 || When you recruit people to your team, how much do you rely on hard data and how much on judgment?

5 || Can you recall a time when your judgment call regarding recruitment panned out well? when it turned out badly? What happened?

6 || What's the difference between intelligence and judgment? How is it possible to be intelligent yet possess poor judgment? Have you ever met a person you would consider poorly educated who was endowed with good judgment? How did that person come to acquire good judgment? What can you learn from that person?

TWENTY-TWO

"I HEARD IT THROUGH
THE GRAPEVINE"

‖ Proverbs 29:12 ‖

I
n 1999, CBS News correspondent Lesley Stahl interviewed Ron Prescott Reagan, the youngest of Ronald Reagan's four children. The fortieth president of the United States had left office in 1989 and was diagnosed with Alzheimer's disease five years later. Stahl asked Ron Reagan what his father was like as a father and a leader.

Ron Reagan replied, "I have never seen him belittle anyone. I have never heard him gossip about anyone or telling stories. He's a nice man to the core and a terribly dignified man. . . . When you're faced with an ethical decision, perhaps, a decision of right or wrong, you could do worse than ask yourself what he might do."[1]

Ron Prescott Reagan, it should be noted, does not agree with his father's political views. Yet despite their political differences, the younger Reagan admired his father as a man and a leader. He paid a tribute to his famous father that I hope my children could say of me: he never belittled anyone, never gossiped about anyone, and he was an example of ethical leadership.

As a leader you set the tone. You shape the culture of your team or organization. Malicious gossip has no place in a healthy and functional organization. A leader who speaks negatively about colleagues, subordinates, competitors, or clients creates a zone of negativity. If your followers hear you passing along malicious gossip about someone, they will follow your lead.

Information flows throughout your organization all the time—in the hallways, at the water cooler, in the lunchroom, in e-mails and text messages, by cell phone, and on and on. That information may be true or false, positive or negative. Some of that information will inspire and encourage your people; some may demoralize and depress them.

Solomon warned in Proverbs 29:12, "When a leader listens to malicious gossip, all the workers get infected with evil" (*The Message*). As a leader you need to take control of the organizational grapevine and make sure that only good grapes grow on it—positive, encouraging, empowering information. Positive talk leads to positive people.

‖ THE DAMAGE OF GOSSIP ‖

What exactly is gossip? Is it always wrong to talk about other people? Of course not. It's not gossip to report neutral or positive information—"Jane Doe has just been promoted to head of the marketing department." But if you spread negative information—"Jane only got that job because she was having an affair with so-and-so"—that's malicious gossip. Before you spread information about someone, ask yourself these questions:

- *Will this information harm someone's reputation?*
- *Am I willing to go to that person privately and discuss the matter?*
- *If I share this information with someone, will that person be in a position to deal with the issue? In other words, am I sharing this information with someone who is directly involved, or am I simply spreading stories to anyone who will listen?*
- *Am I breaking a confidence? If someone trusted me with confidential information, do I have good reason to betray that trust? (For example, if someone tells you that he or she is planning suicide, you should report that information to the appropriate authorities.)*
- *Am I willing to be held accountable for the accuracy of the information? Am I willing to be identified as the source?*

> - *What are my motives? Do I enjoy the sense of power and the attention that comes with sharing a really juicy story?*
> - *In sharing this information with others, am I obeying the Golden Rule? How would I feel if the situation were reversed and people were saying this about me?*

Blogger Desiree Kane, in her Heroes Rising Blog, recalls, "I used to gossip in the workplace. A lot." One day Kane decided that it simply wasn't in her best interests to spread office gossip or even to listen to gossip. She was tired of worrying that someone might find out that she was the source of an office rumor—and damaging the reputations of other people simply didn't make her feel like a good person.

One day a coworker (and longtime gossip buddy) came by her cubicle with some juicy news to dish—but Desiree refused to listen. After the coworker left, the lady in the next cubicle poked her head up and said, in effect, "You know, Desiree, I really respect you for not gossiping with her. I don't think people realize how much other people can overhear in these cubes. You've really matured by squelching that gossip. Good for you."[2]

Few of us stop to think how much harm malicious gossip causes in teams and organizations. Not only does rumormongering harm reputations; it takes a heavy toll on organizations through lost productivity and eroding morale. Gossip is divisive and destroys the teamwork necessary to organizational success. Gossip can spread to customers and clients and out into the community, destroying the reputation of your organization. As management expert Harvey Mackay once observed, "If we could measure the damage to corporations from gossip, it might be more than the GNP of the Third World."[3]

Gossip is the height of injustice, because when people talk about you behind your back, you have no way to defend yourself. You don't even know it's going on. Your reputation and even your career can be completely ruined—and you might never even know why.

People sometimes defend their right to spread gossip, saying, "But if it's true, it isn't gossip." Wrong. Even if it's true, spreading negative information about people is still gossip. If it's untrue, it's even worse, because it's slander as well as gossip. True or false, spreading negative information about someone is malicious gossip—and it's destructive.

If you want to spread positive information, affirming information, edifying information about someone, feel free. Spread all the good news you want—even behind people's backs, if you like. But if the news is hurtful, destructive, or just plain juicy, keep it to yourself.

|| SQUELCHING GOSSIP IN YOUR ORGANIZATION ||

John C. Maxwell once wrote:

> It's been said that great people talk about ideas, average people talk about themselves, and small people talk about others. That's what gossip does. It makes people small. There really is no upside to gossip. It diminishes the person being talked about. It diminishes the person who is saying unkind things about others, and it even diminishes the listener. That's why you should avoid not only spreading gossip but also being a recipient of it. . . . Besides, whoever gossips to you will gossip about you.[4]

What can you, as a leader, do to squelch gossip in your team or organization? Here are some suggestions.

1. Set an anti-gossip policy.

People engage in gossip for all sorts of reasons. Some exchange gossip as a way of maintaining their power and their position in the pecking order. They like to show that they are in the know by always dishing the latest news. Some use gossip to manipulate events or to undermine people they perceive as rivals or enemies. Some try to elevate their own status by putting others down. The act of spreading negative information about others is always a destructive act. Don't allow it.

Tell your people that negative scuttlebutt and character assassination are a violation of the culture and policy of your organization. Then enforce that policy and confront those who violate it. If you confront rumormongers about their behavior and they refuse to change their ways, then let them go for the good of the organization.

2. Set an anti-gossip example.

Don't let anyone hear you running down other people—not even your competitors and critics. Set a positive tone in your organization, and you will begin to see your people following your lead. Make a point of praising the actions of your subordinates. Call them heroes. Tell positive stories about them. Your "good talk" will set a standard for everyone in your organization to aim for.

If someone comes to you with a complaint about another person, respond with a positive comment. For example, if someone says, "Tom is so awkward and shy," respond with, "You know, I have always admired Tom's humility. He works hard and never has an unkind thing to say about anyone." Or if someone says, "Joan is always bossing the rest of us around," respond with, "She's a natural leader, and she has a strong work ethic and a lot of energy. It's not always easy to be around people like Joan, but I admire those traits."

When people are inclined to think the worst of others, show them how to think the best of others. Turn every negative into a positive.

3. Correct false or misleading impressions.

If you discover that a false rumor is circulating about your organization or your people, act quickly. Call a meeting and address your people face-to-face. Don't resort to an impersonal form of communication like e-mail. Don't just say, "The rumor you heard is untrue." Replace faulty information with accurate information before the rumors have time to do much damage.

Gossip tends to flourish in an information vacuum. If you fill that vacuum with accurate information, gossip dies. If you keep plenty of high-quality, accurate information in your organizational pipeline, people will not be so tempted to fill the pipeline with misinformation.

4. Welcome criticism.

Invite people to come to you directly with any complaints about your leadership. When they know they can voice any concern without fear of retribution, they will have less need to complain about you on the office grapevine. In fact, they will praise you behind your back for being so approachable.

Create an organizational structure that allows the periodic airing of problems, criticisms, and grievances. Don't just sit behind your desk and say, "My door is always open." Go out among your people and solicit their opinions. Walk around the office, the factory, or the locker room, and ask questions. Let people know you truly welcome their concerns and that you're there to solve problems.

‖ CHANGE YOUR ORGANIZATION'S ATMOSPHERE ‖

"Gossip can take on a life of its own," warns Annette Simmons.[5] The president of Group Process Consulting, Simmons wrote *A Safe Place for Dangerous Truths*. Office gossip, she says, can seriously damage an organization. When people in the workplace believe they are being targeted by gossip, they may perceive themselves as victims of discrimination working in a hostile environment—and they may retaliate with sabotage or legal action.

Simmons recalls serving as a consultant regarding problems at a manufacturing plant. She found the workplace to be a hotbed of hostility and backstabbing. "People were saying all sorts of nasty things behind each other's backs," she said.

So she called a meeting and invited both union and management leaders to speak candidly about their issues. Top of the agenda: gossip. In the course of the discussions, it became clear that of the thirty-three people present in the room, thirty-one resented the rampant gossip in the organization. Two people in the room defended the practice of spreading rumors—but the thirty-one made it clear to the two rumor-mongers that dissension and slander would not be tolerated.

It was the first time these problems had been discussed openly in the company. Until that meeting, each person felt alone in his or her distaste for workplace gossip. Once the issue was discussed openly, it became clear that the vast (but silent) majority hated gossip—and wanted it stopped. Simmons concluded, "It changed the entire atmosphere."

In Proverbs 16:28, Solomon observed, "A perverse man stirs up dissension, and a gossip separates close friends." Solomon understood the destructive nature of malicious gossip, so he refused to spread it, receive it, or allow it in his court. Perhaps it's time for you to change the atmosphere in your organization. Perhaps you need to bring the problem of gossip out into the open.

May you and I be as wise as Solomon in protecting our followers from gossip's destructive power.

GET WISDOM, GET UNDERSTANDING
QUESTIONS FOR PERSONAL REFLECTION OR GROUP DISCUSSION

1 || Recall a time from your leadership experience when gossip produced destructive results. How were you personally affected by that gossip? How did that incident shape your view of gossip?

2 || Is it ever justified to talk about other people behind their backs? Explain why or why not.

3 || Before you spread information about another person, you should consider the seven questions on page 187. Explain how each of those questions can help you decide whether or not to spread information about someone.

4 || How does gossip adversely affect the health of an organization or team?

5 || List several actions that you, as a leader, can take this week to safeguard your organization from the destructive effects of gossip. What are some actions that are specific to the needs and issues of your particular organization?

6 || List two or three specific actions you can take to change the atmosphere in your organization and build habits of spreading good news instead of gossip.

TWENTY-THREE

THE COMPASSION AND FAIRNESS
OF A GREAT LEADER

Proverbs 29:14

I visited Richmond, Virginia, for a speaking engagement in October 2009. I arrived a day early, and my host for the event, knowing I'm a Civil War buff, set up a guided tour of the Museum of the Confederacy. During the tour I was completely immersed in the Civil War era—the worst and bloodiest period in U.S. history but a time rich in leadership lessons.

As I walked through the museum, viewing artifacts, letters, and photographs of General Robert E. Lee, I was struck by the many contradictions of this fascinating leader.

Though he led the army of the Confederacy, General Lee loved the Union and detested slavery. In a letter to his wife in 1856—five years before the war began—Lee wrote, "In this enlightened age, there are few I believe, but what will acknowledge, that slavery as an institution, is a moral & political evil in any Country."[1] He did not want to see the United States broken in two. In 1854, he wrote to his son, Lieutenant Custis Lee: "I can anticipate no greater calamity for the country than a dissolution of the Union."[2] But when his beloved Commonwealth of Virginia seceded from the Union, Lee sided with the South. "I could take no part in an invasion of the Southern States," he said.[3]

Robert E. Lee was a man of war, a professional soldier who carried out his duties to the best of his ability. He fought on the wrong side of history, but he was a complex man and a leader of great compassion. One incident from the darkest days of that war tells us much about General Lee.

At the Battle of Gettysburg, the Army of the Potomac defeated General Lee's Army of northern Virginia, ending the Confederate invasion of the North. During the battle, at a place called Cemetery Ridge, a Union soldier was shot in the leg by a Confederate musket ball. As the young soldier lay on the ridge, his leg shattered, he heard the sound of approaching Confederate soldiers and officers. Lifting his head, he recognized General Lee. Though weak from loss of blood, he raised his fists and shouted, "Hurrah for the Union!"

General Lee dismounted and walked over to the wounded man. The soldier later recalled, "I thought he meant to kill me. But as he came up he looked at me with such a sad expression upon his face that I wondered what he was about."

Robert E. Lee reached down to the Union soldier and grasped his hand. "My son," he said, "I hope you will soon be well."

The soldier later recalled, "If I live a thousand years I shall never forget the expression on General Lee's face. There he was, defeated, retiring from a field that had cost him and his cause almost their last hope, and yet he stopped to say words like those to a wounded soldier of the opposition who had taunted him as he passed by!"[4]

Leadership that is worthy of respect demonstrates compassion and fairness toward those who are powerless and in need. Solomon wrote, "Leadership gains authority and respect when the voiceless poor are treated fairly" (Proverbs 29:14, *The Message*). A great leader is the champion of the underdog. He speaks for those who cannot speak for themselves.

‖ THE MEANING OF COMPASSION ‖

Another great leader in the Civil War was President Abraham Lincoln. He often left the White House to visit hospitals where wounded soldiers were treated. During one such visit the president encountered a young man who was blind and dying of his wounds.

"Son," he asked, "is there anything I can do?"

"I wish you would write to my mother," the soldier replied.

So the president wrote as the young man dictated, signing his own name to show that he had written the letter on the soldier's behalf. He read the letter back, including the closing sentence, "This letter is written by Abraham Lincoln." The soldier was surprised and asked if he was indeed the president of the United States.

"Yes," Lincoln replied. "Is there anything more I can do for you?"

"Nothing more—unless you would hold my hand and see me through."

So President Lincoln remained beside the cot, holding the soldier's hand until he had passed from this life into the next.[5] That's the compassion of an authentic leader.

For some people the words *leadership* and *compassion* don't seem to go together. The stereotypical uncaring leader has only two emotions: cold indifference and hot anger. But that's not a leader. That's a boss doing a poor job. Bosses like that care about efficiency and profit and lines on a chart. But an authentic leader has empathy for human beings. Some bosses are incapable of genuine compassion. Bosses who are real leaders are compelled by it.

THE MEANING OF FAIRNESS

Genuine leaders also demonstrate fairness. They treat people equally, whether rich or poor, powerful or powerless, and without regard to gender, race, or social status. A leader of authentic fairness listens to problems and complaints and helps resolve them impartially and with respect toward everyone concerned.

Don Miers, a former executive in the Detroit Tigers farm system, told me about an incident from his experience as a Little League baseball coach. At the start of the season, Don explained the rules to the players and parents. He told parents that they were not to interfere with the coaches nor go near the dugout during practices and games. They were also expected to call out only positive encouragement from the stands, never any catcalls or criticism. If a parent violated the rules, his or her child could be benched.

At one game, a player's dad started screaming when Don took the boy out of the game. Don went over to the bleachers and asked the man to be quiet. The man agreed to calm down but demanded to see Don after the game.

After the game the irate father told Don, "I don't understand how a coach can care so little about winning! You took my son out of the game, and he's the most talented player you've got!"

"I'm all for winning," Don replied, "but I'm here to teach twelve boys how to play baseball, work together as a team, and have fun while they're doing it. At our preseason meeting, I explained that all players would get equal playing time, regardless of ability, as long as they came to practice and put in the effort."

"I thought that applied to the other kids. I'm going to the Little League board about this."

"If you don't agree with the way I handle the team, you should talk to the board."

"I'll do that—and I'll tell them I want my son on another team!"

But the boy didn't want to change teams. In fact, he liked the way the team worked, with all the players in an equal rotation.

"The dad and I shook hands," Don concluded, "and we've been friends ever since."

Great leaders are fair to everyone—the highly talented, the modestly talented, the powerful, and the powerless. They stand up to the pressures and temptations to show favoritism.

‖ "A GOOD REPUTATION TO LIVE UP TO" ‖

Former Dodgers manager Tommy Lasorda is a good friend and a proponent of Solomonic leadership principles.

He recalls:

A guy asked me one time what are the number one qualities a manager or a leader should have. It was difficult to put it down in a certain category, but I went to church and I heard the priest give a sermon. He talked about Solomon, who was the paragon of truth, and he was pleasing to the Lord. The Lord said to Solomon, "I want to give you any gift you want," and Solomon said,

"The greatest gift you can give me, Lord, is an understanding heart." I think that's what every manager or coach needs—an understanding heart.[6]

Every winter I catch in the New York Yankees Fantasy Camp in Tampa, Florida. I put on the catching equipment and play ball with former Major Leaguers against the campers who come from all over to live out their boyhood fantasies. At the camp in mid-November 2009, I caught twenty-four innings. Gil Patterson pitched for the Yankee regulars. Gil was the number one draft choice of the Yankees in 1975. He moved through their farm system very rapidly. In 1976, his second year of pro ball, he was playing for the AAA club Syracuse Chiefs in the International League.

While we were sitting in the dugout during the Yankees Fantasy Camp, I asked him who his manager was in Syracuse.

"Bobby Cox," Gil said.

One of the top managers in professional baseball, Cox had gone on to manage the Atlanta Braves for two decades. So I said, "Gil, back in 1976, would you have said that Bobby Cox was a Hall of Famer in the making?"

Without hesitation he replied, "Absolutely."

"Really! Why do you say that?"

"Bobby was always demanding, but never demeaning. He was critical, but always supportive. Because of that, you wanted to play as hard for him as you did for yourself."

I thought to myself, *Now,* that *is the essence of leadership and coaching.*

At around the same time, in mid-November 2009, the new NBA season was getting underway. The Orlando Magic was off to a decent 9–3 start. We were winning, but something was missing. Our guys lacked enthusiasm and fire. Coach Stan Van Gundy knew something was wrong—but what was it? He went to Dwight Howard, our star center, and took him aside.

"What's wrong, Dwight?" he asked. "Why aren't these guys fired up?"

"Coach," Dwight replied, "you're too negative with us. You focus too much on our mistakes. We love you, but we don't like it when you knock us."

After that conversation, a big change came over the Magic. The Oklahoma City Thunder came to Orlando and faced a suddenly re-energized Magic. Our guys silenced the Thunder with a huge home-court win.

The next day, Stan Van Gundy told reporters about his conversation with Dwight Howard. He said that the Magic center "was right. . . . You've seen my press conferences. It was all negative. I think that was affecting our team, so . . . [I've] got to balance being real demanding and not being as negative."[7]

Magic shooting guard J. J. Redick said that Coach Van Gundy's new approach gave the Magic the winning edge in the game against the Thunder. "It was our most energetic game of the year," Redick said. "I don't think it was a coincidence. . . . Stan's an intense guy, we all know that. But he told us that we had to go out now and play with energy and fun—including himself."[8]

I interviewed leadership teacher Dr. Hal Urban for my 2008 book *Coaching Your Kids to Be Leaders*. He said that leaders need to exemplify Dale Carnegie's advice: "Give the other person a good reputation to live up to." Instead of finding fault with our followers, we need to "develop the skill of catching people doing things right, then building on it. Too many young people hear more about what they do wrong than what they do right. . . . Whether you are a parent, teacher, coach, or manager in business, your primary responsibility is to bring out the best in the people you lead."

How do you treat those who have no voice, no power, no wealth, no talent, no prestige, no advantages whatsoever? Solomon says that your leadership is only worthy of respect when you treat everyone with compassion and fairness.

‖ "IT'S THE RIGHT THING TO DO" ‖

Sara Tucholsky played softball at Western Oregon University for four years and had never hit a home run.[9] On April 26, 2008, as Sara and her team took the field for the second game of a doubleheader against Central Washington University, she knew the season would soon come to an end—and with it, her college softball career.

Sara and her teammates had won the first game that afternoon. In the top of the second inning of game two, there was no score. Western Oregon had two runners on base, and five-foot-two Sara Tucholsky was at bat.

She swung at the first pitch—and missed. She took a swing at the second pitch—and the ball soared over the center field fence. It was gone, a three-run homer.

Sara took off, but in her excitement she rounded first without tagging the base. Realizing her mistake, she pivoted to go back and tag it properly.

Meanwhile, Sara's coach, Pam Knox, was coaching third base. She high-fived the first two runners as they rounded third, heading for home—then she spotted Sara on the ground between first and second, her face twisted in pain.

In her haste to double back, Sara had twisted her knee, tearing a ligament. Her knee would no longer support her weight, so she crawled agonizingly back to first base. She had just hit her one and only career home run, but if she couldn't run the bases, she wouldn't score the run.

Coach Knox knew that if any of Sara's teammates or coaches touched her, the home run would be invalidated. Sara had to touch every base on her own—yet she couldn't run, couldn't even stand.

As Sara clutched first base, the umpires conferred over the rule book, then announced that, under the circumstances, Western Oregon would have to replace Sara with a pinch runner at first, and the hit would go down as a two-run single, not a three-run homer. It seemed there was no choice.

Then someone shouted, "Excuse me!" All eyes turned to the Central Washington first baseman, Mallory Holtman. "Would it be OK if we carried her around and she touched each bag?"

Everyone on the field was stunned. The rules prevented Sara's own teammates from helping her—but the rules said nothing about Sara's *opponents* helping her. So Mallory Holtman and shortstop Liz Wallace went to Sara, lifted her off the ground, and carried her to second base, touching Sara's left foot to the bag. Then to third base. Then home.

Up in the stands, fans of both teams cried, cheered, and gave the trio a standing ovation. The game went on. In the end, Western Oregon held on for a 4–2 victory.

"I will never, ever forget this moment," Coach Knox said later. "It's changed me, and I'm sure it's changed my players."

Great leaders are people of compassion and fairness. When no one else on the field knew quite what to do, the first baseman stepped up and offered a suggestion that was compassionate and fair. Asked why she did it, Mallory Holtman simply said, "It's the right thing to do."

GET WISDOM, GET UNDERSTANDING
QUESTIONS FOR PERSONAL REFLECTION OR GROUP DISCUSSION

1 || Name a leader you admire who speaks for "the voiceless" and treats everyone fairly. What are some of that leader's specific character traits that you want to build into your own leadership life?

2 || Recall a time when a leader showed compassion and fairness toward you. How did that leader's behavior impact your life?

3 || Human beings have a natural tendency to favor those who seem the most talented, the most attractive, the most charming, the most influential. Do you treat everyone—including those who are less talented and attractive—in a fair and equitable way? How? If not, why not? What specific steps can you take this week to demonstrate compassion and fairness to those who are less talented and attractive?

4 || On a scale of 1 to 10, how would you rate yourself in your ability to be demanding without being demeaning? On that same scale, how would your subordinates and followers rate you?

5 || If you think something is amiss in an organization, consider going to one of your subordinates (as Stan Van Gundy went to Dwight Howard.) Ask for honest feedback that might reveal flaws in your leadership style. Imagine such a scenario, and jot down what you think the person might say.

6 || Think of some of the less prominent, less successful members of your organization. How can you encourage them and motivate them? How can you give them a better reputation to live up to?

7 || Choose one person in your organization to show compassion to this week. If you are studying this book in a group, ask at least one member of the group to hold you accountable for following through on that decision.

TWENTY-FOUR

THE LIMITS
OF LEADERSHIP

|| **Proverbs 29:26** ||

In 1962, I began my professional sports career as a catcher with a Phillies farm team, the Miami Marlins of the Florida State League. It was a long way from the big leagues, but for two years I got to play pro baseball. After my second season, however, I had to give up my boyhood dream of playing Major League Baseball.

In 1964, I worked in the front office, where I was mentored by general manager Bill Durney. He took me under his wing and taught me leadership lessons I still apply today. The following year I was offered a job running the Phillies farm club in Spartanburg, South Carolina.

I began that venture by renovating the ballpark, doing much of the painting and refurbishing with my own hands. Driven by a fear of failure, I worked seven days a week, eighteen hours a day. When I wasn't hammering or painting, I was selling ad space, getting tickets printed, and meeting with civic leaders. I brainstormed wild promotional ideas to draw crowds to our games—a Miss Spartanburg Phillies pageant, a watermelon eating contest, a cow milking contest, donkey baseball games, and more.

At the end of my first season in Spartanburg, our attendance was way up—and so were profits. I was named Executive of the Year in the Western Carolinas League.

But I wasn't satisfied. Our team hadn't played well. All the praise from the Phillies head office, from the community, and from the media meant little to me next to the fact that we weren't winning enough games.

During the off-season, I phoned one of my mentors, legendary baseball owner and promoter Bill Veeck. I told him I was disappointed in the Spartanburg Phillies' performance on the field.

After I poured out my tale of woe, Bill asked, "How many fans did you draw?"

"A hundred fourteen thousand."

"How many radio listeners did you have?"

"I don't know. Thousands, I guess."

"Pat, you made a lot of people happy and showed them a good time. They had fun at your games, didn't they? Sure, winning is important, but never forget this: You're in the entertainment business. Compete hard for that entertainment dollar, and don't ever apologize for it."

Bill Veeck gave me a lot more good advice over the years, and I took notes on everything he ever said. But the most important thing he taught me was to simply accept the limits of leadership. No leader can do it all. No leader can succeed every time he competes. No leader can make everything right. Every leader should know his limitations, even while continually trying to improve.

Solomon wrote, "Everyone tries to get help from the leader, but only GOD will give us justice" (Proverbs 29:26, *The Message*). Sometimes we drive ourselves crazy by second-guessing every decision, berating ourselves for our mistakes and limitations. Leaders are only human. We can only do so much. Once we've done all we can, it's time to leave the results to God.

‖ KNOWING OUR LIMITS ‖

People tend to put leaders on a pedestal, to treat them as superhuman, to expect them to produce miracles on demand. We see this demonstrated every time we elect a new president. Those who supported the new president, donated to his campaign, attended the rallies, and cheered for him now expect him to work miracles.

But after the inauguration, the new president must roll up his sleeves and get down to business. He has to find common ground with the Congress—535 people who all think they should have his job. Soon his policies are attacked by the press and by the opposing party. One by one his great ideals and campaign promises fall by the wayside. The mood of the nation sours, and approval ratings fall.

Professor Larry J. Sabato, director of the University of Virginia Center for Politics, put it this way: "Presidents are tempted to try to do everything—a recipe for failure. Understand your limitations as a leader and a human being. At most, you'll get a few top priorities adopted. Choose them wisely and focus like a laser on them while you still have political capital. After your glorious victory, you imagine you'll have capital for a long time. You are wrong, as your predecessors can tell you."[1]

Just as a leader's followers will learn to accept his limitations, so must the leader himself. Sometimes when obstacles and frustrations mount, leaders doubt themselves and their ability to lead. And that's when they end up broken and discouraged. So it's important for leaders to learn that they can only do what they *can* do—the final results are in God's hands. Here are some practical takeaways for recognizing our limitations as leaders.

1. Adopt a humble attitude.

To be humble is to have a clear-eyed acceptance of our personal limits, plus a willingness to give credit to our followers and subordinates for the successes of the organization. Humility also protects us from accepting more blame than we deserve. A humble leader says, "We win as a team and we lose as a team." A leader who cannot accept his own limitations will blame himself for every defeat, whether blame is deserved or not.

In July 2009, retired UCLA basketball coach John Wooden was named (at age 98) the greatest coach of all time by the *Sporting News.* The following month he was honored with a ceremony before the sports media and many of his old players. One of Coach Wooden's former players, Andy Hill, told me that Coach gave a brief speech, closing with the words, "I only wish I could have done more for you all."

He wished he could have done more! Coach Wooden not only made his players champions in the game of basketball but also helped shape their lives and their values. He taught them how to be successful in the game of life. What more could he have done?

"That was vintage Coach Wooden," Andy told me. "He was always humble, and he continually taught us what the character of a leader should look like. I glanced around the room when Coach said that, and there wasn't a dry eye in the place." This respect for Coach Wooden was echoed in the media, loud and clear, at the time of his death in June 2010.

An attitude of humility will keep you from being puffed up by praise or deflated by criticism. Learn the lessons of the criticism, and let the praise roll off you like water off a duck's back. Stay grounded, stay focused, stay humble.

2. Give up the need to be perfect.

Perfection is unattainable. Unrealistic expectations of continuous success will set you up for failure even before you begin. Even when perfectionists succeed, they never seem to enjoy their success, because there's always something to find fault with.

Perfectionists are easily frustrated—and easily angered. Perfectionistic leaders often speak harshly when angered—hurting the people around them, damaging relationships, and burning personal and professional bridges. The decisions you make under the influence of anger and frustration tend to be poor-quality decisions that you later regret. Instead of becoming frustrated when things don't go according to plan, adjust your expectations.

3. Don't try to please everybody.

Accept the fact that you will disappoint people from time to time—and it's not your fault. It's simply one of the limitations of leadership. Don't get caught in the trap of people pleasing. People may criticize you for not fulfilling their expectations, but that's their problem, not yours. Don't let anyone make you feel inadequate simply because you don't fit their notion of what a leader should be.

Comedian Bill Cosby put it this way: "I do not know the secret of success, but I know the secret of failure: Try to please everybody."[2]

4. Stop trying to win with a losing strategy.

Great leaders know the difference between cutting their losses and compounding them. Though perseverance is a vital character trait in any great leader, you have to draw the line between genuine perseverance and sheer mule-headed stubbornness. Sometimes the best way to persevere is to back away from a problem and attack it from a different angle. Great leaders don't hesitate to revise a strategy that's not working.

On March 20, 2003, multinational forces led by the United States and Great Britain launched Operation Iraqi Freedom, an invasion of Iraq that liberated the country from the tyrannical rule of dictator Saddam Hussein. My Marine Corps son David was in the first wave of forces that routed the Iraqi army and liberated the country. It seemed at first that Allied forces had won a quick, decisive victory.

Soon, however, it became clear that we faced a new enemy—an insurgency composed of guerrilla-like militias, foreign fighters, and terrorists. The enemy carried out a war of attrition against the U.S.–led coalition and the new Iraqi government. Over time, the numbers of American dead and wounded continued to mount.

In the United States, opposition to the Iraq War grew more strident. President George W. Bush responded by stating his determination to "stay the course" in Iraq. Soon, opponents of the war began mocking the phrase "stay the course," while accusing the president of a stubborn refusal to rethink his Iraq policy.

Then in early 2007, President Bush announced a strategy that became known as "The Surge." It involved sending more than twenty thousand additional troops to Iraq under the command of General David Petraeus. The strategy also involved employing teams of reconstruction experts to rebuild towns, establish city governments, renovate hospitals, and provide loans and grants for small business start-ups.

The additional troops and civilian reconstruction won the hearts and minds of the Iraqi people and helped stabilize Iraqi society. As the Iraqis turned against the insurgents, U.S. security forces and Iraqi police rooted out the bad guys. Within six months of President Bush's announcement of a new strategy, the situation in Iraq had dramatically improved. Soon, the Shiites, Sunnis, and Kurds in Iraq were cooperating more harmoniously than the Republicans and Democrats in Washington!

The moral to the story: When Plan A isn't working, don't "stay the course." Find a new strategy and keep moving forward.

5. Don't try to do it all yourself.

In my early years as a professional sports executive, I thought a leader was someone who could do it all and didn't need anybody's help. When I ran the Spartanburg Phillies, I kept the keys on my belt and unlocked the facility. I did all the selling and handled all the publicity. I set out the brooms and cleaning supplies for the cleaning crew. I personally took the gate receipts to the night deposit at the bank. I didn't delegate anything because I was afraid that if I didn't handle it personally, it wouldn't get done right.

I took many of those same habits with me to the Philadelphia 76ers and the Chicago Bulls. For years, I pounded out press releases on my own typewriter when I could have delegated that task to others—who would have done a better job!

I gradually realized that I needed to hand off those tasks to other people. I needed to train others to be leaders and let them gain experience in making decisions. As I learned to delegate less important tasks, I discovered that more important opportunities came my way. Though I was aware of the details, I entrusted those details to others so I could focus on the larger issues.

You are a leader, not a one-man band. Surround yourself with followers who are as talented as you (or better yet, *more* talented). The best way to transcend your limitations is to recruit people whose skills and competencies far exceed your own. They will supply what you lack—and when *they* succeed, *you'll* succeed.

|| THE WOUNDED LEADER ||

Marine Lieutenant Clebe McClary shipped out for Vietnam shortly after marrying his sweetheart, Deanna. He served as a platoon leader with the 1st Recon Battalion.

In the early morning hours of March 3, 1968, when Clebe and his platoon patrolled Hill 146, deep in enemy territory, a vicious firefight broke out. In the thick of battle, a grenade hurtled toward Clebe. He put up his hands as the grenade exploded. His right eye was saved, but the blast shredded his right hand, destroyed his left arm, tore out his left eye, and burst his eardrums. Wounded as he was, he got on the radio and called in artillery fire.

Another grenade exploded, knocking Clebe to the ground. Shrapnel had ripped his legs, rendering them useless. He continued shouting orders until he blacked out. His last thoughts were for his wife, Deanna.

A medevac helicopter airlifted Clebe McClary to safety. He survived—and underwent thirty major surgeries over the next two and a half years. After returning to the States, Clebe wondered how his wife would react when she saw him. His body was a mass of torn flesh and gaping wounds, held together with stitches and staples. Clebe had heard that the majority of wives of wounded veterans couldn't handle the sight.

But when Deanna first saw him, she had only one thought: Clebe was home and he was alive. Later she often tiptoed into the hospital in violation of the rules, just to be near him and tell him she loved him.

Today Clebe and Deanna McClary are in great demand as motivational and inspirational speakers. They talk to youth conventions, military groups, medical groups, corporations, and sports teams. I met them at one such event. During Clebe's talk, he mentioned that he was starting to lose feeling and dexterity in his remaining hand.

Afterwards, I asked Deanna, "What will happen if Clebe loses the use of that hand?"

She answered without hesitation. "He knows I love him," she said, "and I'll always be there to help him, no matter what."

Clebe McClary symbolizes the kind of leader Solomon spoke of in Proverbs 29:26. He demonstrated his commitment to his leadership role on Hill 146. Even after his body was ripped apart by grenades, he continued to lead his men.

Clebe is a wounded warrior, and his wounds are the limitations he has learned to accept. But he continues to lead, inspire, and motivate wherever he goes. A day may come when he must accept even more stringent limitations, when his one good hand will no longer function, when his own strength will not be enough. When that day comes, he can still rely on Deanna. She'll be there for him, no matter what.

───────────────

We all must accept our limitations. We must rely on our followers to supply what we lack. People will place demands on you. They will expect you to do miracles for them. Do what you can, accept your limitations, and then leave the results to God.

GET WISDOM, GET UNDERSTANDING
QUESTIONS FOR PERSONAL REFLECTION OR GROUP DISCUSSION

1 || Have you ever felt driven by the fear of failure? How did that drivenness affect your life?

2 || Have you ever felt overwhelmed by your responsibilities as a leader, so that you doubted whether you were qualified to lead? Explain how that felt. Describe how that situation impacted your life.

3 || If you are still stuck in that situation, what would help you overcome your sense of being overwhelmed and unqualified?

4 || Are you a perfectionist? If yes, how do your perfectionist tendencies interfere with your effectiveness as a leader? If no, have you ever worked for a perfectionist boss or leader? How has that person's perfectionism impacted your life?

5 || Have you ever stuck by a losing strategy for too long? What was the impact of that losing strategy on you and your organization?

6 || How can you tell when perseverance turns to stubbornness, when "stay the course" turns into "stuck in the mud"?

7 || How are you at delegating responsibilities to others? Cite specific examples of how you delegate well—or poorly. What specific changes can you make to become more effective at delegating?

8 || As a leader, do you currently find it difficult to accept your limitations? Why or why not? How would you and your organization change if you were to decide to accept your limitations and leave the results to God? What holds you back from doing so?

TWENTY-FIVE

LEADERSHIP WISDOM
FROM NATURE

|| Proverbs 30:24-28 ||

A nts have conquered the world. While you and I were focused on various world crises or sporting events or just trying to make a living, billions of ants have been quietly, patiently achieving their goal of world domination.

Here is an excerpt from the report by Matt Walker, editor of *Earth News,* on the BBC:

A single mega-colony of ants has colonised much of the world, scientists have discovered. . . . Argentine ants (*Linepithema humile*) were once native to South America. But people have unintentionally introduced the ants to all continents except Antarctica. . . .

In Europe, one vast colony of Argentine ants is thought to stretch for 6,000 km (3,700 miles) along the Mediterranean coast, while another in the US, known as the "Californian large," extends over 900 km (560 miles) along the coast of California. A third huge colony exists on the west coast of Japan. . . .

Whenever ants from the main European and Californian super-colonies and those from the largest colony in Japan came into contact . . . they acted as if they all belonged to the same colony, despite living on different continents separated by vast oceans. . . .

"The enormous extent of this population is paralleled only

by human society," the researchers write in the journal *Insect Sociaux*.[1]

You see? I wasn't joking. Ants truly have conquered the world. There is a lot that we, as leaders, can learn by studying creatures as small and overlooked as the ant.

In Proverbs 30:24-28 the writer employed four observations from nature to illustrate some hidden truths about leadership. He wrote, "There are four small creatures, wisest of the wise they are—ants—frail as they are, get plenty of food in for the winter; marmots—vulnerable as they are, manage to arrange for rock-solid homes; locusts—leaderless insects, yet they strip the field like an army regiment; lizards—easy enough to catch, but they sneak past vigilant palace guards" (*The Message*).

Ants. Marmots. Locusts. Lizards. From these small creatures the author of Proverbs 30 derived important leadership lessons.

Proverbs 30:1 attributes the author of this passage to be Agur, son of Jakeh. However, according to historians J. Frederic McCurdy and Louis Ginzberg, *Agur* is a play on words, denoting a compiler, the one who gathered the proverbs together into a book. They state that Agur was commonly understood to be another name for Solomon himself.[2] While a case can be made that the writer was a wise Israelite named Agur, we will assume it was Solomon.

In any case, God has inspired the writer to examine four creatures from nature—four forms of animal life we might otherwise pass by without noticing. And in Yoda-like fashion, he said, "Wisest of the wise they are." Let's take a closer look and discover some leadership wisdom from nature.

‖ THE WISDOM OF ANTS ‖

A man could step on an anthill, crushing scores of ants with a single step, and not even notice the death and destruction he had caused to the ant colony. Yet ants possess amazing strength. A single ant can carry an object (such as a morsel of food) weighing ten to fifty times the ant's own weight—the equivalent of you or me carrying several tons. But ants possess an even more amazing strength: they are programmed to work hard and prepare for the future.

In Proverbs 6:6-8, Solomon has more to say about the industriousness of the ant. Issuing a warning to those who are too lazy to prepare for the future, he writes, "You lazy fool, look at an ant. Watch it closely; let it teach you a thing or two. Nobody has to tell it what to do. All summer it stores up food; at harvest it stockpiles provisions" (*The Message*).

Ants are constantly busy aboveground in the summertime, gathering food and carrying it down into the tunnels. Ants burrow as far as six to nine feet below the ground. The deeper their tunnels, the better protected they are from freezing in the winter months. Ants go into a torpor, a sleepy and lethargic state, during the cold winter. In the spring, as the ground is warmed, ants revive and busy themselves with egg tending, feeding new larvae, and so forth.

From ants we learn positive character traits we need as leaders—and traits we should look for in the followers we recruit. Ants are diligent. They work continuously in pursuit of their goals and are committed to their tasks. They tirelessly carry a load much bigger than they are. Ants are self-starters. No one needs to tell them what to do or when to do it. They are inwardly programmed to carry out their tasks. If an ant thinks at all, it has just one thought: *Teamwork!* Every action of every ant is dedicated to the greater good of the entire ant community. That is the leadership wisdom of the ant.

Ants are programmed to prepare for the future. Of course, ants do not think rationally or make decisions. The progression of the seasons and the changing temperatures, along with the ants' own biochemistry, control their behavior and cause them to focus their efforts on providing for the future. When winter comes and food is scarce, the ants have everything they need because they spent the summer preparing for winter.

If only human beings were as well programmed as ants! We all know people who live only for the moment and give no thought to the future. They make no preparations for seasons of hardship, for times of adversity. They figure that if times get tough, someone will bail them out—their parents, their neighbors, or the government.

The time to think of tomorrow is today. Not someday. Not "when I get more time" or "when I get around to it." *Today.* Great leaders know that time is a precious resource. Invest your time wisely today, and you will reap huge dividends in the future. You have to prioritize your efforts *today* in order to reach your goals tomorrow. That is the wisdom of the ants.

|| THE WISDOM OF MARMOTS ||

Solomon continued, "Marmots—vulnerable as they are, manage to arrange for rock-solid homes." Marmots are members of the rodent family and are closely related to squirrels and groundhogs. They are found in mountainous regions of Europe, North America, and Asia, and live on a diet of grasses, flowers, mosses, and berries.

Marmots live in social communities with other marmots, making their homes in burrows under rocks or in high rocky crevices. These are the "rock-solid homes" Solomon referred to. Marmots care for one another, and when one marmot senses danger, it whistles an alarm to warn the rest of the community. Marmots are not designed for fighting; they're made for hiding among the rocks. They fit into crevices where predators cannot follow. They wisely hide themselves within the safety of their rocky fortresses.

If you have the wisdom of a marmot, you will know where your safety and security is found. Marmots must leave their rocky burrows in order to forage for food, but they don't take foolish chances. They instinctively understand their own weakness and their need for the strength of the rock. That is the wisdom of the marmot.

Every organization needs a sense of security, a rocklike fortress to serve as a habitat. Don't risk your organization on foolish gambles. Make sure you provide adequate security for perilous times. Build your organization on a firm and rock-solid foundation of good character, ethical practices, sound policies, prudent money management, and strong leadership.

Marmots recognize their need for each other. They live by the credo "All for one and one for all." When a marmot spots a predator, he sounds the alarm—and *all* the marmots scatter. They look out for one another and protect one another. That too is the wisdom of the marmot.

‖ THE WISDOM OF LOCUSTS ‖

"Locusts—leaderless insects, yet they strip the field like an army regiment." Under the right conditions they breed rapidly, migrate in vast swarms, and feed voraciously, completely destroying fields and crops over a vast area.

Exodus 10:13-15 tells how Moses, at God's direction, summoned a plague of locusts against Pharaoh and the land of Egypt:

> Moses stretched out his staff over Egypt, and the LORD made an east wind blow across the land all that day and all that night. By morning the wind had brought the locusts; they invaded all Egypt and settled down in every area of the country in great numbers. Never before had there been such a plague of locusts, nor will there ever be again. They covered all the ground until it was black. They devoured all that was left after the hail—everything growing in the fields and the fruit on the trees. Nothing green remained on tree or plant in all the land of Egypt.

Locusts have been a source of terror and destruction at all times and in all parts of the world. Pearl S. Buck's Pulitzer-winning novel *The Good Earth* (1931) includes a scene where the protagonist, Wang Lung, sees a small cloud hanging in the sky. The cloud descends, darkening everything, and is revealed to be a swarm of locusts. And in one of her Little House on the Prairie novels, *On the Banks of Plum Creek,* Laura Ingalls Wilder describes a swarm of locusts so vast that it blocked out the sun, attacking the fields of the Ingallses' Minnesota homestead.

One locust by itself can do very little. It is one of the least significant creatures on God's earth. But a swarm of locusts is a plague. A single swarm can damage or destroy the economy of a region—and even bring starvation to thousands of people. The strength of the locust is in numbers. The wisdom of the locust is that even tiny creatures can accomplish much when all work together at the same time.

Locusts were not created to work alone, and neither were we. Human beings are social creatures who work best and achieve their highest potential in an atmosphere of community and cooperation. One person, working alone, can build a doghouse or a brick barbecue. Many people, working together, can build a skyscraper, tunnel under the English Channel, or send human beings to the moon.

Notice too that Solomon calls locusts "leaderless insects," yet they are devastatingly effective at stripping a field of its vegetation. Now, if a swarm of leaderless insects can do so much damage, think of the good that can be accomplished by an organization with a wise leader at the helm and all its members working together to achieve a grand vision.

Such an organization could change the world.

Solomon employed the wisdom of the locusts as he governed Israel. In 1 Kings 5 we see that when Solomon began his greatest construction project, the magnificent temple in Jerusalem, he started a peacetime draft. He conscripted workers from all over Israel, a total of 30,000 men. He sent them in shifts of 10,000 to Lebanon to fell the cedar trees for the rich paneling and strong timbers of the temple structure. Each shift of 10,000 men would work on the temple for a month, then return home for two months before returning for the next shift. Everyone contributed, but no one suffered undue hardship. Solomon also employed 70,000 carriers to transport construction materials; 80,000 stonecutters in the quarries; and 3,300 foremen to oversee the work.

Unlike locusts, the workers of Israel were not leaderless. They had one of the greatest leaders of all time directing them toward a single goal: the construction of the great temple of Jerusalem.

THE WISDOM OF THE LIZARD

Solomon concluded, "Lizards—easy enough to catch, but they sneak past vigilant palace guards." Our family has lived in Florida for well over twenty years. And there are certain things you have to adjust to:

no snow in the winter, 100 percent humidity all summer, and lizards everywhere.

They are harmless little fellows, but they are ubiquitous in the Sunshine State. If you leave your door open for very long, count on having lizards in your house.

Solomon lived in a palace, and he marveled that his home—a place of incredible splendor, furnished with gold and silver, cedar wood and jewels—was also a home to lizards. Undoubtedly, he had seen many lizards dashing across his floors or flitting along the palace walls.

No matter how many royal guards you post at every entrance, you can't keep lizards out of the palace. Lizards are small, quick, and furtive. They can wriggle into spaces where human hands can't reach. Lizards can't tell the difference between the royal palace and a poor man's house, and that's why they're found in both.

As Solomon observed, lizards are fairly easy to catch and remove from the premises. My guess is that Solomon didn't bother removing them. Instead, he observed the behavior of these uninvited guests and learned wisdom from them.

From the humble lizard we learn that the quick and the nimble survive. A roaring lion is a thousand times more powerful than a lizard, but if a lion bounded through the open doorway of the king's palace, he would instantly attract the attention of the palace guards. The lion wouldn't stand a chance.

But the humble lizard can slip past palace guards without attracting any notice. He has the run of the palace precisely because he is small and powerless. Whether you are the leader of a corporation, a military organization, a church, a nonprofit organization, or a sports team, you probably know that it is often better to be a lizard than a lion, to fly under the radar rather than be in the gun sights. Bigger is not always better.

Before you build your organization into a big roaring lion, remember the wisdom of the lizard. Find your niche. Be quick and nimble. You can accomplish much by going unnoticed. If you lead by the wisdom of the lizard, you may find yourself in the palace of the king.

"There are four small creatures," Solomon tells us, "wisest of the wise they are." We can't help but gain wisdom from all the things God built into the nature around us . . . if we'll only observe and learn.

GET WISDOM, GET UNDERSTANDING
QUESTIONS FOR PERSONAL REFLECTION OR GROUP DISCUSSION

1 || Solomon draws leadership lessons from four small creatures in the natural world: ants, marmots, locusts, and lizards. Which of these four creatures yields the most relevant leadership lessons for your life today? Explain your answer.

2 || Ants are programmed by their Creator to work hard in the summertime, storing up food for the winter. Ants prepare for the future. They are diligent self-starters. They act unselfishly on behalf of the entire community. Is there a situation in your organization that requires you to implement the wisdom of the ants? Explain your answer.

3 || Marmots are rodents that live in burrows under rocks or in high rocky crevices. They look out for each other. When one senses danger, he warns the rest of the community; and they all scramble to the high rocks and hide. Marmots practice teamwork. Is there a situation in your organization that requires you to implement the wisdom of marmots? Explain your answer.

4 ‖ Locusts find their power and their wisdom in large numbers of individual creatures working together as one. Locusts are leaderless—but human beings can adopt the wisdom of locusts by working together under the direction of a visionary leader. Is there a situation in your organization that requires you to implement the wisdom of locusts? Explain your answer.

5 ‖ Lizards are small and have no strength to speak of, yet they are quick and nimble. They can wriggle into tiny spaces beyond human reach. And that is why lizards are able to live in palaces with kings. Is there a situation in your organization that requires you to implement the wisdom of lizards? Explain your answer.

6 ‖ Solomon learned leadership lessons by observing various creatures in the animal kingdom. What does this passage from Proverbs say to you about the importance of observing the world around you? Have you learned any life lessons, especially leadership lessons, by observing nature? Explain your answer.

TWENTY-SIX

THE LEADER AND
SEXUAL TEMPTATION

‖ Proverbs 31:2, 3 ‖

In January 1998, the president of the United States delivered one of the most famous sound bites in American history: "I want to say one thing to the American people. . . . I did not have sexual relations with that woman, Miss Lewinsky. I never told anybody to lie, not a single time—never. These allegations are false."[1]

But as history records, the allegations were true. The president of the United States did, in fact, have a sexual relationship with "that woman." Because the president's conduct included false testimony and obstruction of justice, the president was later impeached by the House of Representatives (though not convicted by the Senate). He was fined $90,000, and his license to practice law was suspended by his home state for five years and by the United States Supreme Court, from which he chose to resign.

The late Dr. D. James Kennedy observed that there are profound leadership lessons to be learned from the Oval Office sex scandal—lessons in character and integrity. Oddly, however, the news media framed the scandal in terms of presidential "stupidity," not a character defect. Kennedy wrote:

> The "lesson" of the Oval Office sex scandal, according to an op-ed piece in the *Dallas Morning News*: "You're never too old to be stupid about sex." . . . *USA Today* led coverage of the scandal

with these words: "The most common response heard . . . was, 'How could he be so stupid?'" Man-on-the-street interviews published by the *Los Angeles Times* included such comments as, "I wonder what [the president] is thinking right now—probably, 'How could I be so stupid?'" . . .

I would submit to you, however, that all of these comments have utterly missed the point of the Oval Office sex scandal. It was not an act of stupidity; it was an act of sin. The president was not *mentally* challenged, but *morally* challenged.[2]

The writer of Proverbs 31:2, 3, identified as King Lemuel, recalls wise words his mother taught him. She warned, "Oh, son of mine, what can you be thinking of! Child whom I bore! The son I dedicated to God! Don't dissipate your virility on fortune-hunting women, promiscuous women who shipwreck leaders" (*The Message*).

It's true: sexual immorality can shipwreck a leader. It can destroy everything you've worked for—your family, your reputation, your career, and your legacy. Whether you are a president or a CEO, a minister or an educator, a man or a woman, you need to maintain firewalls in your life against sexual temptation.

‖ THE PERILS OF LEADERSHIP ‖

In any organization the leader has the most visible role. You are the public face of your organization. You are in the spotlight. As a leader you have the big megaphone. Everyone hears your voice. You speak for the organization. That's as it should be.

The visibility of the leader is advantageous when the leader is a person of strong moral character. But if the leader is morally weak, then that visibility becomes a liability. A spotlight of fame can become a searchlight of shame. When a leader's moral indiscretion becomes public knowledge, everyone suffers. You owe it to yourself, your family, your organization, and God to maintain your integrity.

Unfortunately, the very drives that propel us into leadership can become twisted. People often seek leadership in order to serve. But somewhere along the way, that desire can become distorted by the praise and attention that often go with leadership. We may begin to crave the adulation, the excitement, the thrill of competition. Some leaders become addicted to risk taking and adventure seeking. Instead of serving others, they feel entitled to be served.

Leaders who become addicted to the adrenaline rush of leadership are easy prey for sexual temptation. If the thrill of leadership grows stale, a leader may seek that same emotional rush through illicit sexual relationships. Flirting with temptation is a foolish gamble. The few moments of guilty pleasure are simply not worth the risk.

‖ THE MODESTO MANIFESTO ‖

In his autobiography Dr. Billy Graham reveals the secret of how he maintained his reputation decade after decade without a single hint of scandal. In 1948, Dr. Graham and his team—George Beverly Shea, Grady Wilson, and Cliff Barrows—drove to Modesto, California, for two weeks of evangelistic meetings. Dr. Graham recalls:

> Cliff, Bev, Grady, and I talked among ourselves about the recurring problems many evangelists seemed to have, and about the poor image so-called mass evangelism had in the eyes of many people. . . . One afternoon during the Modesto meetings, I called the Team together to discuss the problem. Then I asked them to go to their rooms for an hour and list all the problems they could think of that evangelists and evangelism encountered.
>
> When they returned, the lists were remarkably similar, and in a short amount of time, we made a series of resolutions or commitments among ourselves that would guide us in our future evangelistic work.[3]

This series of resolutions focused on several areas. The Graham team resolved not to manipulate people with emotional appeals, misuse funds, or exaggerate successes or the size of the crowds. But the most important resolution dealt with the issue of sexual temptation. Dr. Graham explained, "We pledged among ourselves to avoid any situation that would have even the appearance of compromise or suspicion. From that day on, I did not travel, meet, or eat alone with a woman other than my wife."[4]

In later years, Dr. Graham's associate, Cliff Barrows, referred to the pact they made as the Modesto Manifesto. Dr. Graham concluded that the Manifesto served to "settle in our hearts and minds, once and for all, the determination that integrity would be the hallmark of both our lives and our ministry."[5]

‖ MORAL FIREWALLS ‖

The Modesto Manifesto is an example of what I call a moral firewall. A firewall is a partition to keep fire from spreading from one place to another. Firewalls are used as protective barriers in buildings and ships, as well as between the engine compartment and passenger compartment of an automobile. The time to put a firewall in place is not after a fire has started. You build a firewall when there is no fire. You hope you never need it—but if a fire starts, you're glad it's there.

A moral firewall can protect you from being scorched by sexual temptation. You don't wait until you're tempted before putting a firewall in place. You do so when you feel morally strong. Then if you ever encounter the "fire" of sexual temptation, it's ready to protect you. Here are some practical guidelines for establishing moral firewalls.

1. Make sure your firewalls are firmly in place.

Like Billy Graham and his team, *decide ahead of time* on a set of rules for your behavior that will keep you out of danger. The Graham team agreed not to place themselves in situations where there might be even a *hint* of moral compromise. They agreed they would not travel, meet, or take meals alone with women other than their spouses.

You may be able to think of additional rules specific to your own situation. For example, if you are a man in a car pool at work, make sure that when it's your turn to drive, you drop off the women first so that you are never alone with a female coworker. If you have a private meeting with an opposite-sex staff member, keep your office door open. Always be aware of appearances. Make sure you can't even be accused of the *appearance* of impropriety.

2. Prioritize time with your family.

If you are a driven workaholic, you need to make an intentional effort to set aside regular time with your family. This time restores your sense of perspective and helps you to remember what you are living for. Your role as a leader in your family far outweighs your role as a leader in your organization. Make sure you have your life in balance and your priorities in the right order.

3. Make yourself accountable to a few trusted counselors.

A wise leader doesn't go it alone. He gathers wise counselors around him, consults with them, admits his struggles to them, seeks insight from them, and invites them to ask probing questions about his behavior.

Many a fallen leader will admit that he had few close friends. He may have had hundreds of acquaintances and thousands of admirers, but there was no one with whom he could be transparent and accountable. You should have at least two or three people who regularly ask tough questions and demand honest answers.

4. Heed your own advice.

Suppose one of your subordinates asked you, "Should I risk everything for the sake of an affair?" Would you respond, "Go for it! Have a good time—just don't get caught"? Or would you say, "What are you thinking? Don't throw everything away for an affair!"

You know the right thing for others to do. Why, then, would you give *yourself* any different advice? Follow your own wisdom—not your emotions. Do what you *know* is right. Take your own best advice and turn your back on temptation.

5. Weigh the consequences.

Leaders know how to envision the future. You know that if you take a certain risk, you stand a good chance of suffering consequences. If you engage in an illicit affair, you could lose your marriage, your relationship with your kids (including their respect and affection), your reputation in the community, your friendships, your position in the organization, your self-respect, your peace of mind, and your relationship with God. Is it worth it? You know it's not.

If, after weighing the consequences, you decide to go ahead and risk everything for the sake of a guilty pleasure, then you're not much of a leader. You're showing that you care only about selfish, sensual pleasure—not your family, your leadership role, your organization, or your followers.

6. Avoid pornography at all costs.

It will destroy you. From time to time, I interview family counselors on my radio show in Orlando. One question I ask on the air is, "What's the number one problem you deal with in your practice?" The answer is always the same: "Pornography. It's a problem of epidemic proportions."

You are never more than a few mouse clicks from the most vile and degrading sexual images imaginable. Pornography is so prevalent that some people are foolish enough to view it at work or at the library. Do you know a pastor or corporate leader who lost his job because of viewing pornography at work? I know plenty of them. Decide today not to be one of them—stay away from pornography.

Pornography is addictive. It can take control of your life. So you have to make a decision that you won't let pornography gain a foothold. You have to put up barricades to keep pornography out of your computer, your TV, your house, and your mind.

7. Pray.

Moral purity is a spiritual battle. Ask for God's help and strength to reject temptation. If you "fall" to sexual temptation, you're not a victim. You are responsible for your choices.

In 1987, I was invited to speak at a Billy Graham event in Syracuse, New York. I spoke before a crowd of nearly fifty thousand people in the Carrier Dome and couldn't believe I was on the same stage with men like Dr. Graham, Cliff Barrows, and George Beverly Shea.

After the event I went back to my room at the Holiday Inn feeling spiritually and morally invincible. I turned on the television to catch up on the sports scores. As I flipped the dial, seeking a sports channel, the screen lit up with a raw pornographic scene.

People have accused me of being naive, of being stuck in the *Father Knows Best* 1950s. Maybe I am. I had no idea that such sexually explicit material was freely available on a hotel room TV. I didn't have to order it—it simply popped up on a free channel! I flipped past a few more channels, but I remembered what I saw.

I think I know how King David must have felt when he looked over the parapet of his palace and saw Bathsheba bathing. He hadn't gone looking for temptation, and neither had I. But once temptation appeared, King David had a choice to make—and so did I.

My first thought was, *Why is this happening? I've just come off the greatest high of my spiritual life!* But the war was on—a spiritual battle royal in a Holiday Inn in upstate New York. I fought that battle with prayer, and ultimately, the Spirit was victorious.

Prayer is your strongest, sturdiest firewall whenever you face the threat of temptation. Ask God for the strength to make wise moral choices in every aspect of your leadership life—and especially in the expression of your sexuality.

‖ THE FAILURE OF A GREAT LEADER ‖

In Proverbs 5:15-21, Solomon wrote these beautiful, poetic words about marital love and sexual fidelity:

> Drink water from your own cistern,
> running water from your own well.
> Should your springs overflow in the streets,
> your streams of water in the public squares?
> Let them be yours alone,
> never to be shared with strangers.
> May your fountain be blessed,
> and may you rejoice in the wife of your youth.
> A loving doe, a graceful deer—
> may her breasts satisfy you always,
> may you ever be captivated by her love.
> Why be captivated, my son, by an adulteress?
> Why embrace the bosom of another man's wife?
> For a man's ways are in full view of the LORD,
> and he examines all his paths.

The tragedy is that Solomon didn't always follow his own advice. In the closing years of his life, Solomon made a series of immoral sexual choices. He didn't completely turn away from God, but he became preoccupied with sexual pleasure. Though he was married to Pharaoh's daughter, he became involved with women from other cultures and religions: "King Solomon, however, loved many foreign women besides Pharaoh's daughter . . . from nations about which the LORD had told the Israelites, 'You must not intermarry with them, because they will surely turn your hearts after their gods.' Nevertheless, Solomon held fast to them in love" (1 Kings 11:1, 2).

Moral defection always begins with an emotional desire. That's the pattern of Solomon's tragedy. The text tells us: "As Solomon grew old, his wives turned his heart after other gods, and his heart was not fully devoted to the LORD his God, as the heart of David his father had been. He followed Ashtoreth the goddess of the Sidonians, and Molech the detestable god of the Ammonites. So Solomon did evil in the eyes of the LORD; he did not follow the LORD completely, as David his father had done" (vv. 4-6).

The women Solomon loved lured him away from God and toward idolatrous religions that practiced human sacrifice—even the sacrifice of infants.

So ended the success of Solomon. God told him, "Since this is your attitude and you have not kept my covenant and my decrees, which I commanded you, I will most certainly tear the kingdom away from you and give it to one of your subordinates. Nevertheless, for the sake of David your father, I will not do it during your lifetime. I will tear it out of the hand of your son" (vv. 11, 12). Isn't that ironic? Solomon had cautioned his own wayward son, yet in the end was himself a shipwrecked leader.

———————|————————|———————

Maintain your firewalls against sexual temptation. If you want to achieve your vision and your goals, and if you want to maintain your success and your reputation, follow the wise advice of Solomon—and be instructed by his tragic example.

GET WISDOM, GET UNDERSTANDING
QUESTIONS FOR PERSONAL REFLECTION OR GROUP DISCUSSION

1 || When you hear about a leader who has been caught in a sex scandal, what is your first thought: *How could he violate his integrity?* or *How could he be so stupid?* Do you see sexual integrity as a serious issue or a minor issue for leaders? Explain your answer.

2 || Does your leadership role provide you with a sense of adventure, excitement, and even thrills? Do you agree or disagree that a leader can become addicted to risk taking and adventure seeking? Why? Do you believe that this is a danger in your own life? Explain.

3 || Do you think that you need moral firewalls in your life as described in the Modesto Manifesto (p. 224)? Why or why not?

4 || Do you have trusted counselors and advisers who will ask you tough questions and hold you accountable for your actions? Why or why not?

5 || What steps can you take to put moral firewalls in place in your life?

6 || What does Proverbs 5:15-21 say to you about the joy and satisfaction of maintaining a life of authentic intimacy and sexual fidelity to your spouse?

7 || The end of Solomon's life was characterized by moral, spiritual, and sexual defection. What does the tragic example of King Solomon say to you about the danger of sexual temptation in a leader's life?

TWENTY-SEVEN

THE LEADER
AND ADDICTION

‖ Proverbs 31:4, 5 ‖

My father taught and coached at Tower Hill School in Wilmington, Delaware, and later worked full-time in the life insurance business. He was a leader in the state of Delaware in many areas of civic life and is still remembered fondly today. I admired him and wanted to be a leader like my dad.

Unfortunately, he also had a problem: he didn't handle alcohol well. He wasn't a heavy drinker. In fact, he didn't drink very often. He was what you would call a social drinker; but when he drank socially, alcohol tended to get the better of him.

There was alcoholism in my extended family. My dad's brother was a full-blown alcoholic and would have drunk himself to death if he hadn't found Alcoholics Anonymous. And my mother's father and uncle were also problem drinkers. Alcoholism seems to run in families—but whether that's a result of genetic or environmental factors, I don't know.

I had just about the best childhood a kid could want. But I do recall a number of times when my father had been to a party with friends. I would find him stretched out on the couch in his rumpled street clothes, either sleeping it off or too hungover to function. He was never mean or abusive when he drank. But it hurt me to see him like that.

I vividly remember one scary moment when I was fourteen or

fifteen. I was accustomed to having Dad get me up for school every morning—but on this particular day, I woke up to the distant clangor of Dad's alarm clock. It just went on and on, and I wondered, *Why doesn't he shut it off?*

My mother was out of town for a few days, visiting relatives, so there was no one in the house except Dad, me, and my younger sister. I got up and went down the hall to his bedroom and found my father lying across the bed with his clothes on. The alarm clock was like a fire alarm, yet he didn't move.

Edging closer, I saw blood on my father's face. That shocked and scared me. For a moment I wondered if he was dead. Then I saw his chest rising and falling, so at least he was alive.

I shut off the alarm and went downstairs and out to the garage. I found Dad's VW Beetle with the front end crushed. He'd had an accident, which explained the blood on his face. I later found out that he had rear-ended a truck.

Since Mom was gone, I called Dr. Briggs, our family physician, and he hurried over. He was able to get my dad upright and check him. Finally, Dr. Briggs said, "Jim, I wouldn't insure you for a nickel right now."

That was a wake-up call for my dad. He lived seven years after that and never took another drink.

Dad was a leader, a good man, and a caring father—but he had a troubled side. It's frightening for a child to see a parent out of control because of alcohol or some other addictive substance. I didn't see my dad out of control very often, but the few times I did left a disturbing impression on me. In our family, we didn't talk about it.

The writer of Proverbs 31:4, 5 warned, "Leaders can't afford to make fools of themselves, gulping wine and swilling beer, lest, hung over, they don't know right from wrong, and the people who depend on them are hurt" (*The Message*).

‖ BEING HONEST WITH OURSELVES ‖

Human beings are prone to addiction. Though the book of Proverbs speaks of the intoxicating effects of wine and beer, there are many forms of behavior that can substitute for alcohol, causing us to hurt the very people who depend on us, both our followers and our families.

Some are addicted to alcohol, illicit drugs, or prescription drugs. Some are addicted to pornography and sexual promiscuity. For some the "drug" of choice is gambling or compulsive spending. Some are addicted to anger or to a lifestyle of drama and continuous chaos. Some have an unhealthy relationship with food. One addiction that particularly affects leaders is workaholism. If there is any behavior in our lives that *controls us* and that *we cannot control,* then we are dealing with an addiction.

Anytime you turn to a behavior to soothe feelings of anxiety, restlessness, boredom, depression, resentment, and so forth, then you are engaging in your addiction. Addictive behavior is how we try to mask our unpleasant moods and painful emotions when we are unwilling to deal squarely with them. When life becomes unmanageable, we anesthetize the pain by taking a drink, swallowing a pill, downing a quart of ice cream, buying something we don't need, or escaping through sex or pornography.

We try to convince ourselves that our addictive behavior isn't really that bad or that we are entitled to a little escape or that we can quit anytime we want to (we just don't want to). But as long as we keep medicating our pain instead of seeking surgery for the underlying cancer in our lives, we keep getting sicker and more addicted.

Look back over the past twelve months of your life and answer these questions honestly:

- *Is there behavior in your life that has caused you to lose time from work?*
- *Do you engage in behavior that disrupts your home life or creates conflict with your spouse?*
- *Is there anything you do that causes you to feel guilty or remorseful afterwards?*
- *Is there behavior in your life that has harmed your reputation or caused you to suffer financial difficulties?*

- *Do you ever crave this behavior and think about it in an obsessive way?*
- *Does this behavior interfere with your sleeping?*
- *Does this behavior erode your effectiveness as a leader?*
- *Is it jeopardizing the success of your business or organization?*
- *Do you engage in this behavior alone and in secret?*
- *Do you engage in it to forget your problems?*
- *Is there behavior that you only do with people of low character?*
- *Is there behavior you indulge in only in low-class environments?*
- *Have you ever neglected your family because of this behavior?*
- *Has it adversely affected your ambitions and goals?*
- *Have you ever been hospitalized or treated by a physician because of this behavior?*
- *Do you do this behavior in order to feel more confident and less insecure?*
- *Has this behavior ever caused you to experience a loss of memory?*

If you answered yes to three or more of those questions, then you may have an addiction problem that is harming you and the people who depend on you. If so, I would encourage you to talk to your doctor or therapist about this behavior. As a leader you need to face those issues courageously and deal with them firmly.

‖ ADDICTED TO POWER, WORK, AND ADRENALINE ‖

Late one night in 1995, Secret Service agents noticed a man staggering on the sidewalk near the White House. Clad only in his underwear, he was trying to flag down a taxi. The agents recognized him as Boris Yeltsin, the president of Russia. A guest of President Bill Clinton, he was staying at Blair House, across Pennsylvania Avenue from the White House. And he was roaring drunk. When the agents questioned him, he told them he was hungry and wanted a pizza.

The embarrassing incident was immediately hushed up. It only became public after the 2009 publication of *The Clinton Tapes: Wrestling History with the President* by historian Taylor Branch.[1]

This was not unusual behavior for Boris Yeltsin. In 1991, when he took the oath of office as the first president of post–Soviet Russia, he gave no formal inaugural address but merely spoke off-the-cuff for less than a minute. His speech was noticeably slurred.

During his eight years in office, Yeltsin became notorious for bizarre behavior, unpredictable outbursts, incoherent statements and policies, and unexplained disappearances. On one occasion he traveled to the village of Uspenskoye to visit a friend. A short distance from his friend's house, he ordered the driver to let him out. The driver did so. Later Yeltsin turned up at a nearby police station, soaked from head to foot. Yeltsin said that he was about to cross a bridge over a river when a car pulled up beside him. The next thing he knew, he said, "I was in the river."

On another occasion Yeltsin attended a ceremony in Berlin to commemorate the withdrawal of Russian forces from Germany. At the ceremony he drank glass after glass of champagne—then took the baton from the hands of the orchestra conductor and proceeded to conduct the orchestra himself.

He sometimes disappeared from the Kremlin for days on end, and no one knew where he was. Once, in February 1994, he was missing for three weeks. His absence was explained as an attack of the flu.

And this man had his finger on the Russian nuclear button.[2]

Boris Yeltsin was a stumbling, staggering example of the truth of Solomon's words. Is there something about the leadership role that attracts addictive personalities? I don't know. Most of the leaders I've known have been steady, stable, committed servants of their organizations. But I have also known a number of bosses (they weren't really leaders) who seemed addicted to power, to arrogance, to an attitude of entitlement, and to ordering others around. For some people, power is a drug. They get high on being the "alpha ape."

Some leaders are addicted to work. They pride themselves on arriving early, leaving late, and never taking a vacation. Though a strong work ethic is an admirable trait, an effective leader maintains balance.

Workaholic leaders put themselves, their families, and their organizations at risk. A healthy leader knows that enough is enough—and that too much is dysfunctional.

Leaders need sleep, exercise, family time, quiet time, and leisure time. You should be training people to step into your shoes and do your job when you're not around. If you are "indispensable" in your organization, you've failed as a leader. If you are addicted to work, it's time to kick the habit.

Leadership guru Patrick Lencioni, founder of The Table Group and author of many best-selling books on management, warns that many leaders are addicted to adrenaline. He writes:

> Executives with adrenaline addiction are the ones always pecking away at their BlackBerries during meetings, talking on their cell phones during every five-minute break from those meetings, and checking e-mail late at night. They go from meeting to meeting to meeting with no time in between for reflection or thought.
>
> Always overwhelmed, adrenaline junkies seem to have a constant need for urgency, even panic, to get them through the day. They cannot grasp the race driver's motto: you have to slow down to go fast. Instead, they keep their foot on the pedal at full throttle, convinced that any deceleration is lost opportunity. . . .
>
> Unlike other addicts whose behaviors are socially frowned-upon, adrenaline addicts are often praised for their frantic activity, even promoted for it during their careers. And so they often wear their problem like a badge of honor, failing to see it as an addiction at all in spite of the pain it causes.[3]

Adrenaline addicts are a major problem in organizations. They stir up chaos, disrupt planning and procedures, and throw the entire organization into crisis mode—simply because they live for excitement and emotional highs. Such leaders are tough on an organization's morale and can cause a once-efficient organization to become highly dysfunctional.

If you are addicted to adrenaline, there is hope. The first step is to admit you have a problem and agree that you want to change. Let the people around you know that you are trying to kick the adrenaline habit—and tell them they have permission to confront you whenever you begin to engage in chaotic, high-drama behavior.

Lencioni encourages us to examine the basic problem underlying our adrenaline addiction. Some leaders, out of a sense of insecurity and self-doubt, feel a need to prove they are worthy of the position they hold. They keep people stirred up and off balance to create the impression of busyness. They mistake a chaotic office for a bustling office. They mistake frenzied activity for effective action. He suggests that time spent in counseling could help the adrenaline-addicted leader kick the habit.

Lencioni concludes, "Executives who are not adrenaline addicts make purposeful decisions about how they spend their time and where they give their attention. . . . Recovering addicts enjoy and understand the need to take a breath from time to time, to step back from their daily grind to assess and reflect where they are professionally, as well as personally."[4]

———————

Great leaders understand who they are and what motivates them. They are self-aware—and self-controlled. They refuse to be mastered by substances or compulsions. They refuse to medicate and anesthetize their pain with behaviors they can't control. They choose growth and maturity, not escape from reality.

Leaders can't afford to make fools of themselves by indulging in addictive behavior. They need to be wise and free from addiction, because a lot of people are depending on them.

GET WISDOM, GET UNDERSTANDING
QUESTIONS FOR PERSONAL REFLECTION OR GROUP DISCUSSION

1 || Addiction comes in a variety of substances and behaviors: alcohol, illicit drugs, prescription drugs, pornography, sexual promiscuity, gambling, compulsive spending, anger, a lifestyle of drama and chaos, overeating, and workaholism. Are there any items on this list that, in your opinion, should not be included? Can you think of substances or behaviors that are not listed but should be? Explain your answer.

2 || If you haven't already done so, ask yourself the questions on page 232. Are you concerned that you may have a problem with some form of addiction? What steps do you need to take this week to deal effectively with those issues? Are there people in your life who could hold you accountable for taking those steps? (Suggestion: Call those people now and ask them to call you at least once a week to check on your progress.)

3 || Is *power* a drug for leaders? Support your answer with examples and personal experiences.

4 || What is the difference between having a strong work ethic and having an addiction to work? How can you tell whether you are a hard worker or a workaholic?

5 || How have you been able to strike a healthy balance between your leadership career and your family life? Would your family members agree with your self-assessment?

6 || Are you "indispensable" to your organization? If you needed to take a few weeks off, or even a few months off, could your organization get by without you? What does your answer say about your success or failure as a leader? What does it say about the health of your organization?

7 || What steps can you take this week to ensure that you are living a self-controlled life—not a life that is mastered by substances or compulsions?

TWENTY-EIGHT

THE LEADER'S
REPUTATION

|| Ecclesiastes 10:20 ||

Carla Barnhill is a publishing executive and an author. She recalls a time near the ten-year mark in her career when she received a phone call from a superior.[1] He wanted to know why a coworker, Helen, would be under the impression that Carla had purchased an airline ticket for personal use with company money.

Carla was shocked. But she realized what had happened: "I had to fly to Oregon for work, my ticket was on Alaska Airlines, and my brother lives in Alaska. So Helen saw the ticket in my inbox, noticed the Alaska part, and jumped to the conclusion that I was on my way to see my brother using the company dime."

Carla explained the misunderstanding to the boss, and he accepted her explanation. But the more Carla thought about it, the more anger she felt toward Helen.

"It was bad enough that she'd gone to my boss without talking to me first," she said. "But what really got me was that she made a very serious accusation of immoral—and illegal—action on my part. . . . What if she told other people and I became the subject of gossip and speculation? What if, in a matter of hours, she managed to ruin a reputation I spent 10 years building?"

As it turned out, Carla Barnhill had such a strong reputation for integrity that no one gave any heed to Helen's charges. But Carla learned that it takes a long time for a business leader to build a reputation for integrity—and a few careless words could destroy that reputation in the blink of an eye.

Both leaders and followers need to take seriously the issue of guarding one another's reputation. In Ecclesiastes 10:20 Solomon wrote, "Don't bad-mouth your leaders, not even under your breath, and don't abuse your betters, even in the privacy of your home. Loose talk has a way of getting picked up and spread around. Little birds drop the crumbs of your gossip far and wide" (*The Message*).

KING SOLOMON OR KING SAUL?

Years before David became king of Israel, he served as an aide to King Saul. But Saul knew that David was destined to succeed him as king. In a fit of jealous rage and madness, Saul swore to kill David.

In 1 Samuel 24, David was on the run from Saul. He led a band of outlaws and hid out in a cave in the wilderness. While David was hiding, Saul arrived with a force of three thousand men, searching for him. David and his small band withdrew to the back of the cave. Moments later, Saul entered the cave "to relieve himself."

David's men whispered to David that his chance to kill Saul had arrived. Surely God had delivered David's enemy into his hands.

So David snuck up behind Saul, raised his blade . . . but did not kill Saul. Instead, he sliced off a corner of Saul's robe. Then he retreated to the back of the cave, telling his men, "The LORD forbid that I should do such a thing to my master, the LORD's anointed" (v. 6).

Saul left the cave, unaware of how close he had come to death. David waited for Saul to walk down the hill from the cave; then he came out and shouted to Saul, "My lord the king! . . . Why do you listen when men say, 'David is bent on harming you'? This day you have seen with your own eyes how the LORD delivered you into my hands in the cave. Some urged me to kill you, but I spared you. . . . I cut off the corner of your robe but did not kill you. . . . I have not wronged you, but you are hunting me down to take my life" (vv. 8-11).

When King Saul realized that the man he hunted had just spared his life, he wept and repented of trying to kill David.

But Saul was an unstable man. Soon he again tried to track David down and kill him. In 1 Samuel 26, David had another opportunity to kill King Saul, this time as the king slept in his encampment. Instead, David took Saul's spear and water jug as proof that he had been there—and that he had again spared Saul's life.

Young David, the aide to King Saul, had one of the worst bosses in the world. I've had some unreasonable bosses in my career, but I've never had a boss who chased me into the desert and tried to murder me. I doubt that you've had such a boss either.

How did David treat his murderous, irrational boss? He treated King Saul with respect. When he had the chance to get revenge, he refused to take it. He spoke well of King Saul and blessed him—not because Saul had earned it, but because it is right to give honor to the leader of the nation. David respected the *office* of the king, so he refused to harm the *person* of the king.

David, Solomon's father, set an example that we should show respect for leaders and guard their reputations. We should avoid saying anything that may do harm. It doesn't matter whether we love the leader or fear him, whether he is a King Solomon or a King Saul.

|| LOOSE TALK ||

Leaders and followers should practice mutual respect. Leaders should defend the reputations of followers, and followers should return the favor. There will be times when leaders and followers come into conflict. A certain amount of dissent is healthy in any organization. In a healthy organization, subordinates are free to point out problems that leaders might otherwise miss.

But followers need to remember to state their views respectfully. Go to the leader directly and state your concerns in a constructive way. Never criticize a leader behind his back. As Solomon said, don't criticize him even under your breath or in the privacy of your own home. Whatever you do, don't criticize your leader on Twitter or your Facebook page. You may think that what you say goes only so far and no further, but as Solomon said, "Loose talk has a way of getting picked up and spread around."

That's what Miss Swann, a young administrator at a marketing company, discovered—much to her regret. She thought her job was "boring," and said so on Facebook (though she didn't mention her company by name). Then she invited her coworkers to check out her comments. Her "loose talk" found its way to her boss, and Miss Swann received notice that her services were no longer required.

A spokesman explained, "Her display of disrespect and dissatisfaction undermined the relationship and made [her job] untenable. We thought that Miss Swann's best interests would be served by working for a company that would more suit her expectations."[2]

Respect benefits everyone—your leader, your organization, and you. If you want to have a successful experience in your organization and a successful career, then protect the reputation of your leader and your organization. In doing so, you will give yourself a good reputation—and improve your chances for a long and happy career. Here are some suggestions to help you maintain that relationship of respect.

1. Remember that no one is perfect.

Your leader is not perfect, and neither are you. Before you point the finger of blame, can you honestly say that *you* are blameless? Instead of criticizing, try being patient and understanding. Think about the tough decisions the leader must make. Can you honestly say you would do a better job if you were on the hot seat?

2. Instead of talking behind the leader's back, offer your support.

You will be amazed at how much the leader will appreciate your encouragement. You'll find that most leaders are eager to repay loyalty with loyalty. Even if you don't agree with his decisions, show your support. You may find that leader to be a valuable friend in your own times of adversity.

3. Don't compare your leader to other leaders you've known.

Don't expect your present boss to do things the same way as your old boss. Don't impose expectations, stereotypes, and preconceived notions on your leader, then criticize him when he doesn't measure up. Every leader is an individual.

4. Give your leader the benefit of the doubt.

You may not always understand a decision your leader makes or an action he undertakes. When we don't understand why people do what they do, we are often quick to judge, criticize, and complain. Be patient and supportive. Wait and see how the leader's decision turns out. He may have information you lack, and his decision may turn out better than you imagine.

5. Practice gossip control.

If someone comes to you with a complaint or gossip, squelch it. Say, "I don't listen to gossip, and you shouldn't spread it. If you have a complaint about the leader, go to him directly." Stand up for the leader and defend his reputation against attack. Whether you agree with the leader is beside the point. You have a moral obligation to stop negative speech in its tracks.

|| YOU CAN'T DEMAND RESPECT ||

Most of this advice has been directed at followers. But this counsel from Solomon also suggests a responsibility on the part of leaders. If you don't want to be criticized and sabotaged behind your back, you must *earn* your followers' respect. Make sure you lead wisely and with integrity. Never abuse the power of your position. Inspire loyalty, not fear. Set an example in everything you do.

Finally, take a page from the experience of Howell Raines.[3] He served as executive editor of the *New York Times* from 2001 until 2003—a twenty-one-month tenure. Why was his stay so short? It wasn't because Raines was incompetent. In fact, the newspaper won seven Pulitzer prizes in a single year during his editorial reign.

Sarah Baxter of the *Sunday Times* of London explained, "Raines's high-handed management style . . . angered and finally alienated his subordinates." Those subordinates, in the end, succeeded in getting Raines fired. His demise, Baxter adds, sounds "a cautionary note to others who share a similar leadership style."

Baxter described Howell Raines's leadership style as "an autocrat who had chosen to shake up" the *Times* with "a star system that put protégés on the fast track to top stories at the expense of more experienced and increasingly mutinous newsroom hands."

One of Raines's protégés was Jayson Blair, a young reporter who wrote newspaper copy that read like fiction—because, as it turned out, much of it *was* fiction. Blair wrote about going to the little town of Palestine, West Virginia, and witnessing the emotions of the father of Jessica Lynch, an American POW who had just been freed in Iraq. Blair reported that Jessica's father "choked up as he stood on the porch here overlooking the tobacco fields and cattle pastures."

The problem was that Blair had never set foot in Palestine, West Virginia, and never met Jessica's father. He invented the entire scene, writing it in his Brooklyn apartment. He later described that particular journalistic scam as his favorite and added, "The description was so far off from reality. I just couldn't stop laughing."

New York Times staffers warned that something didn't ring true in Blair's reporting. They begged Howell Raines to put the brakes on Jayson Blair and warned that Raines's personal biases were lowering the standards of the "newspaper of record." When the Jayson Blair scandal broke, many people, both inside and outside the organization, called for Raines's resignation. He vowed to continue on.

The internal battle at the *Times* spilled over onto the Internet. A Web site hosted by a respected journalism school became the place where *Times* staffers posted their grievances against Howell Raines, pouring out "gossip and venom" against him, wrote Sarah Baxter.

The civil war at the *Times* over Howell Raines became so rancorous that Raines's chief advocate at the paper, publisher Arthur Sulzberger, was reluctantly forced to fire him. It was a humiliating episode for the *New York Times*. Ultimately, it was Raines's own autocratic leadership style that did him in. As a leader he made many enemies and few friends. When the storms of criticism raged around him, there was no one to provide any shelter.

―――――

If you are a follower, then give your leader the respect he is due, simply because of the position he holds. It's the right thing to do.

And if you are a leader, don't expect your followers to do the right thing. Don't expect subordinates to respect you (even though they should). Don't expect people to defend your reputation (even though they should). The unfortunate truth is that, all too often, if you fail to meet their expectations, they will probably gossip about you and criticize you behind your back. They may even rake you over the coals in e-mails and blogs. It goes with the territory. You can't demand respect. But you can *earn* it. And that's what great leaders do.

GET WISDOM, GET UNDERSTANDING
QUESTIONS FOR PERSONAL REFLECTION OR GROUP DISCUSSION

1 || King Saul was one of the worst bosses in history, but David showed respect to him and refused to take revenge. Compare the story of King David and King Saul to your own situation, either in the past or present. What does David's example teach you about how to respond to your own boss?

2 || As a leader, do you think you receive the respect from your followers and subordinates that is your due? Why or why not? Do you give them the respect that they are due? Why or why not?

3 || If you are a follower, do you think you receive an appropriate level of respect from your leader? Explain your answer. Do you give your leader the respect that is his or her due? How so?

4 || Describe a time when you defended the reputation of a leader (or follower) when someone else was tearing down his or her reputation. When you defended that person, what was the result?

5 || Would you defend the reputation of a leader (or follower) even if you didn't like that person? Why or why not?

6 || As a leader, how are you earning your followers' respect? List two or three specific actions you can take this week to earn their respect.

MENTORED BY SOLOMON

World War II ended in Europe on V-E Day, May 8, 1945. Though the war would continue in the Pacific for four more months, the defeat of Nazi Germany was, in the words of Winston Churchill, "the signal for the greatest outburst of joy in the history of mankind."[1]

The following month, Churchill invited one of the chief architects of the victory, General Dwight D. Eisenhower, to speak at a celebration in London. Eisenhower—ever the reluctant and humble hero—didn't want to be glorified. But at Churchill's persistent urging, Eisenhower finally agreed. So on June 12, 1945, General Eisenhower stood before a vast audience in the bomb-scarred Guildhall. After the Lord Mayor of London presented him with the sword of the Duke of Wellington, Eisenhower spoke.

"No man alone," he said, "could have brought about [the victory]. Had I possessed the military skill of a Marlborough, the wisdom of Solomon, the understanding of Lincoln, I still would have been helpless without the loyalty, vision, and generosity of thousands upon thousands of British and Americans."[2]

What was true of Eisenhower is true of you and me. Even if we possess the wisdom of Solomon, we are helpless without the followers we depend on every day. Though leaders give vision and direction to their followers, the followers make a leader what he is.

King Solomon depended on thousands and thousands of followers to turn his vision into a reality. He had followers at every level, from the generals and administrators and priests in his government to the tradesmen at the construction sites, the laborers in the quarries, and the sailors on the ships. Solomon demonstrated leadership, but the people of Israel transformed the nation.

|| TWENTY-EIGHT STRATEGIES ||

In the fall of 2009, I toured Fort Monroe—a key fort during the Civil War—on the coast of Virginia. Abraham Lincoln visited there in the spring of 1862. Confederate President Jefferson Davis was incarcerated there for two years after the war. It's still an active training base for the Army.

Near the end of the tour, I saw a building with a sign over the door. It read, "Leadership Excellence." I asked the guide what it meant. He said, "Here is where we train young men and women to be leaders. We want them to be the very best they can be."

Leadership excellence. Isn't that what Solomon is trying to teach us? Isn't that what he wants us to strive for? What is your dream, your grand vision of the future? Remember that Solomon's success began with wisdom. He didn't ask for glory or wealth, for long life or victory over his enemies. He asked for wisdom—and God gave him the wisdom he asked for.

Solomon shared his leadership wisdom with us in passages from Proverbs and Ecclesiastes. We've looked at twenty-eight practical strategies for leading with integrity. Let's review those principles.

1. Listen to the voice of wisdom.

Solomon portrayed wisdom as a lady who speaks to us—but not all of us hear her voice. If we seek her, we will find her—and she will be our friend for life.

Become a sponge for wisdom. Cultivate a hunger for wise sayings, especially from the Bible's wisdom literature. Memorize wise insight and build a reservoir of wisdom to tap into in times of need. Seek counsel from wise advisers and mentors. Make the search for wisdom your lifelong quest.

2. If you think you are leading, make sure someone is following.

Others have a choice—they don't have to follow your leadership. You can't demand their loyalty; you have to inspire it and earn it.

Leadership is a process of attraction, not coercion. The best way to attract followers is by showing you care.

If you want to know how well you are doing as a leader, look at your followers. Are they growing in character and commitment? To measure yourself, measure the people you lead.

3. To be a great leader, become a great motivator.

A good leader does not mislead, manipulate, or exploit his followers. There's nothing wrong with extrinsic motivation (money, recognition, and so forth). But if you *really* want to inspire your followers, use intrinsic motivation. Find a way to light a fire within them.

4. Maintain a strong moral foundation.

Commit to doing what is right. The Ten Commandments form the moral bedrock of our laws and ethical principles—a basic moral code that will enable you to tell right from wrong in any situation.

5. Always speak the truth—and always expect the truth.

As a leader you need clear channels of information between you and your followers. If you receive inaccurate information, how can you make informed decisions? A healthy and functional organization is characterized by honesty. When problems and issues are covered up or denied, organizations become dysfunctional.

What is the "elephant in the room" of your organization? Your job is to expose elephants so everyone can speak freely about those issues. Let your followers know that you welcome problems, bad news, and dissent, and that you expect everyone to speak the truth.

6. Beware of toxic bosses.

Toxic, dysfunctional bosses can be egotistical, angry and intimidating, lacking in empathy for others, and deceptive. Many are insecure and feel threatened by the talents of others. Some are charming and charismatic on the surface but scheming and manipulative underneath. There is very little anyone can do to change a toxic boss. Solomon's advice: "You're smart to stay clear of someone like that."

7. Be a complete leader.

Solomon speaks of "good-tempered leaders" who are invigorating "like spring rain and sunshine." Such leaders know how to inspire, energize, and motivate their followers. Complete leaders possess the Seven Sides of Leadership: vision, communication skills, people skills, good character, competence, boldness, and servanthood.

If you lack any of those traits, don't worry; they are learnable. The more complete you become in *all* those qualities, the more likely your subordinates are to say, "My boss is a prince!"

8. Communicate to inspire and motivate.

Effective communication is a two-way process, so practice good listening habits. Keep your communication simple and focused. Avoid big words, bureaucratese, and jargon. Whenever possible, communicate face-to-face. Keep your communication positive and empowering—and always tell the truth.

9. Learn to manage your anger.

Don't become a mean-tempered, "mad dog" leader. It's normal to feel anger from time to time, but it's destructive to unleash anger against your subordinates. Deal with your anger in a constructive way.

Anger can cloud your thinking and prompt you to make rash, unwise decisions. So count to ten, taking a few moments to gain a healthy perspective. Practice self-control; don't let anger control you. Resolve your anger as quickly as possible.

10. Beware of bosses with explosive tempers.

If you have a quick-tempered boss, maintain your professionalism. Devote yourself fully to your duties; deliver excellent service to the organization. If you make a mistake, apologize—don't make excuses or defend yourself. Always be respectful and controlled, even if your boss is not.

Document everything; keep notes, e-mails, voicemails, and so forth. Think twice about reporting your boss to superiors (innocent whistleblowers often suffer more than guilty bosses). Find a mentor or a support group to advise you. If necessary, change jobs.

11. Focus on quality and excellence.

Never settle for the cheap or slipshod. Inspire a passion for quality throughout your organization and build a quality-minded team. Inform every individual that he or she is responsible for the excellence of the entire organization. Welcome competition, because your competitors push you to improve. Maintain consistency; if you are only excellent ninety-nine times out of a hundred, the remaining 1 percent will cost you. Deliver speed with excellence and maintain attention to detail. Inspire excellence by making it fun, not by instilling fear.

12. Assemble a great team—and remove rebels and slackers.

A great leader knows his people—their talents, skills, attitudes, and character traits. Some leaders focus on talent alone, then wonder why their teams are dysfunctional. The best talent in the world can be undermined if your people are disrespectful, uncoachable, or undisciplined.

Great leaders know the importance of recruiting not only great talent but also strong character.

13. Love your followers.

Solomon said, "Sound leadership is founded on loving integrity." Your followers and subordinates are not mere cogs in a machine—they are real people with real needs. A leader loves his followers and cares about their personal and emotional needs, career advancement, character growth, physical and spiritual well-being, and families.

14. Maintain your spiritual health.

Leaders should be directed by God. People of faith believe that God expects them to live moral and ethical lives. Good character traits are anchored in a strong moral and spiritual foundation.

15. Demonstrate character qualities that will make you a friend of "kings."

Seek out prominent people as mentors. Be willing to pay your dues and serve an apprenticeship. Be humble and teachable, gracious and sincere. Demonstrate gratitude for the help others give you.

16. Be respectful to your leaders.

If you show respect today, you'll have a generous friend to help you tomorrow. Life is uncertain, but respect will pave the way to your own future as a leader. So build bridges of respectful relationships; don't burn them.

17. Expand your horizons and deepen your understanding.

Never settle for the narrow and the shallow. Instead, continually seek wider knowledge and a deeper understanding of the truth. An authentic leader is a lifelong learner.

18. Remove corrupt people from leadership.

Those who abuse power for the sake of dishonest gain or sex or power itself are disqualified from leadership. Corrupt acts include nepotism, plagiarizing the work of others, cruelty, exploitation, intimidation of subordinates, and so forth. When corrupt leaders are allowed to remain in power, the entire organization is discredited. Take the hint and avoid becoming a bad leader yourself.

19. Remain steady in times of crisis.

A crisis is the acid test of leadership. When plans are upset and chaos reigns, great leaders radiate confidence, cut through the clutter of conflicting advice, and reassure those who are panicking. They lay out a winning strategy and make good decisions under pressure.

Prepare ahead for emergencies. For every Plan A, have a Plan B. Drill your people for various contingencies. Make sure your followers see you in command. After the crisis, sit down with your followers, discuss what happened, and learn the lessons of the crisis.

20. Put moral and ethical guardrails in place.

Be sure that you never fall into scandal and corruption. Never compromise your character. Be ethical and upright in your public and private life. Whenever you face an ethical dilemma, ask yourself these questions:

> *1. Is this decision permissible and legal?*
> *2. Is it edifying (does it build people up)?*
> *3. Is it fair to everyone?*
> *4. Is this a decision I can be proud of?*
> *5. Is it consistent with the Golden Rule?*

21. Exercise good judgment.

A leader must often make judgment calls based on very little data. Leaders must sometimes weigh hunches and "fuzzy data" along with cold, hard facts in order to exercise good judgment.

22. Squelch gossip.

Gossip is destructive to the life of an organization. You, as the leader, set the tone for the organization. So refuse to participate in gossip in any way. Don't receive it, spread it, or give it any credence. Set an anti-gossip policy—and set an anti-gossip example.

23. Treat your followers compassionately and fairly.

Be a champion of the underdog. Treat people equally, whether they are rich or poor, powerful or powerless. Resolve conflict in the organization impartially and respectfully toward everyone concerned.

24. Accept the limits of leadership.

A leader does what he can, he but can't do everything—so don't second-guess yourself or doubt your calling as a leader. Do the best you can, and then leave the results in God's hands.

25. Learn leadership wisdom from nature.

From the ants we learn that diligence and persistence move us toward our goals. If you want to be prepared for tomorrow, set your priorities today. From the marmots we learn the importance of caring for others in the community; marmots look out for their teammates—and so should we. The wisdom of the locusts is that an organization can accomplish much when all your members work together. From the lizards we learn that it's not the large and powerful who prevail, but the quick and nimble who will one day live in palaces.

26. Maintain firewalls against sexual temptation.

When a leader yields to immorality, organizations and families reap the negative consequences. Flirting with sexual temptation is a foolish gamble—and those few moments of guilty pleasure are not worth risking everything you treasure. Maintain your integrity.

27. Don't let addictions and compulsive behavior destroy you as a leader.

People look up to you and depend on you. If you struggle with compulsive or addictive behavior, get the help you need and conquer your addiction—before it conquers you.

28. Guard the reputation of your leader, followers, and organization.

Show respect to everyone, regardless of rank or status. Don't permit loose talk and criticism to harm the reputation of your leader or your organization. Instead of tearing down your leader, offer your support. As a leader, earn the respect of your followers every day.

‖ A CERTIFICATE OF LEADERSHIP WISDOM ‖

Author and satirist Malcolm Muggeridge once appeared on NBC's *Tonight Show* with host Jack Paar. When Paar asked Muggeridge about his politics, Muggeridge confessed that he had only voted once in his life. Paar asked what prompted him to vote on that one occasion.

"I just had to," Muggeridge replied. "There was this one candidate who had been committed to an asylum and upon discharge was issued a Certificate of Sanity. Well, now, how could I resist? What other politician anywhere has an actual medical report that he is sane? I simply had to support him!"[3]

I can't give you a Certificate of Sanity. But I know where you can obtain a Certificate of Leadership Wisdom. In fact, I guarantee that if you will immerse yourself in these twenty-eight leadership strategies, you can consider yourself officially certified as a Wise Leader.

These are the leadership principles that made Solomon the wisest and greatest leader of all time, the principles that produced Israel's golden age of peace and prosperity. These are the leadership principles Solomon wrote down and imparted to his own sons, his military commanders, his administrators and managers, his priests and aides. These principles will make you a more successful CEO, a more effective manager, a more motivational coach, a more inspirational pastor, a more outstanding educator, or a more dynamic military leader.

⊢—————⊣

Don't just read through this book once and forget it. Let Solomon be your teacher and counselor. Return to these pages again and again. Underline and highlight. Record your thoughts and insights in the margins.

Live with these principles day after day—and be mentored by the wisest and greatest leader who ever lived.

EPILOGUE: ALL THE WISDOM
IN THE WORLD

The Greek philosopher Thales lived in Miletus in Asia Minor about six hundred years before Christ. He is one of the Seven Sages of Greece, and Aristotle named him the first of the Greek philosophers. Thales was well known for his wisdom. But there were some in the city of Miletus who mocked him. They said, "Yes, Thales is wise—but all his wisdom has failed to make him rich."

When Thales heard that some were openly taunting him, he took his meager savings and spent it all to purchase every olive press in the city. He had studied the weather and the seasons, and he knew that the olive trees would produce a record crop of olives that year.

When the time came to harvest the olives, the olive growers discovered that one man had a monopoly on all the olive presses. If they wanted to make a profit from their harvests, the growers had to rent their olive presses from Thales. The philosopher charged an extortionate rate for each press he rented out, and the olive growers gladly paid it in order to press their olives and cash in their bumper crops.

At the end of the harvest, Thales sold all the presses and returned to being a poor but wise philosopher. He proved that he could have chosen riches—but he preferred wisdom instead. He had made his point, and no one ever mocked him again.[1]

The moral of the story: Wisdom can make you successful and prosperous—but wisdom is its own reward. In the closing years of Solomon's life, apparently he forgot this simple truth. Through his wisdom, Solomon had become wealthy and powerful. I suspect that, as a result, Solomon gradually forgot the reason God made him wise.

He thought that God had given him wisdom so that he could accumulate power and riches. But Solomon was mistaken. God made Solomon wise because wisdom is its own reward. Don't seek wisdom for the sake of becoming rich. Seek wisdom for the sake of becoming wise.

|| BITTER IRONY ||

Solomon's life ended on a tragic and cautionary note. Remember Solomon's first leadership principle? *Listen to the voice of wisdom.* Solomon asked, "Do you hear Lady Wisdom calling?" (Proverbs 8:1, *The Message*). In his youth, his early adulthood, and on toward middle age, he listened to the voice of wisdom. But when he became older, something changed. He made a choice to put his hands over his ears and ignore wisdom's voice. He became involved with foreign women who tempted him with foreign ideas. His affection shifted away from God and away from wisdom. Solomon wandered from the very strategies that he taught us in these twenty-eight leadership principles.

God told Solomon, "Since this is the way it is with you, that you have no intention of keeping faith with me and doing what I have commanded, I'm going to rip the kingdom from you and hand it over to someone else. But out of respect for your father David I won't do it in your lifetime. It's your son who will pay—I'll rip it right out of his grasp" (1 Kings 11:11, 12, *The Message*).

This is the bitter irony of Solomon's life. He was the wisest and most successful leader in the ancient world and perhaps in all of history—next to Jesus. There has never been a kingdom like Solomon's kingdom. Perhaps he became conceited because of his success. Perhaps he thought, *Everything I have ever done has been successful. Every decision I've made has been the right decision. Every plan I have made, every project I have initiated, every policy I have decreed has brought peace and prosperity to the land. I can do no wrong.*

That, I suspect, was the moment he decided he no longer needed to listen to the voice of wisdom. That was when he decided to listen to his own will and his own wants and his own lusts instead. He even shut out of his mind the words he himself had written—wise words, brilliant words, leadership insights of such genius that even the Queen of Sheba was astonished in his presence. His wisdom *literally* took her breath away.

God had freely given it all, but Solomon let it all be taken from him.

‖ STAY ON COURSE ‖

What about you? Perhaps you have already achieved some great things and hope to achieve even greater things as a leader. Your plans have been successful. You've made a series of very good decisions. And perhaps you have begun to think, *I can do no wrong.*

If so, you are in great danger. Your wisdom is no match for Solomon's—yet you see how his story ended. If even a wise man like Solomon could suffer a disastrous fall at the end of his career, what chance do you and I have?

The leadership wisdom of Solomon—as valid today as it was in ancient times—is yours for the taking. But remember, all the wisdom in the world is useless if you refuse to listen to it. All the wisdom in the world is worthless if you neglect to live by it.

Listen to the voice of wisdom, my friend. Listen every day and stay on course for the rest of your life. Wisdom will protect your integrity and revolutionize every aspect of your leadership.

Lead on!

GET WISDOM, GET UNDERSTANDING

QUESTIONS FOR PERSONAL REFLECTION OR GROUP DISCUSSION

1 || Of Solomon's twenty-eight strategies for leading with integrity found in this book, name two or three of these strategies that you feel are already your best leadership strengths. Citing specific examples from your experience, explain why you feel these are your strong points.

2 || Name two or three of these strategies in which you need the most improvement. Explain why you feel these are your weak points.

3 || List two or three actions you can take this week to become stronger in the areas in which you are now weak. If you have an accountability group, ask someone in the group to hold you accountable on a regular basis for improvement in those areas.

4 || The Seven Sides of Leadership are: vision, communication skills, people skills, good character, competence, boldness, and servanthood. Which of these leadership traits are your two or three greatest strengths? Which are your two or three weakest traits?

5 || List at least one action you can take this week to improve those weaknesses in your arsenal of leadership skills. If you have an accountability group, ask someone in the group to hold you accountable on a regular basis for your improvement in those areas.

6 || Do you view wisdom as a means to an end—or as an end in itself? Explain your answer.

7 || Is it possible, in your opinion, to *possess* wisdom yet refuse to *listen* to wisdom's voice? Explain your answer.

8 || If a wise man like Solomon could turn away from the wisdom he spent a lifetime accumulating, what does this say about you? What chance does anyone have of securely holding on to wisdom for life? List two or three specific steps you can take to stay on course, both now and in the future.

ACKNOWLEDGMENTS

With deep appreciation I acknowledge the support and guidance of the following people who helped make this book possible:

Special thanks to Bob Vander Weide and Rich DeVos of the Orlando Magic.

Hats off to my associates, Andrew Herdliska and Latria Leak; my proofreader, Ken Hussar; and my ace typist, Fran Thomas.

Thanks to my writing partner, Jim Denney, for his superb contributions in shaping this manuscript.

Hearty thanks also go to my friends at Standard Publishing, Dale Reeves and Lynn Pratt. My thanks to them and the entire Standard team for their vision, their editorial insight and oversight, and for believing that we had something important to share in these pages.

And finally, special thanks and appreciation go to my wife, Ruth, and to my wonderful and supportive family. They are truly the backbone of my life.

INTRODUCING THE MOST SUCCESSFUL LEADER IN HISTORY

1. Jon Meacham, *American Gospel: God, the Founding Fathers, and the Making of a Nation* (New York: Random House, 2007), 173.

2. Ibid.

3. There is some variation in the possible dates suggested for the beginning of King Solomon's reign. Here are a few sources: Shira Schoenberg, "Solomon," Jewish Virtual Library, http://www.jewishvirtuallibrary.org/jsource/biography/Solomon. html; http://www.answers.com/topic/king-solomon; http://www.biblearchaeology. org/post/2008/02/22/Amenhotep-II-as-Pharaoh-of-the-Exodus.aspx (all accessed February 4, 2010).

4. For examples of viewpoints regarding Solomon's age, see: Frederick E. Greenspahn, *When Brothers Dwell Together: The Preeminence of Younger Siblings in the Hebrew Bible* (New York: Oxford University Press, 1994), 78, note 199; http://www.1911encyclopedia.org/Solomon and http://74.125.95.132/ search?q=cache:uV7AZW0hqpoJ:www.bible.ca/archeology/bible-archeology-exodus-route-date-chronology-of-judgeshtm+solomon+became+king+at+age+20&c d=20&hl=en&ct=clnk&gl=us&client=firefox-a (both accessed February 4, 2010).

5. Author uncredited, "Megiddo—The Solomonic 'Chariot City,'" Israel Ministry of Foreign Affairs Web site, November 20, 2000, http://www.mfa.gov.il/ MFA/History/Early%20History%20-%20Archaeology/Megiddo%20-%20The%20 Solomonic%20Chariot%20City (accessed December 1, 2009).

INTRODUCING THE WISEST LEADER IN HISTORY

1. John W. Hill, *Abraham Lincoln—Man of God* (Original edition: New York: Putnam, 1920; reprint edition: Millerton, NY: Sedgwick Press, 2008), 276–277.

2. Ibid., 282–283.

3. Abigail Van Buren, www.thinkexist.com.

4. *Strong's Exhaustive Concordance* entry for 1 Kings 10:5, http://www. biblestudytools.com/OnlineStudyBible/bible.cgi?word=1+Kings+10%3A5&section =0&version=str&new=1&oq=&NavBook=2ch&NavGo=9&NavCurrentChapter=9 (accessed December 1, 2009).

ONE || "I, WISDOM"

1. Clifton Fadiman, ed., *The Little, Brown Book of Anecdotes* (Boston: Little, Brown and Company, 1985), 221.

2. Charles Colson, "The Problem of Ethics," speech at Harvard Business School, published January 1, 1992, http://www.breakpoint.org/features-columns/

articles/12145-the-problem-of-ethics (accessed December 1, 2009).

3. Ibid.

TWO || WHO'S FOLLOWING?

1. Stephen Ambrose, *Undaunted Courage: Meriwether Lewis, Thomas Jefferson, and the Opening of the American West* (New York: Simon & Schuster, 1997), 233–234.

2. Quoted by Chief Master Sergeant James Morman, "Lead: Develop Future Leaders," McConnell Air Force Base Web site, June 24, 2008, http://www.mcconnell.af.mil/news/story.asp?id=123104205 (accessed December 1, 2009).

3. Fred Smith Sr., "Ask Fred," *Leadership* Web site, July 1, 2005, http://www.ctlibrary.com/le/2005/summer/18.40.html (accessed December 1, 2009).

4. David Ogilvy, "Confessions of an Advertising Man," 5, Tallieu Marketing Web site, http://www.namti-online.com/TailieuMarketing/doc_view/75-confessions-of-an-advertising-man.raw?tmpl=component (accessed December 1, 2009).

5. John C. Maxwell, *Be a People Person* (Colorado Springs, CO: David C. Cook, 2007), 90.

THREE || THE LEADER AS MOTIVATOR

1. Michael Rowland, "Churchill's Greatest Speeches: Winston Churchill's Wartime Speeches to Parliament," Suite101.com, March 29, 2008, http://greatthinkers.suite101.com/article.cfm/churchills_greatest_speeches (accessed December 1, 2009).

2. Zig Ziglar, "Motivation, Manipulation and Leadership," Florida Department of Corrections Web site, September 1999, http://www.dc.state.fl.us/pub/compass/9909/page03.html (accessed December 1, 2009).

3. Bob Nelson, *1001 Ways to Reward Employees* (2d ed; New York: Workman, 2005), 48.

4. John Baldoni, *Great Motivation Secrets of Great Leaders* (New York: McGraw-Hill, 2005), 5, http://govleaders.org/motivation_secrets.htm (accessed December 1, 2009).

5. Quoted on contact page, Executive Leadership & Management Coaching Web site, http://www.executive-leadership-management-coaching.com/contact.html (accessed December 1, 2009).

6. "Lombardi," Anecdotage.com, http://www.anecdotage.com/index.php?aid=1948.

7. Ibid.

FOUR || THE LEADER'S MORAL FOUNDATION

1. Quoted by Harold Myra and Marshall Shelley, *The Leadership Secrets of Billy Graham* (Grand Rapids: Zondervan, 2005), 61.

2. John H. Dalton, Secretary of the Navy, "Take Care of Your Morals First," Address to U.S. Naval Academy Class of 2002 Plebes, U.S. Holocaust Museum, August 13, 1998, http://www.navy.mil/navydata/people/secnav/dalton/speeches/holo0813.txt (accessed December 1, 2009).

3. Charles W. Colson with Anne Morse, *Burden of Truth: Defending the Truth in an Age of Unbelief* (Carol Stream, IL: Tyndale House, 1998), 55–56.

FIVE || TRUTH, INC.

1. Oren Harari, *The Leadership Secrets of Colin Powell* (New York: McGraw-Hill, 2002), 47–48.

2. Ibid., 38.

3. Ibid.

4. Ibid., 36.

5. Pat Summitt with Sally Jenkins, *Reach for the Summit* (New York: Broadway Books, 1999), 51–52.

6. Bob LaMonte with Robert L. Shook, *Winning the NFL Way* (New York: HarperBusiness, 2004), 77.

7. Ibid., 77–78.

SIX || "MY BOSS IS A MADMAN!"

1. Portfolio.com, "Portfolio's Worst American CEOs of All Time," No. 6-Al Dunlap, CNBC.com (accessed December 1, 2009).

2. Ibid.

3. Jean Lipman-Blumen, *The Allure of Toxic Leaders: Why We Follow Destructive Bosses and Corrupt Politicians—and How We Can Survive Them* (New York: Oxford University Press, 2006), 18.

4. Information in this section was taken from Gerri Willis, "Dealing with an Abusive Boss—Five Tips: How to Make Your Workplace More Pleasant," Money/CNN, October 15, 2004, http://money.cnn.com/2004/10/15/pf/saving/willis_tips/index.htm (accessed December 1, 2009).

5. Melissa Korn, "Toxic Cleanup: How to Deal With a Dangerous Leader," December 19, 2007, http://www.fastcompany.com/magazine/88/things-leaders-do.html (accessed December 1, 2009).

6. Frank Pellegrini, "Person of the Week: 'Enron Whistleblower' Sherron Watkins," *Time,* January 18, 2002, http://www.time.com/time/nation/article/0,8599,194927,00.html (accessed December 1, 2009).

7. Author uncredited, "Enron Scandal," MedLibrary.org, http://medlibrary.org/medwiki/Enron_scandal (accessed December 1, 2009).

8. Quoted in "Enron's Ken Lay: Captain of a Modern-day Titanic?" Knowledge@Wharton, July 28, 2004, http://knowledge.wharton.upenn.edu/printer_friendly.cfm?articleid=1015 (accessed December 1, 2009).

SEVEN || "MY BOSS IS A PRINCE!"

1. J. Richard Chase, "Three Traits of a Leader," *Church Leader Gazette,* September 8, 2009, http://churchleadergazette.com/clg/2009/09/three-traits-of-a-leader-by-j.html (accessed December 1, 2009).

EIGHT || THE COMMUNICATOR IN CHIEF

1. Peggy Noonan, "Pull the Plug on ObamaCare," *Wall Street Journal,* August 20,

2009, http://online.wsj.com/article/SB100014240529702048840457436297134
9563340.html (accessed December 1, 2009).

2. Quoted by Library of Congress, "American Presidents," Churchill and the
Great Republic Library of Congress Interactive Exhibit, http://www.loc.gov/
exhibits/churchill/interactive/_html/2_06_00.html (accessed December 1, 2009).

3. Carlo D'Este, "The Power of Oratory: Why Churchill is Still Relevant,"
George Mason University's History News Network, January 19, 2009, http://hnn.
us/articles/60046.html (accessed December 1, 2009).

4. Jon Gruden with Vic Carucci, *Do You Love Football?!* (New York:
HarperCollins, 2003), 67–68.

5. Whitey Herzog with Jonathan Pitts, *You're Missin' a Great Game: From Casey to
Ozzie, the Magic of Baseball and How to Get It Back* (New York: Berkley, 2000), 172.

6. Quoted by Ray Blunt, "Courage in the Corridors," GovLeaders.org Web site,
http://govleaders.org/courage.htm (accessed December 1, 2009).

TEN || HOW TO HANDLE AN ANGRY BOSS

1. "I Hate My Boss," product advertisement on ShareWareConnection.com, http://
www.sharewareconnection.com/i-hate-my-boss.htm (accessed December 1, 2009).

2. Marshall Goldsmith, quoted in "Tom Peters: Apology is Nothing Short of
Strategic Competence," John Kador's Apology Matters Blog, April 25, 2009, http://
blog.effectiveapology.com/2009/04/tom-peters-apology-is-nothing.html (accessed
December 1, 2009).

ELEVEN || QUALITY AND EXCELLENCE

1. Quoted by APC Newsletter, Administrative Professionals Conference Web
site, June 2006, http://www.apcevent.com/newsletter_archives/6_2006.html
(accessed December 1, 2009).

2. Norman R. Augustine, *Augustine's Laws* (Reston, VA: American Institute of
Aeronautics and Astronautics, Inc., 1997), 78.

3. G. Kingsley Ward, *Letters of a Businessman to His Son,* Scribd Web site, http://
www.scribd.com/doc/4805980/Letters-of-a-Businessman-to-His-Son-Kingsley-
Ward?autodown=txt (accessed December 1, 2009).

4. Chris Widener, "Secrets of Successful Teams," IRJ Business, http://www.
insiderreports.com/storypage.asp?storyID=20000336&ChanID=BZ (accessed June
28, 2010).

5. Quoted by Mike Freeman, *Bloody Sundays: Inside the Rough-and-Tumble World
of the NFL* (New York: HarperCollins, 2003), 65.

6. Jim Calhoun with Richard Ernsberger Jr., *A Passion to Lead: Seven Leadership
Secrets for Success in Business, Sports, and Life* (New York: Macmillan, 2007), 27.

7. Quoted by Michael Treacy and Fred Wiersema, *The Discipline of Market
Leaders: Choose Your Customers, Narrow Your Focus, Dominate Your Market* (New
York: Perseus Books, 1997), 75.

TWELVE || THE LEADER AND HIS TEAM

1. Pat Summitt, *Reach for the Summit,* 146.

2. Quoted by "Sports Quotes," Josephson Institute Center for Sports Ethics, http://josephsoninstitute.org/pdf/sports_quotes.pdf (accessed December 1, 2009).

3. Patrick M. Lencioni, *The Five Dysfunctions of a Team: A Leadership Fable* (San Francisco: Jossey-Bass, 2002), 91–93.

THIRTEEN || LEADING THROUGH LOVE

1. Chad Lewis information in this section, as told to Doug Robinson, was taken from "Reflections: Memories Include a Friendship with President Bush," *Deseret Morning News,* July 31, 2006, http://www.deseretnews.com/article/640198917/Reflections-Memories-include-a-friendship-with-President-Bush.html (accessed December 1, 2009).

2. Quoted by Stefan Fatsis, "The Young and the Tactless: Why Are So Many New NFL Coaches Such Boorish Tyrants?" *Sports Illustrated,* October 19, 2009, http://sportsillustrated.cnn.com/vault/article/magazine/MAG1161264/index.htm (accessed December 1, 2009).

3. "Forrest Gregg," Pro Football Hall of Fame, http://www.profootballhof.com/hof/member.aspx?PlayerId=81 (accessed December 1, 2009).

4. Lisa McLeod, "Leadership—What's Love Got to Do With It?" Ezinearticles.com, http://ezinearticles.com/?Leadership---Whats-Love-Got-to-Do-With-It?&id=2792034 (accessed December 1, 2009).

5. Quoted by Pat Townsend with Joan Gebhardt, *Quality Makes Money* (Milwaukee: Quality Press, 2005), 133.

6. Sun Tzu, translated by Thomas Cleary, *The Art of War* (Boston: Shambhala Publications, Inc., 1988), 137.

FOURTEEN || THE SPIRITUAL DIMENSION OF LEADERSHIP

1. Marvin Olasky, "Out of Spiritual Slavery," *World Magazine,* February 8, 1997, http://www.worldmag.com/articles/675.

2. Quoted by Marc Lacey, "Looking Back at a Day in Selma, 35 Years On," *New York Times,* March 6, 2000, http://www.nytimes.com/2000/03/06/us/looking-back-at-a-day-in-selma-35-years-on.html?n=Top/Reference/Times%20Topics/Subjects/E/Elections (accessed March 25, 2010).

3. Jacob M. Appel, "Interview with Peter Singer: Philosopher as Educator," Education Update Online, July 2004, http://www.educationupdate.com/archives/2004/july/html/spot-interviewwithpete.htm (accessed December 1, 2009).

4. Scott Klusendorf, "Peter Singer's Bold Defense of Infanticide," *Christian Research Journal,* 2001, http://www.equip.org/articles/peter-singer-s-bold-defense-of-infanticide# (accessed December 1, 2009).

5. Peter Singer, *Practical Ethics* (New York: Cambridge University Press, 1993), 169–170.

6. Ronald Bailey, "The Pursuit of Happiness: Peter Singer interviewed by Ronald Bailey," *Reason,* December 2000, http://reason.com/archives/2000/12/01/the-pursuit-of-happiness-peter (accessed December 1, 2009).

FIFTEEN || HOW TO REACH THE HEART OF A LEADER

1. Quoted by Eric Lichtblau and Eric Lipton, "Senator's Aid After Affair Raises Flags over Ethics," *New York Times,* October 1, 2009, http://www.nytimes.com/2009/10/02/us/politics/02ensign.html (accessed December 1, 2009).

2. Quoted in "Thoughts on the Business of Life," Forbes.com, http://thoughts.forbes.com/thoughts/experience-harold-geneen-in-the-business (accessed December 1, 2009).

SIXTEEN || RESPECT—PAVING THE WAY TO YOUR FUTURE

1. Vince Lombardi Jr., *What It Takes to Be #1: Vince Lombardi on Leadership* (New York: McGraw-Hill, 2003), 210.

2. Ibid., 210–211.

3. Ibid., 211.

4. Ibid.

5. Ibid., 212.

6. Ibid.

7. Nigel McCrery, *Still Waters* (New York: Vintage, 2009), 172.

8. John Wooden with Steve Jamison, *Wooden on Leadership* (New York: McGraw-Hill, 2005), 74–75.

SEVENTEEN || THE BREADTH AND DEPTH OF A GREAT LEADER

1. John C. Maxwell, *The 21 Irrefutable Laws of Leadership* (Nashville: Thomas Nelson, 2007), 29–30.

2. Ibid., 25.

3. Ibid.

4. Charles Stewart Given, *A Fleece of Gold: Five Lessons from the Fable of Jason and the Golden Fleece,* http://infomotions.com/etexts/gutenberg/dirs/etext05/7jasn10.htm (accessed December 1, 2009).

5. John C. Maxwell, *The Maxwell Daily Reader: 365 Days of Insight to Develop the Leader Within* (Nashville: Thomas Nelson), 92.

6. Quoted by The Taylor Group, "Professional Development," TaylorGroup.com, http://www.taylorgroup.com/prodev.php (accessed December 1, 2009).

7. Rick Warren, "Recovering Your Joy," sermon delivered November 8, 2009, Saddleback Church, Lake Forest, California, transcribed from audio file archived at http://www.saddleback.com/mediacenter/services/currentseries.aspx?site=yDi0V4EwP58=&s=Fvi62yA1ax0= (accessed December 1, 2009).

8. Sheila Murray Bethel, *A New Breed of Leader: Eight Leadership Qualities That Matter Most in the Real World* (New York: Penguin, 2009), 260.

EIGHTEEN || WHEN LEADERS GO BAD

1. Jim Jones, Transcript of Interview, Tape Number Q 134, Jonestown Audiotape Primary Project: Transcripts, Transcript prepared by Fielding M. McGehee III, The Jonestown Institute, http://jonestown.sdsu.edu/AboutJonestown/Tapes/Tapes/TapeTranscripts/Q134.html (accessed December 1, 2009).

2. John Hall, *Gone from the Promised Land: Jonestown in American Cultural History* (Edison, NJ: Transaction Publishers, 2004), 17–18.

3. Ibid., 54.

4. Ibid., 47.

5. Ibid., 146.

6. Jim Jones, Transcript of Interview, Tape Number Q 622, Jonestown Audiotape Primary Project: Transcripts, Transcript prepared by Fielding M. McGehee III, The Jonestown Institute, http://jonestown.sdsu.edu/AboutJonestown/Tapes/Tapes/TapeTranscripts/Q622.html (accessed December 1, 2009).

7. Jim Jones, quoted at http://en.wikiquote.org/wiki/Jim_Jones (accessed June 23, 2010).

8. Ibid., 3.

9. Daniel J. Flynn, "Top Ten Skeletons in the Left's Closet," *FrontPage Magazine,* May 16, 2008, http://97.74.65.51/readArticle.aspx?ARTID=30964 (accessed December 1, 2009).

10. NBC Bay Area TV, "Through a Daughter's Eyes: Remembering Leo Ryan," November 19, 2008, http://www.nbcbayarea.com/news/local-beat/Through-a-Daughters-Eye-Remember-Leo-Ryan.html (accessed December 1, 2009).

11. Denice Stephenson, ed., *Dear People: Remembering Jonestown: Selections from the Peoples Temple Collection at the California Historical Society* (Berkeley, CA: Heyday Books, 2005), 140.

12. Henrik Ibsen, *An Enemy of the People* (Stilwell, KS: Digireads.com Publishing, 2005), 88.

NINETEEN || LEADERSHIP IN TIMES OF CRISIS

1. Uri Bar-Joseph, "The 1973 Yom Kippur War," Jewish Virtual Library, May 2009, http://www.jewishvirtuallibrary.org/jsource/isdf/text/barjoseph.html; Mitchell Bard, "The Yom Kippur War," Jewish Virtual Library, http://www.jewishvirtuallibrary.org/jsource/History/73_War.html (accessed December 1, 2009).

2. "Golda Meir (1898–1978)," Jewish Virtual Library, http://www.jewishvirtuallibrary.org/jsource/biography/meir.html; "Golda Meir, 1898–1978," Israel Ministry of Foreign Affairs, http://www.mfa.gov.il/MFA/Facts+About+Israel/State/Golda+Meir.htm (accessed December 1, 2009).

3. Yaakov Hasdai, "Sorry, Golda: We owe Golda Meir an apology; resignation following 1973 war was admirable," YNet Israel Opinion, April 30, 2007, http://www.ynetnews.com/articles/0,7340,L-3393255,00.html (accessed December 1, 2009).

4. "Golda Meir on the Palestinians," Jewish Virtual Library, http://www.jewishvirtuallibrary.org/jsource/Quote/meirq.html (accessed December 1, 2009).

5. Scott Pelley, "The Day Reagan Was Shot: Haig's Famous Statement," CBS News, April 24, 2001, http://www.cbsnews.com/stories/2001/04/23/60II/main287292.shtml (accessed December 1, 2009); Author uncredited, "Alexander Haig," *Time,* April 2, 1984, http://www.time.com/time/magazine/article/0,9171,954230,00.html (accessed December 1, 2009).

6. Quoted by John Cook and Leslie Ann Gibson, *The Book of Positive Quotations* (Minneapolis: Fairview Press, 2007), 412.

TWENTY ‖ AVOIDING THE FALL

1. A&E Television, "Dennis Kozlowski Biography," Bio True Story, http://www.biography.com/articles/Dennis-Kozlowski-234610 (accessed December 1, 2009).

2. Annelena Lobb, "Shop like Dennis K," CNN/Money, September 24, 2002, http://money.cnn.com/2002/09/23/pf/saving/q_tyco/ (accessed December 1, 2009).

3. Thomas M. DeFrank, "A Regular Guy: Gerald Ford, 1913–2006," *New York Daily News,* December 27, 2006, 7.

4. John C. Maxwell, *There's No Such Thing As Business Ethics: There's Only One Rule for Making Decisions* (Nashville: Center Street, 2003), xi.

5. William Greider, *Come Home, America: The Rise and Fall (and Redeeming Promise) of Our Country* (New York: Rodale Books, 2009), 190.

6. Raymond V. Gilmartin, "Commencement: Remarks by Raymond V. Gilmartin," Union College, June 13, 1999, *Union News,* http://www.union.edu/N/DS/s.php?s=3382 (accessed December 1, 2009).

7. "Ethics Quotes," University Ethics Office, University of Illinois Web site, http://www.ethics.uillinois.edu/resources/quotes.cfm (accessed December 1, 2009).

TWENTY-ONE ‖ A LEADER OF GOOD JUDGMENT

1. "Jamestown Colony," *Encyclopedia Britannica,* 2009, Encyclopedia Britannica Online, http://www.britannica.com/EBchecked/topic/300134/Jamestown-Colony/247840/Representative-democracy-and-slavery-1619 (accessed December 1, 2009).

2. Doris Kearns Goodwin, *Team of Rivals: The Political Genius of Abraham Lincoln* (New York: Simon & Schuster, 2005), 206–207.

3. Ibid., 207–208.

4. Gil Troy, *Leading from the Center: Why Moderates Make the Best Presidents* (New York: Basic Books, 2008), 74.

5. Quoted by Maureen Dowd, "Moved by a Crescent," *New York Times,* October 22, 2008, http://www.nytimes.com/2008/10/22/opinion/22dowd.html (accessed December 1, 2009).

6. John William Gardner, *On Leadership* (New York: Simon & Schuster, 1993), 49.

7. Peter F. Drucker, *The Effective Executive* (Burlington, MA: Elsevier, 2007), 134.

8. Noel M. Tichy and Warren G. Bennis, *Judgment: How Winning Leaders Make Great Calls* (New York: Penguin, 2007), 3–5.

9. Tom Davenport, "Robert S. McNamara's Good Brain—and Bad Judgment," Harvard Business Publishing, Voices (blog page), July 7, 2009, http://blogs.harvardbusiness.org/davenport/2009/07/robert_s_mcnamaras_good_brain.html (accessed December 1, 2009).

TWENTY-TWO || "I HEARD IT THROUGH THE GRAPEVINE"

1. Rebecca Leung, "Morris: 'Reagan Still A Mystery'—Lesley Stahl Talks To Edmund Morris, Reagan's Official Biographer," CBS News, June 9, 2004, http://www.cbsnews.com/stories/2004/06/09/60II/main622051.shtml (accessed December 1, 2009).

2. Desiree Kane, "GenY Women in the Workplace: Gossip," Heroes Rising Blog, October 9, 2009, http://heroesrising.wordpress.com/2009/10/09/geny-women-in-the-workplace-gossip/ (accessed December 1, 2009).

3. Quoted by Hal Urban, *Positive Words, Powerful Results: Simple Ways to Honor, Affirm, and Celebrate Life* (New York: Fireside, 2004), 154.

4. John C. Maxwell, *The 360 Degree Leader Workbook: Developing Your Influence from Anywhere* (Nashville: Thomas Nelson, 2006), 173.

5. Information in this section was taken from Jacelyn Tse, "Gossip poisons business—HR can stop it," Human Resources Web site, June 1, 2005, http://www.humanresourcesonline.net/news/4246 (accessed December 1, 2009).

TWENTY-THREE || THE COMPASSION AND FAIRNESS OF A GREAT LEADER

1. Roy Blount Jr., "Making Sense of Robert E. Lee," *Smithsonian,* July 2003, http://www.smithsonianmag.com/history-archaeology/robertlee.html?c=y&page=2 (accessed December 1, 2009).

2. The American Civil War Web site, Civil War Quotes, General Robert E. Lee, http://www.brotherswar.com/Civil_War_Quotes_4b.htm (accessed March 24, 2010).

3. Stratford Hall Plantation Web site, "General Robert E. Lee 1807–1870," http://www.stratfordhall.org/learn/lees/robert_e_lee.php (accessed June 14, 2010).

4. Gamaliel Bradford Jr., "The Spiritual Life of Robert E. Lee," *Atlantic Monthly,* Vol. CVIII (Cambridge, MA: The Riverside Press, 1911), 512. Seen at http://books.google.com (accessed June 23, 2010).

5. *Indianapolis Journal,* "Lincoln's Tenderness: The Letter He Wrote for a Dying Soldier Boy and That to the Mother Bereaved of Five Sons," *New York Times,* June 1, 1902, 15, http://query.nytimes.com/gst/abstract.html?res=9F04E3DD113DEE3 2A25752C0A9609C946397D6CF (accessed December 1, 2009).

6. Quoted by Pat Williams, *Paradox of Power* (Nashville: Warner Faith, 2002), 82.

7. Brian Schmitz, "Stan Van Gundy Vows To Limit Negativity After Private Meeting With C Dwight Howard," *Orlando Sentinel,* November 19, 2009, http://www.orlandosentinel.com/sports/os-orlando-magic-1120-20091119,0,1594533.story (accessed December 1, 2009).

8. Ibid.

9. Information in this section was taken from Graham Hays, "Central Washington Offers the Ultimate Act of Sportsmanship," ESPN.com, April 28, 2008, http://sports.espn.go.com/ncaa/columns/story?columnist=hays_ graham&id=3372631 (accessed December 1, 2009).

TWENTY-FOUR || THE LIMITS OF LEADERSHIP

1. Larry J. Sabato, "Be Brutally Honest," *Reader's Digest,* January 2009, http://www.rd.com/your-america-inspiring-people-and-stories/be-brutally-honest/article113174.html (accessed December 1, 2009).

2. Quoted by Robert E. Johnson, "Bill and Camille Cosby: First Family of Philanthropy," *Ebony,* May 1989, 25.

TWENTY-FIVE || LEADERSHIP WISDOM FROM NATURE

1. Matt Walker, "Ant Mega-Colony Takes Over World," *Earth News,* BBC, July 1, 2009, http://news.bbc.co.uk/earth/hi/earth_news/newsid_8127000/8127519.stm (accessed December 1, 2009).

2. J. Frederic McCurdy and Louis Ginzberg, "Agur Ben Jakeh," JewishEncyclopedia.com, http://www.jewishencyclopedia.com/view.jsp?artid=927&letter=A&search=agur (accessed December 1, 2009).

TWENTY SIX || THE LEADER AND SEXUAL TEMPTATION

1. Bill Clinton, "Response to the Lewinsky Allegations (January 26, 1998)," Video and Transcript, Miller Center of Public Affairs, University of Virginia, http://millercenter.org/scripps/archive/speeches/detail/3930 (accessed December 1, 2009).

2. D. James Kennedy, *Led by the Carpenter* (Nashville: Thomas Nelson, 1999), 31.

3. Billy Graham, *Just As I Am* (New York: HarperCollins, 1997), 127–128.

4. Ibid., 128.

5. Ibid., 129.

TWENTY-SEVEN || THE LEADER AND ADDICTION

1. Tim Reid, "Secret Service Picked Up Drunken Yeltsin During Washington Visit," *Times* (London), September 22, 2009, http://www.timesonline.co.uk/tol/news/world/us_and_americas/article6842763.ece (accessed December 1, 2009).

2. Martin Ebon, "Yeltsin's V.I.P. Depression," 1996, Healthier You Web site, http://www.healthieryou.com/exclusive/yeltsin.html (accessed December 1, 2009).

3. Patrick Lencioni, "The Painful Reality of Adrenaline Addiction," Kravis Leadership Institute, *Leadership Review,* Winter 2005, 3–6, http://www.leadershipreview.org/2005winter/LencioniArticle.pdf (accessed December 1, 2009).

4. Ibid.

TWENTY-EIGHT || THE LEADER'S REPUTATION

1. Information in this section was taken from Carla Barnhill, "Women of Integrity," BuildingChurchLeaders.com, October 21, 2008, http://www.buildingchurchleaders.com/articles/2008/womanofintegrity.html (accessed June 30, 2010).

2. SkyNews, "Sacked For Calling Job Boring On Facebook," SkyNews.com, February 27, 2009, http://news.sky.com/skynews/Home/UK-News/Facebook-Sacking-Kimberley-Swann-From-Clacton-Essex-Sacked-For-Calling-Job-Boring/Article/200902415230508?lpos=UK_News_Article_Related_Content_

Region_4&lid=ARTICLE_15230508_Facebook_Sacking%3A_Kimberley_Swann_
From_ (accessed December 1, 2009).

3. Information in this section was taken from Sarah Baxter, "Editor falls to bloggers' rapid poison," *Sunday Times* (of London), June 8, 2003, http://www.timesonline.co.uk/tol/news/world/article1139946.ece (accessed December 1, 2009).

MENTORED BY SOLOMON

1. Stephen E. Ambrose, *Eisenhower: Soldier and President* (New York: Simon and Schuster, 1991), 205.

2. Ibid., 206–207.

3. "Malcolm Muggeridge: Loopy Reasoning," Anecdotage.com, http://www.anecdotage.com/index.php?aid=8454 (accessed December 1, 2009).

EPILOGUE: ALL THE WISDOM IN THE WORLD

1. Clifton Fadiman and Andre Bernard, *Bartlett's Book of Anecdotes* (New York: Little, Brown and Company, 2000), 529.

ABOUT THE AUTHOR

Pat Williams is a best-selling author of more than sixty-five books, a sought-after motivational speaker, and senior vice president and co-founder of the Orlando Magic. Pat and his wife, Ruth, have nineteen children—including fourteen adopted from four different countries.

Jim Denney has collaborated with Pat Williams on numerous books. Jim is a full-time freelance writer with eighty published books to his credit. He and his family reside in California.

Contact Pat Williams at:
> Pat Williams
> c/o Orlando Magic
> 8701 Maitland Summit Boulevard
> Orlando FL 32810
> 407-916-2404
> pwilliams@orlandomagic.com

Visit Pat's Web site at:
> www.PatWilliamsMotivate.com

To set up a speaking engagement for Pat Williams, contact:
> Andrew Herdliska
> 407-916-2401
> aherdliska@orlandomagic.com

We would love to hear from you. Please send your comments about this book to Pat Williams at the above address or in care of our publisher at:
> Dale Reeves, editor
> Standard Publishing
> 8805 Governor's Hill Drive, Suite 400
> Cincinnati OH 45249

Read what Pat Williams has to say about marriage. Order *Happy Spouse . . . Happy House* at www.standardpub.com or from your local retailer.